D1523341

SCHOLASTIC MEDITATIONS

STUDIES IN PHILOSOPHY
AND THE HISTORY OF PHILOSOPHY

General Editor: Jude P. Dougherty

Studies in Philosophy
and the History of Philosophy　　Volume 44

Scholastic Meditations

Nicholas Rescher

THE CATHOLIC UNIVERSITY OF AMERICA PRESS
Washington, D.C.

The paper used in this publication meets the minimum requirements of
American National Standards for Information Science—Permanence of Paper
for Printed Library materials, ANSI z39.48-1984.
∞

LIBRARY OF CONGRESS CATALOGING-IN-PUBLICATION DATA
Rescher, Nicholas.
Scholastic meditations / Nicholas Rescher. — 1st ed.
        p. cm. — (Studies in philosophy and the history of philosophy ; v. 44)
   ISBN 13: 978-0-8132-1410-8 (cloth : alk. paper)
   ISBN 10: 0-8132-1410-6 (cloth : alk. paper)
    1. Scholasticism. I. Title. II. Series.
   B21.S78 vol. 44
   [B839]
   100 s—dc22
   [189´.4]
                                                    2004014859

For Norris Clarke

Contents

Preface

These studies are collectively entitled *Scholastic Meditations* on the obvious precedent of Husserl's *Cartesian Meditations.* I have also been tempted to entitle the book *Scholastic Mediations* because these studies endeavor to intermediate between Scholastic concerns and contemporary philosophical issues. For while the present deliberations are always closely linked to historical sources of inspiration, their main preoccupation is generally with philosophical problems as such.

From the way in which philosophers have been inclined to talk after the era of "modern" philosophy inaugurated by Descartes in the seventeenth century, no one would guess that the Scholastic era of philosophy from Abelard (1079–1142) to Suarez (1548–1617) was one of the golden ages of Western philosophizing. And yet any open-minded and candid attention to the matter soon reveals that this was indeed the case. It was then, in fact, more than at any other stage of history, that philosophy stood at the center of academic and intellectual culture. And most of the complaints made about the thinkers of the era—their preoccupation with subtle distinctions and logic chopping, for example—fail to do justice at once to the seriousness of their concerns and to the fact that their subtleties generally served a clear and present purpose with regard to the clarification of significant philosophical issues.

Be this as it may, however, the studies gathered together in this present volume seek to do homage to the spirit of Scholasticism. They all address key issues relating to this important sector of philosophical tradition—partly on the historical side and partly on matters of substantive concern. They are written in the conviction that there is much to be learned from a preoccupation with the Schoolmen because even where one fails to agree with their positions on the issues, the methods they employed and their commitment to their projects have much to teach us about the proper conduct of philosophizing. And not only to teach, but to inspire as well.

The essays comprising this volume are pretty much balanced between historical and systematic. Five of them have their roots in earlier publications as acknowledged in the footnotes, while the remaining five are quite new. The author gives thanks to the journals involved for their permission for this material to be included here.

I am grateful to a reader of a draft of this text (who wishes to remain anonymous) for making various points that have enabled me to improve the book. And I also want to thank Estelle Burris for her patient help in producing a manuscript suitable for the printer's needs.

SCHOLASTIC MEDITATIONS

Chapter 1

CHOICE WITHOUT PREFERENCE
The Problem of "Buridan's Ass"

A logical theory may be tested by its capacity for dealing with puzzles, and it is a wholesome plan, in thinking about logic, to stock the mind with as many puzzles as possible, since these serve much the same purpose as is served by experiments in physical science.
—*Bertrand Russell*

In things which are absolutely indifferent there can be no choice and consequently no option or will, since choice must have some reason or principle.
—*G. W. Leibniz*

1. INTRODUCTION

The idea that the reasoned life, although rewarding, is not all that simple is already prominent in the earliest speculations on "wisdom" *(sophia)* out of which philosophy *(philo-sophia)* was to grow. Nor is this surprising. After all, a choice that is *reasoned* is more difficult to arrive at than a choice made haphazardly when, in the blithe manner of Mark Twain's dictum, "you pays your money and you takes your choice." But such reflections lead to the puzzle posed by the question: How is a reasoned choice among fully equivalent alternatives possible? We here confront the problem of *choice without preference:* a reasoned choice must proceed from a reasoned preference, but a reasoned preference among fully equivalent objects is patently impossible.

There are puzzles and puzzles—"idle" ones that can at best amuse a sated imagination, and "profound" ones that can lead the intellect into a deeper appreciation of the nature of things. The Buridan's Ass puzzle of equivalent choices is of the second kind, seeing that its analysis provides an occasion both for insight into the logic of reasoned choice and for a better understanding of some important issues in the history of philosophy.

As is generally the case in matters of this sort, it is useful to consider the historical background. In elucidating the substantive philosophical contexts in which the problem of choice without preference has figured, and for which it has been viewed as fundamentally relevant, a historical survey brings to light primarily the three following issues: first, its role in Greek science, originally in cosmological discussions of the Earth's place in the physical universe, and ultimately in more general considerations regarding physical symmetries (cf. Axiom 1 of Archimedes' treatise *On Plane Equilibria*); second, its role in philosophico-theological discussion among the Arabs regarding the possibility of explaining God's actions in ways acceptable to reasoning men; and third, its role in the medieval Scholastic ethico-theological discussions of man's freedom of the will.

So much for a preview of the historical aspects of our problem. With regard to the theoretical findings of the analysis, let it suffice to note here in a preliminary way that a study of choice without preference forces upon us a clear recognition of the difference between *reasons*, on the one hand, and inclining *motives*, on the other. We shall see that an indifferent choice must be made (in effect) randomly. Now, when a random selection among indifferent objects is made by me, I do have a reason for my particular selection, namely, the fact that it was indicated to me by a random selector. But I have no *preference* or psychological motivation of other sorts to incline me to choose this item instead of its (by hypothesis indifferent) alternatives. Such absence of psychological preference does not entail the impossibility of a rationally justifiable selection. A choice can therefore be vindicated as having been made reasonably even though it cannot be traced back to any psychological foundation. In short, we can have *reasons* for a choice even where there is no inclining *motive*. Thus, despite the seemingly abstruse and esoteric character of the issue, the puzzle of a reasoned choice among fully equivalent alternatives is not lacking in instruction from both the theoretical and the historical points of view.

2. THE PROBLEM

Can a reasonable agent choose a course of action, or an object, without a preference? It certainly appears on first view that this question has to be answered negatively. By the very concept of a "reasonable agent," it is requisite that such an individual have *reasons* for his actions. And when a reasonable choice among alternatives is made, this must, it would seem, have to be based upon a *preference* for the object actually chosen vis-à-vis its available alternatives. Where there is no *preference*, it would appear that no *reason* for a selection can exist, so that there apparently cannot be a *reasonable* way of making a choice. This line of reasoning seems to establish the precept: *No reasonable choice without a preference*.

However, despite the surface plausibility of this argument, it cannot be accepted as fully correct. For there is a well-known, indeed notorious, counterexample: the dilemma or paradox of Buridan's Ass. This mythical creature is a hypothetical animal, hungry, and positioned midway between essentially identical bundles of hay. There is supposed to be no reason why the animal should have a preference for one of the bundles of hay over the other. Yet it must eat one or the other of them, or else starve. Under these circumstances, the creature will, being reasonable, prefer having-one-bundle-of-hay to having-no-bundle-of-hay. It therefore *must choose one* of the bundles. Yet there is, by hypothesis, simply no *reason* for preferring either bundle. It appears to follow that reasonable choice must—somehow—be possible in the absence of preference.

It should at once be noted that the problem of the Identity of Indiscernibles, famous because of its prominent role in the philosophy of Leibniz, has no bearing upon the issue. For what is at stake in cases of choice without preference, such as the example of Buridan's ass, is not there being *no difference* between the objects of choice (i.e., that they be strictly indiscernible), but merely that such differences as do admittedly exist are either entirely *irrelevant* to the desirability of these items (as the mint markings of coins in current circulation have no bearing upon their value or worth), or else are simply *unknown* to the chooser. Thus strict indiscernability is not so much at issue here as effective indistinguishability qua objects of choice—value symmetry, in short—so that every identifiable reason for desiring one alternative is equally a reason for desiring the others. There is consequently no need for the issue of the identity of indiscernibles to concern us in the present context.

In the main, the problem of choice in the absence of preference is a theoretical, not a practical, problem. Real-life situations do not often confront us with strictly indifferent choices. Such situations do, however, appear to exist. For example, if a person were offered a choice between two fresh dollar bills, the only perceptible difference between which is that of their serial numbers, we would be greatly astonished if this selector could offer us a "reason" for choosing one of them rather than the other that could reasonably be regarded as cogent. While a difference between the bills does indeed exist, it simply does not constitute a valid difference as regards their preferability as objects of choice. And again, when purchasing a stamp at the post office, one is utterly indifferent as to which one on the sheet the agent gives one (for *him*, to be sure, this indifference is eliminated by such factors as ease of access, etc., so that the overall *situation* is not one of indifference). However, while situations of totally indifferent choice are comparatively rare, the problem of choice without preference does, nevertheless, have the status of an interesting question in the theory of reasoned choice. And as such it also has—as we shall see—significant philosophical implications and consequences, as well as a venerable history in philosophic thought.

3. THE HISTORY OF THE PROBLEM OF "BURIDAN'S ASS"

The problem of nonpreferential choice has a long philosophical, and even literary, history. Its most noteworthy parts will be sketched in this section. The interest of this historical excursus lies both in the view that it provides of various formulations of our puzzle, and in its indication of the alternative philosophical problem contexts in which it has played a significant role.

Anaximander (ca. 610–ca. 545 B.C.)

According to a report of Origen, certain of the early Greek cosmologists had held "that the Earth is a celestial object [*meteôron*], supported [in the heavens] by nothing whatsoever, and remaining in its place on account of its equidistance from all."[1] From Aristotle we learn that just this was the position and the line of reasoning of the pre-Socratic philosopher Anaximander of Miletus:

There are some who name its [i.e., the Earth's] equipoise [*homoiotês*] as the cause of its remaining at rest, e.g., among the early philosophers Anaximander. These urge that that which is situated at the centre and is equably related to the extremes has no impulse to move in one direction—either upwards or downwards or sideways—rather than in another; and since it is impossible for it to accomplish movement in opposite directions at once, it necessarily remains at rest.[2]

And this idea was endorsed by Socrates in Plato's *Phaedo:*

"I am satisfied," he [Socrates] said, "in the first place that if [the earth] is spherical, and located in the middle of the universe, it has no need of air[3] or any oth-

---

1. Origin, *Philosophoumena*, c. 6; my translation.
2. Aristotle, *De caelo*, II 13, 295b10; trans. W. K. C. Guthrie in the Loeb Classical Library Series. Regarding this passage and its bearing on Anaximander, see E. Zeller, *Philosophie der Griechen*, vol. 1, 7th edition, ed. W. Nestle (Leipzig: O. R. Reisland, 1923), p. 303, notes.
3. According to Aristotle (*De caelo*, II 13, 294b14), Anaximenes, Anaxagoras, and

er force of that sort to make it impossible for it to fall; it is sufficient by itself to maintain the symmetry of the universe and the equipoise of the earth itself. A thing which is in equipoise and placed in the midst of something symmetrical will not be able to incline more or less towards any particular direction; being in equilibrium, it will remain motionless."[4]

In the thought of Anaximander, then, that an object "placed in the midst of something symmetrical will not be able to incline more or less towards any particular direction" we have the conceptual origin, the germ as it were, of the problem of Buridan's Ass.[5] But this is only the start, and a further step was required to reach our actual problem: the move to the concept of a psychological cancellation or balance among opposing motivations of equal strength, to a *psychological equilibrium of motives*, in short. This step was already taken by Aristotle.

Aristotle (384–322 B.C.)

In criticizing as inadequate the very view we have just considered that the Earth is sustained in space through the equipoise of the surrounding heavens, Aristotle contrasts this view with his own theory of *natural place*, to the distinct advantage of this latter theory:

The reason [for the Earth's position] is not its impartial relation to the extremes: that could be shared by any other element, but motion towards the center is peculiar to earth. . . . If . . . the place where the Earth rests is not its natural place, but the cause of its remaining there is the constraint of its "indifference" [*isorropia*] (on the analogy of the hair which, stretched strongly

---

Democritus held that the Earth stays in place "owing to the air beneath, like the water in *klepsydrae.*"

4. Plato, *Phaedo*, 108 E; trans. R. S. Bluck (London: Routledge & Kegan Paul, 1955). This reasoning is endorsed also by Parmenides and by Democritus (see *Aetios*, III, 15, 7), who are also reported to have characterized the state resulting from the Earth's equidistance from the cosmic extremities as one of *isorropia* (equilibrium; the term used by pre-Socratics and by Plato in the citation). Again, according to a report of Achilles (*Eisagôgê*, 4; ed. V. Arnim, vol. 2, p. 555), "The Stoics . . . [hold that] the earth will remain in the center, being kept in equilibrium by the pressure of air from all sides. And again, if one takes a body and ties it from all sides with cords and pulls them with precisely equal force, the body will stay and remain in its place, because it is dragged equally from all sides." (I take the reference and the translation from S. Samfrom S. Samburskury, *Isis*, vol. 49 [1958], pp. 331–35.) Cf. the "explanation" given in medieval times by eager Christians anxious to refute the supposed miracle that Mohammed's coffin had floated unsupported in midair: they claimed that it was made of iron and was supported just midway between two precisely equal magnets.

5. Cf. Archimedes' axiom: "I postulate that equal weights at equal distances balance, and equal weights at unequal distances do not balance, but incline towards the weight which is at the greater distance" (*On Plane Equilibria*, trans. Ivor Thomas, in *Greek Mathematics* [Cambridge, Mass.: Loeb Classical Library, Harvard University Press, 1939]), vol. 2, p. 207, Axiom 1).

but evenly at every point, will not break, or the man who is violently but equally hungry and thirsty, and stands at an equal distance from food and drink, and who therefore must remain where he is), then they [i.e., Anaximander and the other supporters of this view] ought to have inquired into the presence of fire at the extremes. . . . Fire when placed at the centre is under as much necessity to remain there as earth, for it will be related in the same way to any one of the points on the extremity; but in fact it will leave the centre, and move as we observe it to do, if nothing prevents it, towards the extremity. . . .[6]

Here, in Aristotle's extension of the mechanical equilibrium cases into his example of the man torn between equal attraction to food and drink, the physical theme of an equilibrium of forces was first transformed into a psychological balance of motives for choice.

The sixth-century Aristotelian commentator Simplicius offers the following discussion on this passage:

The sophists say that if a hair composed of similar parts is strongly stretched and the tension is identical throughout the whole, it would not break. For why would it break in this part rather than that, since the hair is identical in all its parts and the tension is identical? Analogously also in the case of a man who is exceedingly hungry and thirsty, and identically so in both, and identically lacking in food and drink, and for this reason identically motivated. Necessarily, they say, this man remains at rest, being moved to neither alternative. For why should he move to this one first, but not that, inasmuch as his need, and thus his motivation, is identical [on each side]. . . . The solution of such examples of identity is hardly surprising. For it is clear that the hair breaks. Even hypothesizing a fictitious thing with parts thus identical, plainly an identical tension at the ends and the middle is impossible. As to the other example, even if the man were equally distant, thirst would press him more. And if neither this nor that presses more, he will choose whatever he first happens on, as when two pleasant sights lie equally in our view. Whatever happens first we choose first. For identity does not completely obviate the choice, but simply makes the drive [toward one alternative] slower by the diversion of the other.[7]

In his discussion of the choice problem, Simplicius rigidly preserves the psychological character of the example as instancing a psychological equilibrium of motives. Simplicius's proposed solution to the problem does, however, offer, an interesting and original suggestion, namely, that indifferent choices can be resolved on grounds of *convenience*, and, in particular, that this can be accomplished by selecting the alternative upon which "we happen first." We shall have occasion to revert to this suggestion below.

6. Aristotle, *De caelo*, II 13, 295b24; trans. W. K. C. Guthrie in the Loeb Classical Library series.

7. *Commentaria in Aristotelem Graeca*, vol. 7, *Simplicii in Aristotelis de Caelo Commentaria*, ed. I. L. Heilberg (Berlin: Royal Prussian Academy, 1894), pp. 533–34; my translation.

Before the definition of the philosophic problem of choice without preference was to attain its ultimate logical sharpness of formulation, it was necessary that the mode of indifference at issue should become transformed from a *psychological* balance among diverse motivations into a strict *logical* indifference: a choice in the face of essentially identical alternatives. This was the step taken by al-Ghazâlî, the Algazel of the Schoolmen, and taken first, it would seem, by him.

Ghazâlî (1058–1111)

In his great work on the *Incoherence of the Philosophers*, the Arabic philosopher-theologian Ghazâlî is concerned, inter alia, to defend the orthodox Moslem theological thesis of the createdness of the world against the view maintained by the Arabic Aristotelians that the universe is eternal.[8] One of the reasonings that Ghazâlî endeavors to refute is an argument against the createdness of the world based on a concept of sufficient reason: Why, if the world is the creation of God, did he elect to create it when he did, rather than earlier or later?[9] Speaking, for the moment, on behalf of the (Aristotelian) philosophers, Ghazâlî presses this question home against the supporters of the createdness of the world:

But we philosophers know by the necessity of thought that one thing does not distinguish itself from a similar except by a differentiating principle, for if not, it would be possible that the world should come into existence, having the possibility both of existing and of not existing, and that the side of existence, although it has the same possibility as the side of non-existence, should be differentiated without a differentiating principle. If you answer that the Will of God is the differentiating principle, then one has to inquire what differentiates the will, i.e., the reason why it has been differentiated in such or such way. And if you answer: One does not inquire after the motives of the Eternal, well, let the world then be eternal, and let us not inquire after its Creator and its cause, since one does not inquire after the motives of the Eternal![10]

8. Al-Ghazâlî, *The Incoherence of the Philosophers*, trans. Michael E. Marmura (Provo, Utah: Brigham Young University Press, 1997). Ghazâlî's work is quoted *in extenso* in Averroes's commentary thereon, *The Incoherence of the Incoherence* (*Tahâfut al-Tahâfut*, trans. S. van den Bergh, 2 vols. [Leiden: Brill, 1954]); all further quotations from *Tahâfut al-Tahâfut* are drawn from van den Bergh's edition.

9. "How will you defend yourselves, theologians, against the philosophers, when they ... [say] that times are equivalent so far as the possibility that the Divine Will should attach itself to them is concerned ... ?"; Averroes, *Tahâfut al-Tahâfut*, vol. 1, p. 18.

10. Averroes, *Tahâfut al-Tahâfut*, vol. 1, p. 18. Cf. R. G. Collingwood's discussion in *The Idea of Nature* (Oxford, U.K.: Clarendon Press, 1945): "Unless God had a reason for His choice [to create the world as He did], it was no choice: it was something of which we have no conception whatever, and calling it a choice is merely throwing dust in our own eyes by pretending to equate it with a familiar human activity, the activity of choosing,

In opposing this argument, Ghazâlî proceeds by a closer examination of the concept of *will*, seeking to establish the drastic-seeming remedy of a denial that the concept of a sufficient reason for action is applicable to the supreme being,[11] whose will can of itself constitute a differentiating principle.[12] We must accept the idea of a "mere" will—of a choice made not conditionally because it subserves some other willed purpose, but categorically—simply and solely because its willer would have it so.[13] It is of the essence of an omnipotent will, Ghazâlî argues, that choice without reason be possible. The divine can provide a substitute for reason out of its own resources: *stat pro ratione voluntas*.[14]

We answer: The world exists, in the way it exists, in its time, with its qualities, and in its space, by the Divine Will and will is a quality which has the faculty of differentiating one thing from another, and if it had not this quality, power in itself would suffice. But, since power is equally related to two contraries and a dif-

---

which we do not in fact conceive it to have resembled. Choice is choice between alternatives, and these alternatives must be distinguishable, or they are not alternatives; moreover one must in some way present itself as more attractive than the other, or it cannot be chosen. [Cf. Averroes and Leibniz below—N.R.] . . . To speak of Him as choosing implies either that He chooses for a reason . . . or else He chooses for no reason, in which case he does not choose. And the dilemma cannot be evaded by a profession of reverent ignorance. You cannot wriggle out of it by saying that there are mysteries into which you will not pry: that God's ways are past finding out, or (if you prefer one kind of humbug to another) that these are ultimate problems. . . . Humbug of that kind arises from a kind of pseudo-religiosity. . . . It is humbug, because it was yourself that began prying into these mysteries. You dragged the name of God into your cosmology because you thought you could conjure with it. You now find you cannot; which proves, not that God is great, but that you are a bad conjurer" (pp. 40–41). Cf. Spinoza, who flatly characterizes the "will of God" as "the refuge for ignorance" (*Ethics*, bk. 1, Appendix).

11. In Christian theology, this was the position of Duns Scotus: "If it be asked why the divine will is determined rather to one of two incompatables than to the other, I reply: it is foolish [*indisciplinatus*] to seek causes and demonstrations for all things . . . there is no cause on account of which the will wills, just as there is no willing to will" (*Opus oxoniensis*, I.vii.5, 23–24). My translation is from the Latin cited by C. R. S. Harris in *Duns Scotus* (Oxford, U.K.: Clarendon Press, 1927), vol. 1, p. 181.

In Jewish theology, this view is espoused by Moses Maimonides: "We remain firm in our belief that the whole Universe was created in accordance with the will of God, and we do not inquire for any other cause or object. Just as we do not ask what is the purpose of God's existence so we do not ask what was the object of His will, which is the cause of the existence of all things with their present properties, both those that have been created and those that will be created" (*Guide for the Perplexed*, trans. M. Friedländer, vol. 3, p. 13 [American edition, New York: Pardes Publishing House, 1946], p. 276).

12. In his controversy with Leibniz, Samuel Clarke maintained just this thesis: "'Tis very true, that nothing *is*, without a sufficient *reason* it is, and why it is *thus* rather than *otherwise*. . . . But *sufficient reason* is ofttimes no other, than the *mere Will of God*" (Second Reply, §1). Leibniz, of course, flatly rejects this line of thought.

13. This idea is not unfamiliar to readers of the *Arabian Nights* as a characteristic feature of the type of medieval oriental despotism there depicted. When one in authority gives as his "reason" for wanting a thing done that "It must needs be so, there is no help for it," this is to be accepted as constituting a very convincing reason indeed.

14. Cf. note 21 below.

ferentiating principle is needed to differentiate one thing from a similar, it is said that the Eternal possesses besides His power a quality which can differentiate between two similars. And to ask why will differentiates one of two similars is like asking why knowledge must comprehend the knowable, and the answer is that "knowledge" is the term for a quality which has just this nature. And in the same way, "will" is the term for a quality the nature or rather the essence of which is to differentiate one thing from another.[15]

Ghazâlî proceeds to illustrate by means of an example that this capacity of differentiating where there is no difference is an essential characteristic power of all will, human as well as divine. This example is the focus of our present interest, and merits quotation in full:

How, then, will you refute those who say that rational proof has led to establishing in God a quality the nature of which is to differentiate between two similar things? And, if the word "will" does not apply, call it by another name, for let us not quibble about words! . . . Besides, we do not even with respect to our human will concede that this cannot be imagined. Suppose two similar dates in front of a man who has a strong desire for them, but who is unable to take them both. Surely he will take one of them through a quality in him the nature of which is to differentiate between two similar things. All the distinguishing qualities you have mentioned, like beauty or nearness or facility in taking, we can assume to be absent, but still the possibility of the taking remains. You can choose between two answers: either you merely say that an equivalence in respect to his desire cannot be imagined—but this is a silly answer, for to assume it is indeed possible—or you say that if an equivalence is assumed, the man will remain for ever hungry and perplexed, looking at the dates without taking one of them, and without a power to choose or to will, distinct from his desire. And this again is one of those absurdities which are recognized by the necessity of thought. Everyone, therefore, who studies, in the human and the divine, the real working of the act of choice, must necessarily admit a quality the nature of which is to differentiate between two similar things.[16]

Here for the first time the problem of choice without preference is given its ultimate logical formulation. The examples in explanation of Anaximander's views involve a physical balance through the equilibrium of forces; and in Aristotle's example we have the psychological balance of contrary drives or motivations of equal intensity. Ghazâlî's formulation, however, sharpens the dilemma to its logical edge: it poses

15. Ghazâlî, as quoted in Averroes, *Tahâfut al-Tahâfut*, vol. 1, p. 19.
16. Averroes, *Tahâfut al-Tahâfut*, vol. 1, p. 21. This is Ghazâli's reply to a hypothetical philosopher opponent who said: "The assumption of a quality the nature of which is to differentiate one thing from a similar one is something incomprehensible, say even contradictory, for 'similar' means not to be differentiated, and 'differentiated' means not similar. . . . If someone who is thirsty has before him two cups of water, similar in everything in respect to his aim, it will not be possible for him to take either of them. No, he

the problem of *the possibility of rational choice in the face of essentially identical alternatives.*

Ghazâlî also poses the problem of an indifferent choice in relation to why God created the universe at one time rather than another.[17] His solution to the problem does not take the simpler line that the creation of the universe is not a creation *in* time but a creation *of* time. Rather, he attributes to God a special "determinative principle" (Arabic *marjah,* i.e., preponderant) which can operate to favor one of two similar objects.[18]

In the Latin translation by Calo Calonymus (ca. 1340) of Averroes's *Tahâfut,* where Ghazâlî's work is cited at length, the definition of the will is rendered as a faculty *"cuius natura sit distinguere rem ab indifferenti absque eo quod sit ibi approprians inclinans actionem unius duorum indifferentium prae alio."*[19] This appears to be the first identifiable text in which the Latin term *indifferentia* is used in relation to the will.[20] However, Ghazâlî's prime concern is not with human free will (which he denies) but with the autonomy of God's will—its being unfettered by any external constraints whatsoever, constraints of reason included.[21] And in this context he put the problem of choice in conditions of symmetric indifference upon the agenda.

By right of historical precedence, then, the problem of Buridan's Ass ought perhaps more appropriately be denominated as that of "Ghazâlî's Dates." But it seems likely—in view of the manner in which Ghazâlî introduces the problem into his discussion—that he found it already in current consideration.[22] He employs it as an example admirably suited

---

can only take the one he thinks more beautiful or lighter or nearer to his right hand, if he is right-handed, or act for some such reason, hidden or known. Without this the differentiation of the one from the other cannot be imagined" (Averroes, *Tahâfut al-Tahâfut,* vol. 1, p. 19).

17. Averroes, *Tahâfut al-Tahâfut,* vol. 1, p. 18.

18. See S. van den Bergh's note in *The Incoherence of the Incoherence,* vol. 2, pp. 17–18, which traces the idea of Stoic *adiaphoron.*

19. Beatrice H. Zedler, ed., *Averroes' Destructio Destructionum Philosophiae Algazelis in the Latin Version of Calo Colonymos* (Milwaukee: Marquette University Press, 1961), p. 89.

20. While Colonymos's text only became available in the 1320s, other translations of Ghazâlî's work were available earlier. For instance, in 1278 the Spanish Dominican Raymond Martin completed a book on "The Battle of Faith against the Moors and the Jews," which contained extensive references to Ghazâlî's work. See B. H. Zedler, *Averroes' Destructio Destructionum Philosophiae Algazelis in the Latin Version of Calo Colonymos,* pp. 21–22.

21. While Ghazâlî's discussion in the *Incoherence* favors human free will, elsewhere—as in the *Book of Faith in Divine Unity and Trust in Divine Providence*—he denies a liberty of indifference to human. For details, see David Burrell, "Al-Ghazâlî on Created Freedom," *American Catholic Philosophical Journal* 73 (1999): 135–58.

22. He may well have owed it to a Syriac or Arabic commentator on Aristotle, presumably in a gloss on *De caelo,* 295b10–35, although the Greek commentators do not seem to have modified Aristotle's formulation of the example (cf. the quotation for Simplicius

to support the concept of a "mere" will—inscrutable from the standpoint of reasons and reasonings, capable of effecting differentiation where there is no difference.[23]

Ghazâlî associates himself with the school of Moslem theologians called Ashᶜarites, after its founder al-Ashᶜari. Opposing the rationalistic Muᶜtazilites, the Ashᶜarites make room for a certain irrationality, or better, nonrationality in matters theological, denying that reason alone is capable of attaining religious truths:

The difference between the Ashᶜarite and Muᶜtazilite conceptions of God cannot be better expressed than by the following passage which is found twice in Ghazâlî . . . and to which by tradition is ascribed the breach between al-Ashᶜari and the Muᶜtazilites:

Let us imagine a child and a grown-up in Heaven who both died in the True Faith, but the grown-up has a higher place than the child. And the child will ask God, "Why did you give that man a higher place?" And God will answer, "He has done many good works." Then the child will say, "Why did you let me die so soon that I was prevented from doing good?" God will answer, "I knew that you would grow up a sinner, therefore it was better that you should die a child." Then a cry goes up from the damned in the depths of Hell, "Why, O Lord, did you not let us die before we became sinners?"

Ghazâlî adds to this: "The imponderable decisions of God cannot be weighed by the scales of reason and Muᶜtazilism."[24]

Ghazâlî's position is that God's will is omnipotent, totally self-sufficient, and free of all constraint—even that of reason.

---

given above and also see C. A. Brandis's edition of the *Scholia in Aristotelem*, published by the Royal Prussian Academy, vol. 4 [1836], p. 507). Thus Léon Gauthier argues that Ghazâlî must have found the example already present in Alfarabi or in Avicenna "because he explicitly states at the end of the first Preamble of the *Tahâfut* that throughout this work, in refuting the doctrines of the Greek philosophers, especially Aristotle and his commentators, he limits his considerations to those ideas taken up and endorsed by their two great Moslem disciples, Alfarabi and Avicenna" ("L'argument de l'Ane de Buridan et les philosophes arabes," *Mélanges René Basset, Publications de l'Institut des Hautes-Études Marocaines*, vol. 10 [Paris, 1923], pp. 209–33; see esp. p. 224).

23. This position was adopted by several of the Scholastics. Johannes Gerson, for example, says that the will *est sibi frequenter sufficiens causa vel ratio* and that it can choose one thing and reject another in such a manner that *nec exterior alia ratio quaranda est: sic volo, sic jubeo; stat pro ratione voluntas* (*Opera Omnia*, ed. M. L. E. Du Pin [Antwerp and Amsterdam, 1706], vol. 3, pp. 443–44). On Gerson's theory of the will, see Hermann Siebeck, "Die Willenslehre bei Duns Scotus und seinen Nachfolgern," *Zeitschrift für Philosophie und philosophische Kritik* 112 (1898): 179–216.

24. S. van den Bergh, p. x of his "Introduction" to the *The Incoherence of the Incoherence.* Cf. St. Paul: "Nay but, O man, who art thou that repliest against God? Shall the thing formed say to him that formed it, Why hast thou made me thus? Hath not the potter

Averroes (1126–1198)

In his book on the *Incoherence of the Incoherence*, a detailed critical commentary on Ghazâlî's *Incoherence of the Philosophers*, Averroes undertook to defend the Arabic Aristotelians against Ghazâlî's onslaught. It is worth quoting in full his criticism of Ghazâlî's example of the dates:

It is assumed that in front of a man there are two dates, similar in every way, and it is supposed that he cannot take them both at the same time. It is supposed that no special attraction need be imagined for him in either of them, and that nevertheless he will of necessity distinguish one of them by taking it. But this is an error. For, when one supposes such a thing, and a willer whom necessity prompts to eat or to take the date, then it is by no means a matter of distinguishing between two similar things when, in this condition, he takes one of the two dates . . . whichever of the two dates he may take, his aim will be attained and his desire satisfied. His will attaches itself therefore merely to the distinction between the fact of taking one of them and the fact of leaving them altogether; it attaches itself by no means to the act of taking one definite date and distinguishing this act from leaving the other (that is to say, when it is assumed that the desires for the two are equal); he does not prefer the act of taking the one to the act of taking the other, but he prefers the act of taking one of the two, whichever it may be, and he gives a preference to the act of taking over the act of leaving. This is self evident. For distinguishing one from the other means giving a preference to the one over the other, and one cannot give a preponderance to one of two similar things in so far as it is similar to the other—although in their existence as individuals they are not similar since each of two individuals is different from the other by reason of a quality exclusive to it. If, therefore, we assume that the will attaches itself to that special character of one of them, then it can be imagined that the will attaches to the one rather than the other because of the element of difference existing in both. But then the will does not attach to two similar objects, in so far as they are similar.[25]

Essentially, then, Averroes's position was that (1) it is necessary to grant the preferability of taking-one-date over against taking-neither-date; but (2) there would be no reasonable way of choosing one particular date were it actually to follow from the hypothesis of the problem that there is no reason for preferring one over the other; however, (3) since there are two distinct dates, they must be *distinguishable* so that there must be some element of difference—at least a difference in *identity*—between them, and the will can and must therefore fix upon such an element of difference as a "reason" for preference. Thus Averroes simply re-

---

power over the clay, of the same lump to make one vessel unto honour and another unto dishonour?" (Romans 9:20–21). Cf. also Omar Khayyám's *Rubaiyât.*

25. S. van den Bergh, trans., Averroes, *The Incoherence of the Incoherence*, vol. 1, pp. 22–23.

asserts—in the teeth of Ghazâlî's example—the impossibility of choice without preference. And he resolves the impasse by holding that a difference will inevitably exist to provide the "reason" for a choice.[26]

The obvious criticism of Averroes's solution is implicit in the quotation marks that have been put about the word *reason*. For it is assumed in the defining statement of the problem that the differences between the objects (whatever they be) are such as to have no rationally valid bearing on the matter of their relative preferability. There consequently is, *by hypothesis*, no legitimacy or validity from the standpoint of reasonableness, in any attempt to base a reasoned preference upon these differences.

St. Thomas Aquinas (ca. 1227–1274)

In discussing "whether man chooses of necessity or freely," Aquinas employed the example of choice without preference as a means of formulating a possible objection to the thesis of freedom of the will (an objection that he subsequently endeavors to refute).

If two things are absolutely equal, man is not moved to one more than to the other; thus if a hungry man, as Plato says,[27] be confronted on either side with two portions of food equally appetizing and at an equal distance, he is not moved towards one more than to the other; and he finds this the reason of the immobility of the earth in the middle of the world.[28] Now if that which is equal-

26. In his highly instructive footnotes on Averroes's text, S. van den Bergh, the learned translator of the *Tahâfut al-Tahâfut* into English, writes: "Averroes misses the point here completely. Certainly the donkey will take one or the other of the two bundles rather than die, but the question is what determines its taking the one rather than the other. Obviously it will take the one that comes first to hand; only, when there is a complete equivalence of all conditions, this is impossible, and Spinoza says bluntly that the donkey will have to die. As a matter of fact, in such cases a complete equivalence of psychological and physical conditions is never reached; no living body even is strictly symmetrical, and if *per impossibile* such an equivalence could be momentarily reached, the world is changing, not static, and the donkey will move and not die" (*The Incoherence of the Incoherence*, vol. 2, p. 20). The point here is twofold: (1) that a complete equilibrium of opposing motivations can never actually be reached, and (2) that even if such an equilibrium, albeit impossible, were to be reached, such a condition would necessarily pass due to an inherent instability. The first of these has been asserted in the present context by numerous writers—Montaigne, Bayle, and Leibniz, among others—and we shall return to it below. However, van den Bergh is the first to urge the second thesis: that a psychological equilibrium would be intrinsically unstable, and would become resolved because "the world is changing, not static." However, since physical equilibrium is in theory possible in a changing world, it would seem that a better case must be made out for this thesis.

27. Aristotle is apparently meant here, though there is a transition to Plato toward the end of this sentence.

28. The text I am quoting reads "and he finds the reason of this in the immobility of the earth in the middle of the world"—which simply does not make sense. The original reads: ". . . , *ut Plato dicit, assignans rationem quietis terrae in medio.*"

ly eligible with something else cannot be chosen, much less can that be chosen which appears the less so. Therefore if two or more things are available, of which one appears to be more eligible, it is impossible to choose any of the others. Therefore that which appears to hold the first place is chosen of necessity. But every act of choosing is in regard to something that seems in some way better. Therefore every choice is made necessarily.[29]

Aquinas thus insists that "every act of choosing is in regard to something that seems in some way better": the will can only choose an alternative adjudged superior by the intellect. (This position is often characterized as Aquinas's "intellectualism.") Observe, however, that this intellectualist position that one must *always* choose whatever reason decisively rules as superior does not of itself entail a rationalistic position holding that the will can *only* choose what reason prefers, so that choice is hamstrung in the absence of rational preferability. So even for the intellectualist, the Buridan-style issue remains unsettled.

After a general discussion of determinism, Aquinas returns briefly to the example of choice among equals, in effect dismissing it summarily:

If two things be proposed as equal under one aspect, nothing hinders us from considering in one of them some [other] particular point of superiority, so that the will has a bent towards the one rather than towards the other.[30]

Thus Aquinas does not view the problem of choice among equals as a hopeless paradox that condemns its victim to utter inaction, since—so he insists—the intellect has the capacity of viewing them under some aspect under which one of them is accorded "some particular point of superiority."

Aquinas's line of thought seems to be essentially as follows: Let it be that I offer you the choice between A and B, these being two wholly indifferent *objects* of choice (be it haystacks, dates, or coins). But let it also be that I offer you a reward for selecting A. You now have a good reason for *choosing* A in the absence of every reason for *preferring* A to B. The operation of such an object-extraneous incentive can clearly break the tie for rational choice in the absence of object preferability in situations of symmetry. It was, apparently, the position of Aquinas—and of Averroes before him—that even in the absence of a difference between the objects of choice the will is *always* able to fix some situational difference to achieve a rational basis of selection.

29. *Summa theologica*, II, i, 13.6; cited from the translation of the Fathers of the English Dominican Province (2d ed., London, 1927). On Aquinas's views regarding free will, see J. B. Kowlee, "Free Will and Free Choice," in Norman Kretzmann et al., eds., *The Cambridge History of Later Medieval Philosophy* (Cambridge, U.K.: Cambridge University Press, 1982), pp. 629–41.

30. *Summa theologica*, II, i, 13.6

Peter John Olivi (1248–1298)

Peter John Olivi was a French-born Franciscan philosopher who ex-pounded an account of the will based on the liberty of indifference much in the manner adumbrated by al-Ghazâlî.[31] Thus, leaning on his date example, Olivi writes:

When there is some number of equivalent things that are equally useful, noth-ing explains the will's adoption of one or the other of them except the freedom by which one is equally able to do this or that. Suppose there are two pieces of fruit or two people that are in every way and through all things similar and equivalent. Nevertheless, the will attaches itself to one of the two and leaves the other . . . It often happens that we want to take one of two coins. We deliberate and ascertain that there is just as good reason to take the one as the other. In these circumstances, we might think that we would be able to take and keep the one coin just as well as the other. Then, when we take one of the two, we mani-festly feel that we do this from freedom of the will alone and not from some greater satisfaction in the one as opposed to the other.[32]

And so Olivi employs reasoning of the Buridan's Ass type to substanti-ate a tie-breaking power not for God's will alone, as per the Arabic Muʿtazilites, but for the human will as well, albeit not for brutes. Olivi was apparently the first to speak explicitly and extensively about the will's capacity to handle matters of indifference *(indifferentia)* in situa-tions of choice.[33] (While Olivi does not flatly say that the baffled beast would starve, the entire tenor of his discussion implies this.[34]) And in making his point he was the first to propose coinage as a realistic, rather then a makeshift, instance of a situation in common life involving essen-tially indistinguishable objects between which choice is thoroughly in-diffcrent.[35] (In this, as we shall see below, he anticipated Thomas Reid by some five hundred years!)

31. For biographical information on Olivi, see the *Stanford [Internet] Encyclopedia of Phi-losophy*, and for further details, see David Burr, "The Persecution of Peter Olivi," in *Trans-actions of the American Philosophical Society* 66, pt. 5 (1976). On Olivi's position on freedom of the will, see Bonnie Kent, *Virtues of the Will* (Washington, D.C.: The Catholic University of America Press, 1995), and Robert Pasnan, "Olivi on Human Freedom," in Alain Boureau and Sylvain Piron, eds., *Pierre de Jean Olivi (1248–1298): Pensée scolastique, dissi-dence sprituelle, et société* (Paris: J. Vrin, 1999), pp. 15–26. Olivi's position in relation to the problem of Buridan's Ass is informatively discussed in Sharon Kaye, "Buridan's Ass and Peter John Olivi" (as yet unpublished), and also in "Why the Liberty of Indifference Is Worth Wanting," *History of Philosophy Quarterly* 21 (2004): 21–42.
32. Fr. Petrus Iohannis Olivi, O.F.M., *Quaestiones in II librum Sententiarum* (Quarrachi: Collegii S. Bonaventurae, 1924), vol. 2, Q. 57, pp. 326–27.
33. See Sharon Kaye, "Why the Liberty of Indifference Is Worth Wanting," 19–20.
34. Ibid.
35. The Skeptics of antiquity were fond of dwelling on the limitations of man's sensory discriminations by adducing the issue of distinguishing between observationally identical

Dante (1265–1321)

Our problem now for the first time steps forth upon the stage of world literature. The events of the *Divine Comedy*, *Paradiso* 3, bring to Dante's mind two perplexing moral problems which—in Canto 4—he wishes Beatrice to clarify for him: Does an evil action performed under duress detract from the moral merit of the agent? Can a good action done in atonement lessen the moral onus of a wrongful deed?

Between two foods alike to appetite, and like afar, a free man, I suppose, would starve before of either he would bite;
So would a lamb, between the hungry throes of two fierce wolves, feel equipoise of dread, so hesitate a hound between two does.
Whence by my doubts alike solicited inevitably, censure can be none, nor commendation if I nothing said.
And I said nothing; but desire upon my face was pictured, questioning as well set forth more fervently than words had done.

So Beatrice replied, and said: "These questions balance equally the beam of thy desire."

In his notes on this passage the translator aptly remarks that "[i]t is in artistic keeping that a Canto dealing so largely with the dilemma of the broken vow should begin with this ancient paradox."[36] Furthermore, it is noteworthy that this problem context of punishment and reward in the world to come in which the example occurs in Dante is essentially the same as in discussions by Arabic philosophers and theologians (see the conclusion of the foregoing discussion of Ghazâlî). However, the problem as presented by Dante is that of conflict among equal desires (or fears—here for the first time), as in Aristotle's formulation, and not that of choice between essentially identical objects, as with Ghazâlî and the Arabs.

Duns Scotus (1265–1308)

As was the case with various of his fellow Franciscan, the philosopher Scotus veers off in a different direction from that taken by Aquinas. For Scotus, the will is not a member of a team, geared systemically to the op-

---

items, such as similar eggs and impressions of the same seal. See Augustine, *Soliloquies*, bk. 1, p. 6; and cf. David Hume's question "What so like as two eggs?" But contrast Leibniz and the linden-tree leaves at Herrenhausen.

36. Dante, *Divine Comedy*, 2:1–26 (with deletions). I quote from the translation prepared by Melville B. Anderson for the Oxford University Press edition of the *Divine Comedy* in "The World's Classics" series. Many of the great philosophical problems and controversies of the age are discussed in the *Divine Comedy*.

eration of reason: it is an independent agent in its own right, a self-mover potentially in conflict with reason. On this basis the will is supreme in matters of decision, predominant insofar as it *praecipit deliberationem* or *eligit praevian deliberatione*, a position it occupies when it acts freely, *quia libere imperat illam deliberationeme et libere eligit.*[37] Scotus thus emphatically endorses the liberty of indifference of the human will.[38] For, as he saw it, the will can indeed choose the lesser of otherwise similar alternatives.

Scotus, like Olivi, employed the term *indifferentia* to characterize the choice situation,[39] contrasting the case of a stymied appetitive bull with that of a tie-breaking rational human being.[40] His discussion of the issues has led some philosophers to credit him with priority over Buridan in relation to the Buridan's Ass problem,[41] though this overlooks the fact that Scotus's position on the issue is substantially the same as that of Al-Ghazâlî and Olivi.

William of Ockham (ca. 1282–ca. 1348)

William of Ockham was another Franciscan voluntarist who, like Olivi and Scotus, defended the liberty of indifference.[42] As he saw it:

37. Duns Scotus, *Opera oxoniensia*, vol. 1, d 39, qq 5, 15, and vol. 3, d 33, qq 1, 22. This work has been edited by P. Mrcanus Fernandez Garcia, O.F.M. (Qarrachi: Collegii S. Bonaventure, 1914).

38. On Duns Scotus, see H. Siebeck, "Die Willenslehre bei Duns Scotus und seinen Nachfolgern," in the *Zeitschrift für Philosophie* 112 (1898): 179–216. Etienne Gilson surmises as follows: "Mais c'est sans doute chez Duns Scot que la spontanéité du vouloir déjà si fortement affirmé par saint Anselme, attaint son expression definitive. . . . La liberté scotiste d'indifference ne fait donc qu'un avec la spontancité du vouloir, qui demeure le seul element possible de contingence devant les determinations de la raison" (*L'ésprit de la philosophie médiévale* [Paris: J. Vrin, 1932], pp. 104–7). See also Mortimer J. Adler, *The Idea of Freedom* (Garden City, N.Y.: Doubleday, 1958–1961), p. 524.

39. John Duns Scotus, *Quaestiones Quoadlibetales*, Q. 18, n. 9, and also QQ. 16–17. For the relevant texts, see Felix Alluntis and Alan B. Wolter, *God and Creatures: The Quodlibetal Questions* (Princeton, N.J.: Princeton University Press, 1975), esp. pp. 369–98; and *Quaestiones in metaphysicam*, 9, q. 15, in Alan B. Wolter, *Duns Scotus on the Will and Morality* (Washington, D.C.: The Catholic University of America Press, 1980), pp. 144–73.

40. "Nam uos vidit berbum, quae movet appetitum suum et ex illo appetitu movet progressive ad herbam; sed in motu illo occurret objectum magis delictabile fortius movens appetitum, et hunc sistitur a primo motu, et tamen nos libere, quia necessario movetur ab illo majore delectabili occurrente, quamquam causaliter occurat" (*Opera oxoniensia*, ed. P. Marcanus Fernandez Garcia, O.F.M. [Quarrachi: Collegii S. Bonaventure, 1914], vol. 2, d. 25, q. 1, pp. 690–91.)

41. See Vernon J. Bourke, *Will in Western Thought* (New York: Sheed & Ward, 1964), p. 85.

42. For his position, see G. Gál et al., eds., *Ockham: Opera Theologica*, 9 vols. (St. Bonaventure, N.Y.: Franciscan Institute, 1967ff.). For an extensive account of Ockham on freedom, see Marilyn McCord Adams, "Ockham on Will, Nature, and Morality," in *The Cambridge Companion to Ockham* (Cambridge, U.K.: Cambridge University Press, 1999), pp.

The [human] will is freely able to will something and not to will it. . . . To deny
every agent this capability for both alternatives alike is to destroy all praise and
blame, all counsel and deliberation, and all freedom of the will [*omnem liber-
tatem voluntatis*]. And then a man will be no more free by his will than an ass by
its sensory appetite.[43]

So here, the ass does at last make its appearance in the context of our
problem. Unhappily Ockham's passage continues "as is shown elsewhere" [*sicut alias ostenditur*], and this elsewhere has not as yet been
found. And here again—as with Olivi—the dialectic is that of a defense
of human free will through a contrast with the sensory determinism
that is taken to prevail with brutes. The "voluntarist" position of an autonomy of the will that is a staple of Franciscan thought is once again in
operation.

Buridan (ca. 1295–1358)

The French Scholastic philosopher Jean Buridan supported a middle
way between the intellectualism of Aquinas and the voluntarianism of
the Franciscans.[44] In view of his extensive discussion of the relevant issues, it has long occasioned astonishment that Buridan's Ass is nowhere
to be met with in Buridan's writings.[45] Among others, Bayle, Schopenhauer, Sir William Hamilton, and Pierre Duhem attest to long hours of
fruitless search.[46] Bayle has even conjectured that the phrase "Ass of

245–72. See also Marilyn McCord Adams, "William Ockham: Voluntarist or Naturalist?,"
in John F. Whippel, ed., *Studies in Medieval Philosophy* (Washington, D.C.: The Catholic
University of America Press, 1987), pp. 203–35; and Jerzy B. Korolec, "Free Will and Free
Choice," in *The Cambridge History of Later Medieval Philosophy*, ed. N. Kretzman et al. (Cambridge, U.K.: Cambridge University Press, 1982), pp. 629–41.

43. Ockham, *Opera philosophia*, ed. Gál et al., p. 321.

44. On Buridan's position regarding intellectual determinism of the will, see Jack Zupko, "Freedom of Choice in Buridan's Moral Psychology," *Medieval Studies* 57 (1995):
75–99; and Edward J. Monahan, "Human Liberty and Free Will According to John Buridan," *Medieval Studies* 16 (1954): 80–108. See also Risto Saarinen, "Moral Weakness and
Human Action in John Buridan's Ethics," in Heikka Kirjavainen, ed., *Faith, Will and Gram-
mar* (Helsinki: Luther-Agricola Society, 1986), pp. 109–39, and *Weakness of the Will in Medieval Thought: From Augustine to Buridan* (Leiden: Brill, 1994), pp. 161–87. See also James
J. Walsh, "Is Buridan a Sceptic about Free Will?," *Vivarium* 2 (1994): 50–61; and Jerzy B.
Korolec, "La philosophie de la liberté de Jean Buridan," *Studia Mediewistyczne* 15 (1974):
120–51.

45. See B. Geyer in the 11th (last) edition of vol. 2, *Die Patristische und Scholastische
Philosophie*, of F. Ueberweg's *Grundriss der Geschichte der Philosophie* (Leipzig: O. S. Reisland,
1929), p. 597. A supposedly complete edition of Buridan's writings was published by
Dullard in Paris in 1500 and was reprinted in ensuing decades.

46. Bayle writes: "The Ass of Buridan was a kind of proverb or example which was long
used in the schools. I do not know if I have determined with precision just what it was, for
I have found no one able to explain it to me, nor any book that enters into detail on this
matter" (*Dictionnaire*, art. "Buridan"). Schopenhauer writes that "one has now been vainly

Buridan" may first have gained currency in connection with an entirely different point of logical difficulty or complexity discussed by Buridan as a *pons asinorum* in logic,[47] and subsequently the phrase came to be shifted in its application to the well-known ambivalence example.[48]

There is no question, however, but that Buridan was familiar, in essence, with the example to which he lent his name. In his unpublished commentary on Aristotle's *De caelo*,[49] in a gloss on the very passage of 2:13 that we had occasion to examine above, Buridan gives the example of a dog—not an ass!—dying of hunger between two equal portions of food.[50] It seems clear, however, that this transposed example in an obscure manuscript could scarcely have been the direct origin of the notorious paradox, and that it must have been associated with Buridan in some more immediate and prominent way.

At any rate, the example of the ass fits in a very natural and congenial way into the problem context of Buridan's theory of the will. In his *Quaestiones* on the *Nicomachean Ethics*, Buridan treats the problem of hu-

---

searching his writings for some hundred years" for the ass of Buridan, and that "I myself own an edition of his *Sophismata*, apparently printed already in the fifteenth century . . . in which I have repeatedly searched for it in vain, although asses occur as examples on virtually every page" (*Prize Essay on the Freedom of the Will*, p. 58 of the original edition). Sir William Hamilton states that "the supposition of the ass, etc., is not, however, as I have ascertained, to be found in his [i.e., Buridan's] writings" (*Reid's Works*, ed. W. Hamilton, vol. 1, p. 38, in the seventh, eighth, and possibly other editions). Pierre Duhem writes: "I have searched in vain for the argument of the ass in all of the writings attributed to Buridan; in those places where it might reasonably occur, we encounter instead wholly different examples" (*Études sur Léonard de Vinci*, 3 vols. [Paris: A. Hermann, 1906–1913], vol. 3, p. 16).

47. This would probably have been the set of rules for determining suitable middle terms in the construction of syllogistic arguments in support of a given conclusion, which have long been ascribed (incorrectly) to Buridan. See B. Geyer's revision of vol. 2 of Ueberweg's *Grundriss*, p. 597.

48. Bayle, *Dictionnaire*, art. "Buridan." Bayle also suggests that the phrase may originally have referred to the "*an*" (Latin) of Buridan—along the lines of *utrum* as common in Scholastic usage—and subsequently metamorphosed into the "asne" (French) of Buridan. This "explanation" is rather far-fetched.

49. I here refer to Buridan's *Expositio textus* of the *De caelo*, and not to the *Quaestiones* that he also devoted to that work. The former is unpublished, and exists in only two manuscript versions: Bruges 477 (210 v–238v), and Vat. lat. 2162 (57r–79r); see Anneliese Maier, *Zwei Grundprobleme der Scholastischen Naturphilosophie* (Rome: Edizioni di storia e letteratura, 1968), p. 205. The *Quaestiones super libris quattuor de Caelo et mundo* has been published by E. A. Moody (Cambridge, Mass.: Harvard University Press, 1942). In this work there is, however, no mention of our example.

50. See the article "Buridan" by L. Minio-Paluello in the *Encyclopedia Britannica* (1956 edition). This almost, though not quite, bears out Schopenhauer's conjecture that Buridan's example was adopted from that of Aristotle's man perplexed by a choice between food and drink, but that Buridan "changed the man to an ass, solely because it was the custom of this parsimonious Scholastic to take for his example either Socrates and Plato, or *asinum*" (*Freedom of the Will*, p. 59). It might seem unseemly to present the greats in perplexity.

man freedom.[51] He asks: "Would the will, having been put between two opposites, with all being wholly alike on both sides, be able to determine itself rather to one opposed alternative than to the other?"[52] As an illustration of a problem of this type, Buridan addresses the situation of two alternative routes leading to the same destination, though not, alas, our ass example.[53] It is highly probable, however, that the example was given by Buridan (in its henceforth traditional description of an ass placed between equally appetizing heaps of hay) in some more memorable manner, possibly in one of his several yet unpublished commentaries on Aristotle, or perhaps it arose in a verbal context, either in his influential lectures, or in oral disputation or discussion.[54]

Buridan's answer to the problem of indifferent choice is given in terms of his theory of the will which sought for a middle way. As he saw it, neither need the will necessarily implement the evaluative rulings of the intellect, nor is it at liberty to overrule and contravene them: it cannot act *against* reason. Instead, it has the suspensive power of inaction, of deferring choice to a later stage. In its relation to the intellect, the will is neither bound to acquiescence and acceptance *(acceptatio)* nor to negation and overruling *(refutatio)*, but autonomously has the power to suspend choice—to defer *(deffere)*.[55] For while if two objects be adjudged by reason as wholly equivalent, the will is unable to act independently to break the deadlock and opt for one or the other, nevertheless it can determine to "wait and see." Buridan grants to the will the status of a *facul-*

51. *Quaestiones super decem libros Aristotelis ad Nicomachum*, III, i.

52. Translated from the quotation given by P. Duhem, *Études sur Léonard de Vinci*, vol. 3, pp. 17–18 (reprint, Paris, 1955). This formulation of the problem of freedom derives from Buridan's master, William of Ockham, who characterizes freedom as *potestas qua possum indifferenter et contingenter effectum ponere, ita quod possum eundem effectum causare nulla diversitate circa illam potentiam facta* (*Quodlibeta*, vol. 1, p. 16).

53. The instance he gives is the following: "I could go from Paris to Avignon either via Lyon or Dun-le-Roy." Ludovico Molina says that "Cyril of Alexandria wrote in the third chapter of his four-book commentary on St. John's Gospel: 'Man is an animal that has freedom, and can choose to elect either the right or the left road (i.e., either virtue or vice)'" (*Concordia liberi arbitrii*, XIV, xiii, 23, §4). Buridan also discusses the problem of choice confronting the mariner in a stormy sea, agonized about whether to jettison his cargo or risk his life; see P. Duhem, *Études sur Léonard de Vinci*, vol. 3, p. 18.

54. This latter possibility would accord well with the oft-voiced conjecture that the example of Buridan's Ass actually derives from an *objection* to Buridan's views; see, e.g., B. Geyer's revision of Ueberweg's *Grundriss*, p. 597. Correspondingly, Sir William Hamilton has plausibly conjectured that "perhaps it [i.e., the example of Buridan's Ass] was orally advanced in disputation, or in lecturing, as an example in illustration of his Determinism; perhaps it was employed by his opponents as an instance to reduce that doctrine to absurdity" (*Reid's Works*, ed. Hamilton, vol. 2, p. 690). We know that for many years Buridan *professa dans l'université de Paris avec une extrême reputation* (Bayle, *Dictionnaire*, art. "Buridan"). Thus Sharon Kaye, in her "Buridan's Ass and Peter John Olivi," also conjectures that Ockham the donkey version of the problem in a public debate against Buridan.

55. See Zupko, "Freedom of Choice in Buridan's Moral Psychology," pp. 94–97.

tas suspensiva which, while it cannot go *counter* to reason, can suspend action. Just this position makes it almost irresistibly tempting to see the ass example as the crux of an argument *against* Buridan.[56]

But matters are not quite so straightforward. For Buridan, ties of indifference between objects of choice, while possible, will arise only because a fallible intellect is unable to comprehend the full complexities of real situations. And then the agent is not stymied like the traditional donkey. For God has made provision that an agent "can, with everything else disposed in the same way, freely determine himself to either of two opposites." But this self-determination is not an intellectual (rational) operation but "is the natural property of a voluntary agent, just as the ability to laugh belongs to man."[57] Brute animals have no free will because they have no will at all: their modus operandi lies in a purely sensuous appetite, whereas willing is an intellectual appetite. (He speaks of *appetitus intellictus, qui est voluntas*.)[58] Buridan supports this view of the will by saying that those who claim free will for man but deny it to animals find themselves in difficult straits:

It seems to me that, to show the difference between the freedom of our will and the lack of freedom to which the actuating faculty of a dog is subject, it would be better to trust to faith than to natural reason.[59] For it would be difficult indeed to show that when our will is wholly indifferent between two opposed acts, then it [in contradistinction to the actuating faculty of a dog] could decide for one or the other alternative without being so determined by some external factor.[60]

In the context of Buridan's theory of will, the ass example can, with its characteristic double-edgedness, serve possibly as a somewhat drastic example in illustration of Buridan's intellectual determinism of the will, or alternately as an example adduced by Buridan's opponents in an attempt to render this doctrine absurd.

In any case, the story of "Buridan's Ass" passed (in various guises) even into the popular lore of all the European peoples. I cite as one instance the Spanish folktale of late medieval vintage:

56. See note 48 above.   57. Ibid., p. 97.
58. Ibid., p. 95, n. 64.

59. This is apparently Buridan's final and considered position on the subject of the freedom of the will: he holds this *not* to be subject to philosophical demonstration or refutation, but a matter of *faith*. See pp. 84–85 of K. Michalski, "Les Courants Philosophiques à Oxford et à Paris pendant le XIVᵉ Siècle," *Bulletin Internationale de l'Académie Polonaise des Sciences et des Lettres* (Classe d'Histoire et de Philosophie, 1919–1920), pp. 59–88.

60. Buridan, *In Metaphysicam Aristotelis Quaestiones*, quoted by P. Duhem in *Études sur Léonard de Vinci*, vol. 3, pp. 20–21. Duhem in this work attributes these *Quaestiones* on the *Metaphysics* to *another* John Buridan, but in the face of manuscript evidence discovered by himself, he subsequently reverses himself (*Le Système du Monde*, vol. 4, p. 126).

EL BURRO DE BURIDÁN: Una día el burro de un filósofo llamado Juan Buridán—y por eso llamado el burro de Buridán—perece de hambre y sed. Teniendo a un lado una gran cantidad de avena y otro un cubo de agua, el burro nunca puede saber si tiene sed o hambre. El burro no sabe que decidir: si comer o beber. En esta horrible vacilación le sorprende la muerte.[61]

Khôdja Zâdeh (1415–1488)

The Turkish philosopher Khôdja Zâdeh, in his reply to Averroes's criticism of the theologians, written in Arabic, again under the title of Ghazâlî's work *Tahâfut al-Falâsifa*, takes up the problem of choice without preference just where Averroes had left it (of course without knowledge of the intervening Western discussions). Taking the part of Ghazâlî against Averroes, Khôdja Zâdeh argues that a genuinely "free" agent can ipso facto resolve the paradox of choice without preference:

> If one puts a loaf of bread before a hungry man, he will begin to eat a certain part to the exclusion of all others, without determination of a volition favoring this part to the rest. You object: "I do not grant that he will begin to eat a part without determination of a volition in its favour; for why would not this volition have for its deciding reason that one part is closer to him, or more appealing, or better baked?" I reply: "By hypothesis it has been assumed that all is, without exception, alike in each part of the loaf. And so the man either cannot start to eat some one particular part and will therefore starve (which is manifestly absurd), or else he will start somewhere to satisfy his desire."[62]

The force of the example is thus presumably to stress the difference between the realm of arational nature where a balance of forces creates equilibrium and the rational realm where a balance of reasons leaves room for free will.

Khôdja Zâdeh then goes on to give a more sophisticated example of choice without preference, which is cited here in Léon Gauthier's epitome:

> If one can demonstrate . . . that in some instance God [in creating the world] must choose among two or more strictly equivalent alternatives, one will have upset in one decisive stroke . . . the premiss on which the argument of the Hellenizing philosophers is founded, the principle of sufficient reason. But there are numerous such instances. . . . Thus with any of the celestial spheres (of Greco-Arabian astronomy) God has an arbitrary choice among an infinity of strictly identical alternatives in selecting the two points which serve as poles or the cir-

----

61. Angel Flores, *First Spanish Reader* (New York: Bantam Books, 1964), p. 2. This balancing of hunger and thirst carries us back to Aristotle.

62. Rendered from the French of Léon Gauthier's translation in "L'argument de l'Ane de Buridan et les philosophes arabes," in *Mélanges René Basset* (Paris: A. Hermann), pp. 209–33; see esp. pp. 227–28.

cle which serves as equator or the line which serves as axis. And again, with respect to the motion of each sphere, a direction of rotation and a particular speed must be chosen arbitrarily; similarly on each eccentric there is an arbitrary choice of a center for the epicyclic sphere and on this sphere itself the place of the planet which it carries must be selected, and so on.[63]

In this astronomical formulation, the example is transformed from a choice between two indifferent alternatives into one among infinitely many, a complication that induces no fundamental change in our problem. Like some Western writers, Khôdja Zâdeh is satisfied with insisting *that* "free will" can resolve a situation of choice among indifferent objects, without explaining *how* this is possible.

Rabelais (ca. 1490–1553)

In Francisco Rabelais's *Gargantua and Pantagruel* our example once again receives a literary treatment:

At Pantagruel's birth, none was more amazed and perplexed than his father Gargantua. On the one hand, he saw his wife Badebec dead, on the other, his son Pantagruel, large as life and much noisier. He was at a complete loss what to say or do. A terrible doubt racked his brain: should he weep over the death of his wife or rejoice over the birth of his son? On either hand, sophistical arguments arose to choke him. He could frame them capitally *in modo et figura*, according to the modes and figures of the syllogism in formal logic. But he could not resolve them. So there he was, fretting like a mouse caught in a trap, or a kite snared in a gin.[64]

Giving full play to his provocative *esprit*, Rabelais devised a highly dramatic and characteristically tragicomic setting for this ancient problem.

Montaigne (1533–1592)

In his *Essais*, Michel de Montaigne discusses the problem of choice without preference—again in Aristotle's formulation—as an intellectual curiosity, a difficulty of the sort that give spice and stimulus to the cultivation of philosophical speculations, that curious pursuit of the paradoxical creature *Homo sapiens*:

63. Ibid., pp. 229–30. Gauthier thinks that Khôdja Zädeh derived the basic idea of his example from the Muslim theologians (pp. 230–31). See also Léon Gauthier, *Ibn Rochd (Averroes)* (Paris: J. Vrin, 1948), pp. 221–22. These astronomical examples are only variations on a theme of al-Ghazali; see S. van den Bergh, trans., *The Incoherence of the Incoherence*, pp. 124, 144.

64. Rabelais, *Gargantua and Pantagruel*, bk. 2, p. 3, translated by Jacques LeClerq (Modern Library edition).

It is a pleasant imagination, to conceive a spirit justly ballanced betweene two equall desires. For, it is not to be doubted, that he shall never be resolved upon any match: Forsomuch as the application and choise brings an inequality of prise: And who should place us betweene a Bottle of Wine and a Gammon of Bacon, with a equall appetite to eat and drinke, doubtlesse there were noe remedy but to die of thirst and hunger.[65]

However, in condemning Buridan's ass to death, Montaigne proposes to draw the venom of the paradox, by reducing it to the status of a strictly abstract and purely fanciful *hypothetical* difficulty that could not possibly arise in a real or *practical* context.

In my opinion, it might . . . be said, that nothing is presented unto us, wherein there is not some difference, how light so ever it bee: and that either to the sight, or to the feeling, there is ever some choise, which tempteth and drawes us to it, though imperceptible and not to bee distinguished.[66] In like manner, hee that shall presuppose a twine-thrid equally strong all-through, it is impossible by all impossibilitie that it breake, for, where could you have the flaw or breaking to beginne? And at once to breake in all places together, it is not in nature.[67]

Montaigne's resolution of the problem flatly maintains that strict identity among objects "is not in nature," so that choice among identicals becomes a purely imaginary complication.

Gataker (1574–1654)

A most interesting discussion of the uses of random selection occurs in *Of the Nature and Use of Lots: A Treatise Historical and Theological* by Thomas Gataker, a sixteenth-century English scholar and divine, first published in London in 1616 (second edition, here cited, published in 1627). Gataker considered a great number of historical examples of the use of lots in the Old and New Testaments (e.g., the selection of a successor to the apostle Judas, Acts 1:23–26); in the assignment of priesthoods and public offices in Greece; in Hebrew, Greek, Roman, and other legal practice; and the like. He defined a "lot" as an "event merely casual purposely applied to the deciding of some doubt" (p. 9), "casual events" being "such as might all out in like sort diversely, and are not determined by any art, foresight, forecast, counsell, or skill of those that either act them, or make use of them" (p. 14). Quoting with approval the dictum that "chance is founded, and dependeth upon Man's ignorance [*fortuna in ignorantia nostra fundatur*]" (p. 37), Gataker criticized

---

65. *Essais*, bk. 2, chap. 14; cited from John Florio's translation (Everyman's Library edition, bk. 2, p. 333).

66. Compare Leibniz's "petites perceptions."

67. *Essais*, bk. 2, chap. 14.

the view that "a Lot discovereth to men God's hidden will" (p. 25), and argued that "Lots are not to be used in [a] question of Fact past and gone . . . for that is no ordinarie Lot able to decide; but where some question is who has the right to a thing; in which case, notwithstanding the Lot is not used to determine who in truth hath right to it, but who for peace and quietnesse sake shall enjoy it" (p. 148). Gataker insisted that "concerning the matter or businesses wherein Lots may lawfully be used, the rule of Caution in general is this, that Lots are to be used in things indifferent onely" (p. 125), for:

> . . . many good things there are that may at sometime be done, where of a man may make chose whether of them hee will doe, being not necessarily tied unto, or enjoyned any one of them: As for a student having divers bookes about him in his study, it is indifferent to choose one, this or that, refusing the rest, for present employment, there being no speciall occasion to urge the use of one more than another: Or for a man that carrieth a pair of knives about him, it is indifferent to draw and use either when occasion requireth (as Plutarch says, *de Stoic, contradict.*). (p. 128)

Gataker's distinguished clerical career was brought into jeopardy by accusations of favoring games of chance, growing out of his defense of the use of lots. He has the distinction of being the first to suggest the employment of random-selection devices as a means of resolving the problem of indifferent choice in public policy situations where some preferential selection is desirable "for peace and quietnesse sake."

Spinoza (1632–1677)

The problem of choice without preference was taken up by Benedict de Spinoza as a source of possible objection to determinism. If two objects of choice are essentially identical (so that there is no difference in the relevant causal factors militating for selection of one vis-à-vis the other), and it is granted that a selection of one of them is possible, would this not reveal a rift in the framework of causal determinism? If choice in situations of indifference were accepted as possible, would this not concede the operation of a free will capable of supplementing causal determinations in such cases, and thus possibly even supplanting them in others?[68]

---

68. This argument underlies use of the phrase "liberty of indifference," regarding which Dugald Stewart writes: "The phrase *Liberty of Indifference*, . . . has been so frequently substituted . . . for the older, simpler, and much more intelligible phrase of *Free-will*. . . . It certainly conveys but a very inadequate notion of the thing meant;—the power, to wit, of choice or *election;* and that not only among things indifferent, but *(a fortiori)* between right and wrong, good and evil" (*Active and Moral Powers*, Appendix on Free Agency, iii). Insistence on the important of *indifference* of will for free (and thus morally responsible) action

It may be objected that if a man does not act from freedom of the will, what would he do if he were in a state of equilibrium, like the ass of Buridanus? Would he not perish from hunger and thirst? and if this be granted, do we not conceive him as a statue of a man or an ass [i.e., rather than as a real human being or animal]? If I deny that he would thus perish, he will consequently determine himself and possess the power of going where he likes and doing what he likes.[69]

Spinoza's imagined opponent here presses the determinist with the objection that surely a *real* agent would not rest inactive in a case of choice under conditions of equilibrium or stalemate among opposing determinations. Spinoza, undaunted by the objection, maintained that—however unreasonable such inactivity might seem—it is just precisely what would actually *have* to happen:

With regard to the objection, I say that I entirely grant that if a man were placed in such a state of equilibrium he would perish of hunger and thirst, supposing he perceived nothing but hunger and thirst, and the food and drink were equidistant from him. If you ask me whether such a man would not be thought as ass rather than a man, I reply that I do not know; nor do I know what ought to be thought of a man who hangs himself, or of children, fools and madmen.[70]

In Spinoza's discussion, then, the problem of Buridan's Ass recurs in its Thomistic setting, in the context of the free-will issue. With Aquinas, however, the example served as part of an (ultimately rejected) argument *against freedom of the will,* while with Spinoza it becomes part of an (ultimately rejected) *objection to a thorough-going determinism* with respect to the choices of responsible agents.[71] For Spinoza makes short shrift of

---

goes back to Duns Scotus; see C. R. S. Harris, *Duns Scotus* (Oxford, U.K.: Clarendon Press, 1927), vol. 2, p. 309.

69. Spinoza, *Ethics*, vol. 2, final Scholion, quoted from the translation of W. H. White and A. H. Stirling (Oxford, U.K.: University of Oxford Press, 1927). This passage does not show Spinoza at his best, since it naively depicts determinism as incompatible with "the power of going where [one] likes and doing what [one] likes." Leibniz agrees with Spinoza in opposition to those who hold that the locus of human liberty of will is to be sought in situations of indifference of choice: "We [can] become as it were masters of ourselves, and make ourselves think and do at the time as we should *wish* to will and as reason commands. But it is always through determined paths, and never *without a reason*, or by means of the imaginary principle of perfect indifference or equilibrium. . . . I here say *without a reason* to mean without the opposition of other inclinations, or without being in advance disposed to turn aside the mind, or without any other means equally explicable. To assert otherwise is to revert to the chimerical, as in the empty faculties or occult qualities of the scholastics, in which there is neither rhyme nor reason" (*New Essays*, II, xxi, 47; my translation largely follows that of A. G. Langley [LaSalle, Ill.: Open Court, various dates]).

70. Spinoza, *Ethics*, vol. 2, final Scholion. "There are more things in heaven and earth, Horatio, than are dreamt of in your philosophy." Spinoza seemingly has the rare candor to admit this with respect to his own system.

71. Note that in both instances the example is used in support of positions that the authors are endeavoring to rebut (though with contrary positions to be sure). It is interesting that the example so often occurs in this manner.

the objection, by insisting that where opposing motivations are actually in strict equilibrium, inaction is the only arguable result. Like Leibniz after him, Spinoza was willing to push the principle of sufficient reason to its logical conclusion.

Leibniz (1646–1717)

Leibniz wrote:

We [humans] are so determined as to choose with the preponderance of reasons or grounds . . . And it is just here that our action is *voluntary*, for otherwise it is not deliberate. Thus while these determinations do not strictly speaking *necessitate*, they do not fail to *incline*. And we will always adopt that choice where there is greater inclination or disposition. For the situation of a perfect indifference—as with the ass of Buridan, dying between two bales—is something imaginary, because a perfect equality on two sides is never to be found.[72]

Two sorts of circumstances would characterize situations of symmetric choice, namely, when

- there is no difference between the choice alternatives

and when:

- there is no *known* difference between the choice alternatives

The former issue of actual (ontological) indiscernibility is one thing, and the second issue of cognitive (epistemic) indiscernment is another. As we have just seen, Leibniz holds that the former situation cannot arise (thanks to the Identity of Indiscernibles). Yet the imperfect condition of humans seems to leave the second case open. However, Leibniz proposes to shut the door on it as well.

The ass of Buridan is immobilized in the setting of Leibniz's philosophy because on Leibnizian principles there must be a *sufficient reason* for all occurrences, and this condition would be violated in the example. Thus in his third letter to Clarke, Leibniz writes:

My axiom has not been fully understood, and . . . the author [i.e., Clarke] while seeming to grant it, has really denied it. "It is true," he says, "that nothing exists without a sufficient reason why it is, and why it is thus rather than otherwise," but he adds that this sufficient reason is often the simple or *mere will* of God. . . . But this is simply maintaining that God wills something without there being a sufficient reason for his will, contrary to the axiom. . . . This is to relapse into

---

72. Gaston Grua, *G. W. Leibniz: Textes inédits* (Paris: Presses Universitaires de France, 1948), p. 479.

the loose indifference which I have amply refuted [in the *Theodicy*] and which I have shown to be absolutely chimerical, even in created beings. . . .[73]

However, Leibniz's Principle of Sufficient Reason would not sentence Buridan's poor animal to death, for a way out of the impasse is made possible by his concept of *petites perceptions*, infinitesimal psychic occurrences beneath the threshold of any conscious awareness, which can act as imperceptible motivations in effecting a choice.

All our unpremeditated actions are the result of a concurrence of *petites perceptions*, and even our habits and our passions, which so much influence our [conscious] deliberations, come therefrom. . . . I have already remarked that he who would deny these effects in the sphere of morals, would imitate those ill taught persons who deny insensible corpuscles in physics. And yet, I see that among those who discuss freedom of the will there are some who, taking no notice of these unperceived impressions which are capable of inclining the balance, imagine an entire indifference in moral actions, like that of the ass of Buridan equally torn between two meadows.[74]

And again, in the *Theodicy*, Leibniz writes:

There is never any *indifference of equipoise*, that is [situations of choice] where all is completely even on both sides, without any inclination towards either. . . . By this false idea of an indifference of equipose the Molinists were much embarrassed. They were asked not only how it was possible to know in what direction a cause absolutely indeterminate would be determined, but also how it was possible that there should finally result therefrom a determination for which there is no source. To say with Molina that there is the priviledge of the free cause is to say nothing. . . . In consequence of this, the case also of Buridan's ass between two meadows, impelled equally towards each of them, is a fiction that cannot occur in the universe, in the order of Nature, although M. Bayle may be of another opinion. . . . For the universe cannot be halved by a plane through the middle of the ass, which is cut vertically through its length, so that all is equal and alike on both sides. . . . Neither the parts of the universe nor the viscera of the animal are alike nor are they evenly placed on both sides of this vertical plane. There will therefore always be many things in the ass and outside the ass, although they may not be apparent to us, which will determine him to go to one side rather than the other. And although man is free, and the ass is not, nevertheless for the same reason it must be true that in man likewise the case of a perfect equipoise between two courses is impossible.[75]

The crux is that a situation of perfectly indifferent alternatives simply cannot arise:

73. §7 of the Third Letter to Clarke.
74. G. W. Leibniz, *New Essays*, II, i, 15. My translation follows that of A. G. Langley (La Salle, Ill.: Open Court, various dates).
75. G. W. Leibniz, *Theodicy*, §§46–49; I quote the translation by Austin Farrer (New

M. Bayle, subtle though he was, has not considered the matter sufficiently, for he believed a situation such as that of Buridan's Ass to be possible, and thought that a man placed in a condition of perfect equilibrium could nevertheless choose. But it must be said that a situation of perfect equilibrium is a mere chimera that cannot arise, the universe not admitting being divided or cut into two equal and entirely similar parts. The universe in not like an ellipse or similar oval which a straight line drawn through the center can cut into two congruent parts. The universe has no center and its parts vary infinitely, so that there will never be a circumstance where different parts are perfectly alike and make the same impression. And even though we cannot always consciously preserve all the minute impressions that conspire to determine our will, there will in fact always be something to decide us between two alternatives, and the situation will never be one of perfect equivalence between them.

> C'est ce que M. Bayle tout subtil qu'il a esté n'a pas assez consideré lorsqu'il a crû qu'un cas semblable à celuy de l'Ane de Buridan, fut possible, et que l'homme posé dans des circonstances d'un parfait equilibre pourroit neantmoins choisir. Car il faut dire que le cas d'un parfait equilibre est chimerique, et n'arrive jamais, l'univers ne pouvant point ester ny parti ny coupé en deux parties egales et semblables. L'univers n'est pas comme une Ellipse ou autre telle Ovale, que la ligne droile menée par son centre peut couper en deux parties congruentes. L'univers n'a point de centre, et ses parties sont infiniment variées; ainsi jamais le cas arrivera, ou tout sera parfaitement egal et frappera egalement de part et d'autre; et quoyque nous ne soyons pas tousjours capables de nous appercevoir de toutes les petites impressions qui contribuent à nous determiner, il y a tousjours quelque chose qui nous determine entre deux contradictorires, sans que le cas soit jamais parfaitement egal d'un part et d'autre.[76]

Thus Leibniz's position is neatly summarized in his correspondence with Clarke:

> In things which are absolutely indifferent there can be no choice and consequently no election or will, since choice must have some reason or principle.[77] To say that the mind may have good reasons for acting when it has no motives, and when things are absolutely indifferent . . . is a manifest contradiction. For if there are good reasons for the course it adopts, the things are not indifferent to it.[78]

Haven, Conn.: Yale University Press, 1932). Cf. also §§302 ff. for Leibniz's critique of Bayle's discussion of indifference of choice.

76. Letter to Pierre Coste of 19 December 1707 (G. P. III, p. 403).

77. §1 of Leibniz's fourth letter.

78. §16 of Leibniz's fifth letter. Cf. also the following passage: "There is indifference, when there is no more reason for one than for the other. The opposite is determination. . . . All actions are determined, and never indifferent. For there is always a reason inclining us to one rather than the other, since nothing happens without a reason. . . . A liberty of indifference is impossible. So it cannot be found anywhere, not even in God. For God is self-determined to do always the best. And creatures are always deter-

Leibniz's solution can be viewed as acceptable only if it is conceded that there are always bound to be actually present factors (possibly unnoticed) which "incline the balance" between the objects of choice. But what if this is not conceded, and the hypothesis of a thoroughgoing similarity of these objects is strictly insisted on? To avert this line of attack, Leibniz would fall back on his Principle of the Identity of Indiscernibles, according to which no two distinct objects can be strictly comparable in the requisite manner.[79] But this is another topic, and a large one, lying beyond the realm of present discussion.

Wolff (1679–1754)

In his *Psychologia Empirica*, Christian Wolff gives as a concrete illustration of choice without preference the example of selection of an individual from a species to provide a specimen to serve as a typical representative for scientific study:

If we neither desire nor are repelled by a know object, we are said to be *indifferent* to it, and the state of mind towards an object thus indifferently considered is called a *state of indifference.* The existence of such states of indifference is attested by experience. For example, some one sees many small stones by a riverside, and regards them without either desire or dislike. He takes some of them up in his hand, to study them more closely, and then throws them away, having wanted them solely for the purposes of examination, without singling out these as preferable to the others, and returning to a state of indifference among them from his examination of the particular specimen.[80]

Wolff rightly appreciates that feature indistinguishability is not a prerequisite for evaluative equivalency.

Reid (1710–1796)

One of the principal interpretations that has been placed upon the example of Buridan's Ass is that an equilibrium of contrary determining motives must, if equal in strength, result in inaction. Such reasoning, according to Thomas Reid, rests upon a spurious analogy:

---

mined by internal or external reasons." From G. W. Leibniz, *Philosophische Schriften*, ed. by C. I. Gerhardt, vol. 7 (Berlin: Werdmann, 1890), p. 109; quoted by B. Russell in *A Critical Exposition of the Philosophy of Leibniz* (Cambridge, U.K.: Cambridge University Press, 1900), pp. 193–94.

79. Cf. §§49, 304, and 307 of the *Théodicée*.

80. Christian Wolff, *Psychologia Empirica*, §585; my translation.

Some philosophers . . . say, that, as the balance cannot incline to one side more than the other when the opposite weights are equal, so a man cannot possibly determine himself if the motives on both hands are equal: and, as the balance must necessarily turn to that side which has the most weight, so the man must necessarily be determined to that hand where the motive is strongest. And on this foundation some of the schoolmen maintained that, if a hungry ass were placed between two bundles of hay equally inviting, the beast must stand still and starve to death, bring unable to turn to either, because there are equal motives to both. This is an instance of that analogical reasoning which I conceive ought never to be trusted. . . . The argument is no better than this—that, because a dead animal moves only as it is pushed, and, if pushed with equal force in contrary directions, must remain at rest; therefore the same thing must happen to a living animal; for, surely, the similitude between a dead animal and a living, is as great as that between a beast and a man.[81]

Reid rightly perceived the conceptual origin of the problem in a physical analogy—an analogy that he regarded as altogether invalid.

In Reid's discussion, the example of Buridan's Ass is treated as a pillar of support for a theory of psychodynamics, denied by Reid, which has it that *action* must take place in a manner proportionate with *motivation*. And he treated the putative invalidity of the supporting scale/will analogy as destroying the case for this thesis:

Cases frequently occur, in which an end that is of some importance, may be answered equally well by any one of several different means. In such cases, a man who intends the end finds not the least difficulty in taking one of these means, though he be firmly persuaded that it has no title to be preferred to any of the others. To say that this is a case that cannot happen, is to contradict the experience of mankind; for surely a man who has occasion to lay out a shilling or a guinea, may have two hundred that are of equal value, both to the giver and to the receiver, any one of which will answer his purpose equally well. To say, that, if such a case should happen the man could not execute his purpose, is still more ridiculous, though it may have the authority of some of the schoolmen, who determined that the ass, between two equal bundles of hay would stand still till it died of hunger.[82]

Reid overlooks the fact that various Schoolmen are entirely in agreement with his own position and deny choice resolution to brutes precisely to emphasize its possession by humans.

81. Thomas Reid, *On the Intellectual Powers*, vol. 1, p. 4; *Reid's Works*, ed. Hamilton, p. 238, of the seventh, eighth, and possibly other editions.
82. Thomas Reid, *On the Active Powers*, bk. 4, p. 4; *Reid's Works*, ed. Hamilton, bk. 2, p. 609.

Kant (1724–1804)

Immanuel Kant nowhere discusses the problem of Buridan's Ass *explicitly*, but it is implicitly present in a behind-the-scenes way in this discussion of will and of the freedom of the will. Kant characterized *will* as of itself a causal agency:

> The *will* is a kind of causality belonging to living things in so far as they are rational, and freedom would be this property of such causality that it can be efficient, independently of foreign causes *determining* it; just as *physical necessity* is the property that the causality of all irrational beings has of being determined to activity by the influence of foreign causes.[83]

Kant distinguished between (1) the Rational Will, which urges those principles of duty that *reasonableness* lays upon men, stipulating objectively and unconditionally how they *ought* to act, and (2) the Elective Will that is operative in making our strictly subjective day-to-day choices. Regarding these modes of will, Kant wrote:

> Laws proceed from the Rational Will; maxims from the Elective Will. The latter is in man a free Elective Will. The Rational Will, which is directed to nothing but the [moral] law alone, cannot be called either free or unfree, because it is not directed to actions, but immediately to the legislation for the maxims of actions. . . . Consequently it [the Rational Will] is absolutely necessary, and is even *incapable* of constraint. It is therefore only the Elective Will that can be called *free*.[84]

The "freedom" of the Elective Will resides in that its choice is only conditioned, and not wholly determined, for an individual by sensuous presentations relating to the objects of choice: "[The free Elective Will] is one which is *affected*, but not *determined* by impulses. . . . The *freedom* of the Elective Will just is that independence of its *determination* on sensible impulses."[85]

This concept of the will as a spontaneous causative agency forms the background of Kant's presentation of the paradox of freedom in the third antinomy of pure reason:

> *Thesis:* To explain . . . appearances it is necessary to assume that there is also another causality, that of freedom.

---

83. Immanuel Kant, *Fundamental Principles of the Metaphysic of Morals*, vol. 3, trans. T. K. Abbott, in *Kant's Theory of Ethics* (London, 1873), p. 65 of third (1883) and subsequent editions.
84. Immanuel Kant, *Introduction to the Metaphysic of Morals*, vol. 4; Abbott, trans., *Kant's Theory of Ethics*, vol. 1, p. 282.
85. Ibid., vol. 1, p. 268.

Proof: . . . We must . . . assume a causality through which something takes place, the cause of which is not itself determined, in accordance with necessary laws, by another cause antecedent to it, that is to say, an *absolute spontaneity* of the cause, whereby a series of appearances, which proceeds in accordance with laws of nature, begins of *itself.* . . .

Antithesis: There is no freedom; everything in the world takes place solely in accordance with laws of nature.

Proof: Assume that there is freedom in the transcendental sense, as a special kind of causality in accordance with which the events in the world can have come about, . . . it then follows that not only will a series have its absolute beginning in this spontaneity, but that the very determination of this spontaneity to originate the series, that is to say, the causality itself, will have an absolute beginning; there will be no antecedent through which this act, in taking place, is determined in accordance with fixed laws. . . . Transcendental freedom thus stands opposed to the law of causality; and the kind of connection which it assumes as holding between the successive states of the active causes renders all unity of experience impossible. It is not to be met with in any experience, and is therefore an empty thought-entity.[86]

Since freedom of the will involves such an antinomy, its status on Kantian principles must be that of a postulate of practical reason.

The freedom of the Elective Will from *complete* determination by its sensuous materials is the distinguishing characteristic of *human* as opposed to *animal* will:

Freedom in the practical sense is the will's independence of coercion through sensible impulses, for a will is sensuous insofar as it is *pathologically affected,* i.e., by sensuous motives; it is *animal (arbitrium brutum)* if it can be pathologically *necessitated.* The human will is certainly an *arbitrium sensitivum,* not, however, *brutum,* but *liberum.* For sensibility does not necessitate its action. There is in man a power of self-determination, independently of any coercion through sensuous impulses.[87]

Thus Kant returns to Buridan's own position that humans, unlike donkeys, would be able to resolve Buridan-type choice situations.

Kant's discussion of the will and its nature thus derives all of its key constituent elements from the historical contexts of the problem of choice without preference:

1. The nature of *will* as a faculty capable of playing a causal role in situations of choice (Ghazâlî, etc.).

---

86. Immanuel Kant, *The Critique of Pure Reason,* trans. N. K. Smith (London: Macmillan, 1929), pp. 409–11.
87. Ibid. "The Antinomy of Pure Reason, Appendix III," p. 465.

2. The concept of *freedom* of the will as involving a lack of complete dependence on the nature of its objects (Ghazâlî, Aquinas, and the *mere will* tradition).

3. Absence of determination by its objects as the essential difference between animal and human will (Buridan).

Schopenhauer (1788–1860)

The problem of Buridan's Ass was adduced by Arthur Schopenhauer as providing conclusive demonstration of the absurdity of the free-will doctrine.

The really profound philosophers of all ages—however diverse their views in other respects—have agreed in asserting the necessity of acts of will in accordance with their motives, and have united in rejecting the *liberum arbitrium*. The incalculably preponderant majority of men, incapable of real thought and ruled by appearances and by prejudice, has at all times stubbornly resisted this truth. Philosophers have therefore been at pains to express it in the most pointed and even exaggerated terms. The most familiar of these devices is the famous Ass of Buridan, for which one has not been vainly searching in his writing for some hundred years. . . .[88]

Schopenhauer thus maintains that the problem of Buridan's Ass reveals the untenability of the thesis of freedom of the will in showing that a selection unconditioned by determining factors is indefensible, indeed, inconceivable.

While the problem context of the puzzle of choice without preference is here again provided by its ancient setting of determinism versus free will, nevertheless, Schopenhauer's particular way of using the problem—as though it gave a plain and incontestable proof of the absurdity of free will—seems to have originated with himself (his claim to the contrary notwithstanding).

Augustus de Morgan (1806–1871)

It is fitting that our ancient paradox is the starting point of Augustus de Morgan's *Budget of Paradoxes*. Here we read:

Buridan was for free-will—that is, will which determines conduct, let motives be ever so evenly balanced. An ass is *equally* pressed by hunger and by thirst; a bundle of hay is on one side, a pail of water on the other. Surely, you will say, he will not be ass enough to die for want of food or drink; he will then make a choice—

88. Arthur Schopenhauer, *Prize Essay on the Freedom of the Will*, p. 58 of the original edition; my translation.

that is, will choose between alternatives of equal force. The problem became famous in the schools; some allowed the poor donkey to die of indecision; some denied the possibility of the balance, which was no answer at all. The following question is more difficult, and involves free-will to all who answer—"Which you please." If the northern hemisphere were land, and all the southern hemisphere water, ought we to call the northern hemisphere an island, or the southern hemisphere a lake? Both the questions would be good exercises for paradoxers. . . .

What we have in this somewhat different but hindered case is also a balance of reasons via a symmetry of arguments.

Lewis Carrol (1832–1898)

In view of the venerable history of our problem, it is not at all surprising that it also has received the (perhaps dubious) honor of humorous treatment. In *Alice in Wonderland* and in *Through the Looking Glass*, Lewis Carroll delights to poke fun at various old and respected pieces of equipment in the logician's arsenal. The problem of Buridan's Ass is up for consideration in the episode of Tweedledum and Tweedledee.

They were standing under a tree, each with an arm around the other's neck, and Alice knew which was which in a moment, because one of them had "Dum" embroidered on his collar, and the other "Dee." "I suppose they've each got 'Tweedle' round at the back of the collar," she said to herself. . . . "I know what you're thinking about," said Tweedledum; "but it isn't so, nohow." "Contrariwise," continued Tweedledee, "if it was so, it might be: and if it were so, it would be; but as it isn't, it ain't. That's logic." . . . Alice did not like shaking hands with either of them first, for fear of hurting the other one's feelings; so, as the best way out of the difficulty, she took hold of both hands at once: the next moment they were dancing round in a ring. This seemed quite natural (she remembered afterwards). . . .[89]

With Rabelais, it is the ludicrous side of the puzzle that appealed to Lewis Carrol.

Frank R. Stockton (1854–1902)

Yet another literary employment of the idea of choice without preference is its role in providing the basis for the plot of Frank R. Stockton's intriguing short story "The Lady, or the Tiger?"

89. Lewis Carroll, *Through the Looking Glass*, chap. 4. In an episode of the television science-fiction series *Star-Trek* broadcast in January 1969, the villain transforms himself into a duplicate of the hero, confronting the latter's collaborators with a vexatious puzzle.

When a subject [of this mythical monarch] was accused of a crime of sufficient importance to interest the King, public notice was given that on an appointed day the fate of the accused person would be decided in the King's arena. . . . [W]hen all the people had assembled in the galleries, and the King, surrounded by his court, sat high up on his throne of royal state on one side of the arena, he gave a signal, a door beneath him opened, and the accused subject stepped out into the amphitheatre. Directly opposite him, on the other side of the enclosed space, were two doors, exactly alike and side by side. It was the duty and the privilege of the person on trial, to walk directly towards these doors and open one of them. He could open either door he pleased: he was subject to no guidance or influence. . . . If he opened the one, there came out of it a hungry tiger, the fiercest and most cruel that could be procured, which immediately sprang upon him and tore him to pieces as a punishment for all his guilt. . . . But, if the accused person opened the other door, there came forth from it a lady, the most suitable for his years and station that his majesty could select among his fair subjects; and to this lady he was immediately married, as a reward of his innocence. . . . This was the King's semi-barbaric method of administering justice. Its perfect fairness is obvious. The criminal could not know out of which door would come the lady: he opened either he pleased, without having the slightest idea whether, in the next instant, he was to be devoured or married.[90]

The choice of the accused, however conditioned by a preference as to ultimate results, is most clearly made without any preference between the doors that are the immediate objects of choice. Here it is in fact *ignorance* that creates a symmetry of arguments; the objects are different enough but what we lack is differentiating information.

Perhaps this lighter note marks a good point for concluding this survey of the historical highlights of the problem of choice without preference. But please do not think, dear Reader, that that's all there is to it. For it would be a grave mistake to pretend to completeness. As a quick look at a search engine from the World Wide Web such as Google indicates, Buridan's Ass has been trotted out hundreds of times in the past few years by writers on all sorts of topics for all sorts of purposes. But *sapienti sat.*

3. A DOCTRINAL PERSPECTIVE

The problem of the Buridan's Ass perplex lies in the consideration that either alternative choice is preferable to inaction, but neither is preferable to the other. The dialectical setting for the Buridan's Ass per-

90. Frank R. Stockton, *Lady, Or the Tiger? and Other Stories* (New York: C. Scribner's Sons, 1884).

plex is thus set by the following aporetic group of individually plausible but collectively inconsistent propositions:

1. Rational choice requires preference: where there is no determinable preferability, a reasoned choice becomes impossible.
2. In Buridan's Ass–style cases there just is no room for preference.
3. In the Buridan's Ass–style cases choice is mandatory: refraining from choice is not a rationally available alternative.

Given that propositions 2 and 3 are simply "facts of life," the inevitable upshot seems to be that proposition 1 must be rejected. And the question, of course, now becomes: Is it the case that a rational creature will act only where a reasoned choice of courses of action is possible?

The doctrinal context of the Buridan's Ass problem is set by the Socratic contention that intelligent beings act *sub ratione boni*, shaping their actions in line with their judgment of what is for the best. The problem then is: What happens when action is clearly necessary and yet there just is no distinguishable best?

As Display 1 indicates, the situation as regards the will's capacity to break an evaluative tie as envisioned by reason admits of four alternatives once we grant that in matters of choice a sapient being can do everything a beast can, and God can do anything that an intelligent creature can manage: these alternative doctrinal positions range from a 1-style across-the-board attribution of liberty of indifference to a 4-style across-the-board denial thereof. To all appearances, none of the Christian medievals took a 1-style position: "Even a dumb beast would not be so foolish as to starve." Most held a 2-style position that contrasted humans and brutes. However, the Arabic theologians generally favored 3 because they equated free choice with creation ex nihilo and saw this power as belonging to God alone, strictly speaking.[91] Moreover, those thinkers who held a 4-style position—such as Averroes, Aquinas, Buridan, and Leibniz—did so by way of holding that Buridan-type situations of total equivalency just cannot arise either because this is inherently impossible (Leibniz) or because the intellect will always *impose* some preference, being able to differentiate through its own resources even where there is no difference in the objects of choice.

And here the Buridan's Ass example lends itself to three realizations, as follows:

A. Even a mere beast (an unintelligent being) would break the tie. Therefore an intelligent agent like man certainly would.

91. On this issue, see David B. Burrell, "Al Ghazali on Created Freedom," *American Catholic Philosophical Quarterly* 73 (1999): 135–57.

DISPLAY 1. Able To Tiebreak?

	Beast	Man	God	Supporters
(1)	+	+	+	None among the historic figures
(2)	-	+	+	Al- Ghazâlî, The Franciscans, (Buridan, Olivi, Scotus)
(3)	-	-	+	Arabic Muctazilites
(4)	-	-	-	Averroes, Aquinas, Buridan, Leibniz

B. An intelligent being like man would certainly break the tie, although a mere brute, lacking intelligence, would not and could not do so.

C. Since the human will is subject to the intellect, man would be unable to break the tie. Only the omnipotent will of God could break the tie.

While moderns may incline to rendering A, none of the premodern discussants did so. The medievals saw mere animals as lacking the intelligence that is required here. Thus in the Christian tradition most discussants favored rendering B. However, in the Islamic tradition (followed only by a few of the Christian Scholastics) there were various exponents of rendering C. As these C-theorists saw it, a will that refuses to subordinate itself to the rulings of intellect was not a weak will (in the tradition of Aristotelian *akrasia*) but rather a strong, powerful, autonomously independent will.

It is clear that in this context, Buridan's Ass–style examples afford a double-edged sword that could be used to illustrate and support various rather different doctrinal positions. But let us now turn to a substantive analysis of the Buridan's Ass puzzle problem and its resolution.

4. CHOICE IN THE ABSENCE OF PREFERENCE

The leading idea that underlies the sensible resolution of the Buridan's choice perplex inheres in the similarity of logical structure between (1) the problem of choice in the case of symmetry of *knowledge*, and (2) the problem of choice in the case of symmetry of *preference*. To establish the kinship that obtains here, let us first examine the problem of choice with symmetric knowledge.

Consider the following example, a simple variant of Frank Stockton's problem of the lady and the tiger: a person is offered a choice between two similar boxes. He is told only that one box contains some prize, and that the other is empty. He is not told which is which. Here there is no problem of absence of preference: the person has a clear preference for the treasure-box. The only lack is one of *information*—the choice is to be made in the face of the absence of any clue as to the *identity* of this treasure-box. While they may differ in other ways (e.g., color or size), with regard to the crucial question—"Which box is empty and which one holds the prize?"—the available information about the boxes is completely *symmetric*.

This example, then, is an instance of the problem of choice under conditions of symmetric information with respect to a particular preferential issue. How, in such cases, can a *reasonable* person go about making a *rationally defensible* choice?

The sensible answer to this question is in fact simple, well known, and uncontroversial. For consider the example of the boxes. By the hypothesis that defines the problem, there is no item of information at the disposal of the chooser that could be embraced by him as a *reason* for selecting one box rather than the other. This person therefore simply cannot *reasonably* incline toward one box vis-à-vis the other. And this fact of itself must accordingly characterize the manner of his choice. In short, if rational, he must make his selection in a manner that does not favor one box over against the other: he must make his selection in a *random* manner.

This is a matter susceptible of reasoned demonstration. Assume that the boxes are labeled *A* and *B*. Given that (by hypothesis) the choice of one box produces a result preferable to the rejection of both, the following three courses of action remain available and are mutually exclusive and exhaustive:

1. To make the choice in some manner that favors selection of Box *A* rather than Box *B*.

2. To make the choice in some manner that favors selection of Box *B* rather than Box *A*.

3. To make the choice by means of a selection process that is wholly impartial as between Box *A* and Box *B*, that is, to choose *randomly*.

Observe, to begin with, that probabilistic considerations as to expected gain do not enter in at all—on the basis of the available information it is *equally probable* that Box *A* holds the treasure as Box *B*, so that the expected gain with *any* of the three procedures (1, 2, or 3) is precisely the same, namely, one-half the value of the treasure. Thus on the sole grounds of expected gain there is no difference among these alternatives. But from the standpoint of *reasonableness* there is a very significant difference among the selection procedures. For by the defining hypothesis of the problem, there is no known reason for favoring Box *A* as against Box *B*, or conversely Box *B* as against Box *A*. This very fact renders it rationally indefensible to adopt 1 or 2. *Per contra*, this symmetry of knowledge *of itself constitutes an entirely valid reason for adopting* 3. This line of reasoning establishes the thesis—pivotal for present purposes— that: *In the case of symmetric knowledge, random choice is the reasonable policy.*

It is be useful to note a corollary of this thesis. When such a problem of choice with symmetric information arises, there is no reason (by the very nature of the problem) why we ought not to regard the *arrival order* in which the choices are given in the formulation or situation of the problem as being purely adventitious, that is, as a random ordering. The following policy would thus be entirely reasonable and justified: whenever confronted with a choice in the face of symmetric knowledge, to select that alternative that is the first[92] to come to view. (Cf. the discussion of Simplicius given above.) Such a policy is defensible as entirely reasonable, since under usual circumstances the arrival order can be taken, by the defining hypothesis of the problem, to be a random ordering.

It is important to note, however, that the matter of a *policy* of choice is very important in this context. When I make a choice among symmetrically characterized alternatives, I *can* defend it, reasonably, by saying, "I chose the first mentioned (or the like) alternative, because I *always* choose the first-mentioned (etc.) in these cases."[93] But I cannot (reasonably) defend the choice by saying, "I chose the first mentioned alternative because this seemed to me to be the thing to do *in this case*, though heaven knows what I would do on other occasions."

The adequacy of such selection policies in the face of indifference based on "subjective convenience" (rather than on objective merit) is of fundamental importance because this alone averts an infinite regress of random selections in cases of indifferent choice. For if such choice had always to be made by a random device, the following regress would at once ensue: We are to choose between the indifferent alternatives *A* and *B*. We take a random instrument, say a coin, as means of resolution (since, by hypothesis, we must have actual recourse to a randomizing instrument). We must now, however, choose between the alternatives:

I. To associate *heads* with alternative *A* and *tails* with alternative *B*.
II. To associate *tails* with alternative *A* and *heads* with alternative *B*.

---

92. Or "the last" or "the second" or "the penultimate," etc.

93. "Why?" "Because this amounts to a random choice." "Why do you choose randomly?" "Because random choice is the only rationally defensible policy in such cases." (Why?—Reread the foregoing!)

It is at once obvious that this is itself an indifferent choice. Thus if the resolution of our initial indifferent choice between A and B requires use of a random device, we must first of all resolve another indifferent choice, that between the alternatives I and II, or their analogues. But now if this choice too must be effected by a random device, it is clear that we shall be faced with another analogous situation of indifferent choice, and so on ad infinitum. Only if we recognize that selections in the face of choice without preference can be effected on the basis of selection policies based on "convenience," and do not invariably necessitate actual employment of actual random devices, can this infinite regress of random selections be circumvented.

It should also be noted, however, that a systematic policy of choice such as, for example, invariable selection of the first-occurring alternative is not a *universally* appropriate substitute for selection by actual outright use of a random device or process. Consider, for example, the following situation of choice. A (fair) coin is tossed. A tries to guess the outcome: heads or tails. B tries to guess A's selection. If B guesses correctly, he wins a penny from A, if incorrectly he pays a penny to him. How is A to chose his guesses? Clearly, it would be a poor proposition for A always to guess heads, even though he is in a position of total ignorance and indifference with regard to the outcome of heads or tails. And the same holds true of any other program of choice, such as always guessing tails, or alternating, or the like. All of these run the risk that B can discern the guessing pattern involved, and then capitalize on this information. The only defensible course, in a situation such as this, is to have outright recourse to a random process or device. (This randomizing instrument may, however, be the human mind, since people are presumably capable of making arbitrary selections, with respect to which they can be adequately certain in their own mind that the choice was made haphazardly, and without any "reasons" whatsoever. To be sure, this process is open to the possible intrusion of unrecognized biases, but then so are physical randomizers such as coins. The randomness of any selection process is a matter which, in cases of importance, should be checked by empirical means.)

Let us now turn from this discussion of choice in the face of symmetric *knowledge* to the problem of symmetric *preference*. It is clear upon careful consideration that the matter of choice without preference—that is, under conditions of symmetric preference—can actually be subsumed under the topic of symmetric knowledge as a special case. For in a case of strictly symmetric preference (two essentially similar dates, glasses of water, bales of hay, ears of corn, etc.), the knowledge or information at our disposal constrains us to regard the objects of choice as

	Course of Action	Reward
(1)	To select neither date for lack of a preference	Nothing
(2)	To fix upon one of the dates by means of some selection	One date procedure which favors one over the other
(3)	To select one of the dates at random	One date

equally desirable, because in the circumstances every possible reason for valuing one applies, *mutatis nomine*, to the other(s). So far as the factor of their value or desirability for us is concerned, our knowledge regarding each object is precisely the same.[94] Problems of choice with symmetric valuation can therefore be regarded as simply a species within the symmetric knowledge genus owing to the equivalence of our relevant information in the symmetric value case.

It thus follows that the device of random selection will also provide the means of resolution appropriate for symmetric preference choices. To test the correctness of this resolution, consider Ghazâlî's example of a man who had the choice between two ostensibly identical dates. Logically, there are three courses of action open to him, with the ensuing reward as indicated.

It is clear that these three courses of action are mutually exclusive and exhaustive. But a reasonable person cannot opt for 1 because its associated reward is of lesser value than that of its alternatives. Further, the defining hypothesis of the example—namely, that there is no known reason for preferring one date to the other—of itself constitutes a reason for rejecting 2. Random selection is the only means of avoiding favoring one alternative over the other. And just this constitutes a valid reason for adoption of 3.

These considerations, then, serve to establish the proposition that: *Random selection is the rationally appropriate procedure for making choices in the face of symmetric preference.* The concept of random selection provides an answer to the problem of choice without preference which is demonstrably its only *reasonable* (i.e., rationally defensible) resolution.

This proposed resolution of the problem of choice without preference is in fact substantially that which was first proposed by Gataker and

94. It is clear, then, that this analysis does not apply in the case of the *psychological* dilemma of a balance among diverse motivations of equal force (e.g., hunger and thirst), but obtains solely with respect to the *logical* dilemma of choice among strictly comparable alternatives.

Bayle as a general means of solution—though in their case without any justifying discussion of the rationale establishing the validity of this solution. Bayle based his suggestion on the fact that when the problem of choice without preference actually arises in real situations—in particular, in the instance of court-precedence cases—resolution by chance selection is generally regarded as acceptable, and indeed has acquired the status of a customary official mode of resolution.[95] But of course custom conformity does not of itself constitute validation but at best supplies some empirical evidence in support of the reasonableness of the proposed resolution.

5. A POSTSCRIPT ON PHILOSOPHICAL ISSUES

In examining the substantive philosophical contexts in which the problem of choice without preference has figured, and for which it has been viewed as fundamentally relevant, our historical survey has brought the three following issues to the fore:

1. Its Greek context in cosmological discussion of the Earth's place in the physical universe (Anaximander, Plato, Aristotle).

2. Its Scholastic context in ethico-theological discussion of man's freedom of will (Aquinas, probably Buridan, and others).

3. Its medieval Arabic context in epistemologico-theological discussion of the amenability of God's choices to reason and to human rationalization, that is, the possibility of explaining God's actions in ways acceptable to reasoning men (Ghazâlî, Averroes).

The entire problem of a choice balanced among indifferent objects originates, historically and conceptually, in an analogy with physical equilibria, such as a body immobile under the pull of opposing forces (see Plato's *Phaedo* 108 E, *vice* Anaximander), or a balance-bar at rest under the pressure of opposed, but equal weights (embodied in Axiom 1 of Archimedes' *On Plane Equilibria*). Here, the issues involved are not properly philosophical, and the definition of the example is still in its embryonic form, dealing either with mechanical equilibrium or with

---

95. According to a *New York Times* report (Monday, 12 January 1959, p. 6), "chance is the arbiter prescribed by Swedish law for breaking tie votes in Parliament." The report states that "a drawing of lots may decide the fate of a controversial pension plan," but goes on to observe that "legislation by lottery has never yet been necessary on any major issue." Again, when Hawaii was admitted as the fiftieth state of the United States, and two new senators were elected, random devices were used by the Senate to decide which of the two new Hawaiian senators would have seniority (decision by a coin-toss), and which would serve the longer term (decision by card drawing). See the *New York Times* front-page report of 25 August 1959.

psychological balance among conflicting motivations of comparable strength. The problem has not yet reached its philosophically pertinent definition as one of selection among *logically* indifferent alternatives, which it achieved only in the Middle Ages.

It is a common occurrence in the history of philosophical concepts that a purely scientific discovery or idea metamorphoses—through application to a novel setting in a more far-reaching context—into a matter of philosophical concern and significance. And just this happened with Aristotle's psychological analogy in the present case. Only with the Aristotelian commentators (in Islam, Ghazâlî and Averroes) did the philosophical problem of choice among strictly indifferent objects reach its ultimate *logical* formulation. Genetically, as already noted by Reid, the philosophic problem of choice without preference descends from a physical problem setting, deriving ultimately from analogy with mechanical equilibrium.

With respect to the free-will context, it must be recognized that use of the Buridan example rests upon, and is inextricably embedded in, the Scholastic identification of *cause* and *reason*.[96] Once we reject this identification, as indeed we must, the bearing of the example changes. For a situation of choice in which a preferring *reason* for a selection is absent need not now be one in which no *cause* (other than the agency of a "free will") is operative in leading to choice. Thus outside the context of Scholastic presuppositions the example becomes incapable of establishing the immobilization that it claims.

It deserves stress that our problem serves also to highlight the difference between *reasons* and *motives*. When a random selection among indifferent objects is made by me, I do have a *reason* for my particular selection, namely, the fact that it was indicated to me by a random selector. But I have no *preference* or psychological motivation of other sorts to incline me to choose this item instead of its (by hypothesis indifferent) alternatives. Such absence of psychological preference does not entail the impossibility of a logically justifiable selection. A choice can therefore be logically vindicated as having been made reasonably even though it cannot be traced back to any psychological foundation. In short, we can have *reasons* for a choice even where there is no *motive* for such a choice.

We come down to the remaining context, the rationalizability of divine choice. Before entering upon a closer consideration of this matter, it is desirable first to take up some other preliminary observations.

---

96. Schopenhauer's monograph on *The Fourfold Root of the Principle of Sufficient Reason* provides an extended critique of this confusion of *logical reason* with real cause.

The solution presented in the foregoing section establishes the central role played by *randomness* in the theory of rational choice and decision. A *rational* person must, by the very meaning of the term, fashion his belief and his action in tune with the *evidence* at his disposal. In symmetric choice situations, therefore, in which the manifold of reasons— the available ramification—bears identically on every side, he must choose—as has been seen—in a random manner. In such cases, the "reasons" for his choice are independent of any distinguishing characteristic of the object of choice. Here, reasonable choice comes to be possible in the absence of preference only by essentially abdicating the right of choice by delegating the selection to a random process, seeing that there simply is *no reasonably defensible way of actually "choosing"* among alternatives in the face of symmetric knowledge. Where there is no basis for preferring, there can be no rational preference. We have either to hand the task of fixing upon a selection over to some random mechanism, by making it contingent upon the outcome of such a device, or else we have to make our selection in accordance with the prescript of some predetermined policy that we can defensibly construe as constituting a random selection process. (E.g., given the serial and sequential nature of human consciousness, the governing rule could be: "Confronted by a choice situation with equivalent alternatives, choose the first that has come to view.")[97]

In any case, in situations of this sort we can be said to have "made a *choice*" purely by courtesy. It would be more rigorously correct to say that we have *effected a selection*—and that, of course, is the rational thing to do. In situations of choice without preference, a reasonable person is not condemned to paralysis and inaction. He can and does select, but does so in a random manner, and thus at the price that "his choice" is "his" in only a Pickwickian sense.[98]

Thus, in a world in which all things are indifferent, all choices are random, and wisdom and morality will alike come to naught. Just this is the criticism advanced by Cicero against the Stoic teaching that all things of this world should be "indifferent" to the wise man. He wrote:

97. We could not always and systematically delegate the choice between indifferent alternatives to a random decision because employment of such a method ("Heads for alternative 1, tails for alternative 2") will always itself involve a choice between indifferent alternatives (why not "Tails for alternative 1, heads for alternative 2"?). So some such other policy of choice management is needed.

98. It should be noted that in games of chance, situations in which *rational* choices of courses of action must be made probabilistically can also arise (when the *optimal* strategy is one that is *mixed*). See any text or treatise on the mathematical theory of games.

If we maintained that all things were absolutely indifferent, the whole of life would be thrown into confusion . . . and no function or task could be found for wisdom, since there would be absolutely no distinction between the things that pertain to the conduct of life, and no choice need be exercised among them.[99]

Consequently the idea of randomness must play a key part in the theory of rational choice. The concept of randomness that is at issue here is not that of mathematics as characterized by the criteria that govern the construction of random number tables. Rather, it is its logical cognate: an alternative is *randomly selected* (in this logical sense) if the selection situation is such that the sum total of the weight of evidence for the selection of the chosen alternative is equal to the weight of evidence for selection of its competing alternatives. (Symmetric information or evidence is a special case of evidence of equal weight.) This concept of randomness as based on evidence is a wholly logical or epistemological concept, which relativizes randomness to knowledge and ignorance.[100]

Another line of consideration is worth noting in this connection. Already Pierre Bayle quite correctly perceived that the problem of choice without preference can take on two forms: (1) selection of one among several (exclusive) alternatives that are essentially identical as regards their desirability status as objects of possession or realization—that is, choice without preference among the *objects* involved (the problem of Buridan's Ass); and (2) selection of one among several alternative claimants, whose claims are indivisible and uncompromisable, and whose claims are essentially identical in strength, and must therefore in fairness be treated alike—that is, choice without preference among the *subjects* involved. Bayle properly recognizes that the device of random selection provides a means of resolution that is entirely appropriate for both cases alike. Random selection, it is clear, constitutes the sole wholly satisfactory manner of resolving exclusive choice between equivalent claims in a wholly fair and unobjectionable manner. Only random, and thus strictly "unreasoned," choice provides an airtight guarantee that there is no answer forthcoming to the question: "Why was this alternative, rather than another, selected?" Random choice thus guarantees that the other alternatives *might just as well* (in the strictest of senses) have designated. Where there is no way of *predicting* the outcome in ad-

---

99. Cirero, *De Finibus*, bk. 3, § 50; I quote H. Rackham's translation in the Loeb Classical Library series.

100. Cf. Hume's thesis that "though there be no such thing as *chance* in the world; our ignorance of the real causes of any event has the same influence on the understanding, and begets a like species of belief or opinion" (*Enquiry*, bk. 6, first sentence). For further explanation of the concept of evidence and of measures of evidential weight, the reader is referred to the writer's paper on "A Theory of Evidence," *Philosophy of Science* 25 (1958): 83–94.

vance, no charge of preferential treatment can possibly be substantiated. Thus random choice affords the appropriate avenue of resolution for selection situations in which considerations of fairness leave no other courses of immediate resolution open as acceptable or as defensible.

This consideration has further implications of philosophical import. For one thing, it is surely a *contingent* fact that random processes and devices exist in the world: it is logically feasible to conceive of a possible universe without them. Now the problem of choice without preference is, in its abstract essentials, a theoretical and not a practical problem. It seems curious that the solution of this *theoretical* problem hinges upon the availability of an instrumentality (viz., random choice) whose existence is *contingent*. Surprisingly, it is thus possible to conceive of circumstances (specifically, symmetric choice situations) in which the possibility of rational action depends upon an otherwise wholly extraneous matter of contingent fact: the availability to rational agents of random selection methods. (The availability of random selection policies does, however, blunt the concept of this consideration.)

Now let us finally return to examining the bearing of the foregoing discussion upon the question—much disputed, alike in medieval Islam, Judaism, and Christianity—as to the reasonableness of God's choices.[101] Here it is—or should be—perfectly clear that as a means of resolving the problem of choice without preference the proposed solution is entirely inapplicable. Orthodox Islamic theology, no less than Christian or Judaic theology, cannot grant that the concept of random selection has any applicability to the divinity. There can be no chance mechanisms or processes whose outcome is not known to an omniscient God, nor need He trouble with weights of evidence: in postulating divine omniscience, no possibility is left open for random choice.[102] God's knowledge being complete and timeless, selection cannot be delegated by Him to some contingently future outcome or to some element of fortuitous ordering, such as "the first" (or "the last") alternative.

It follows that the proposed resolution of the problem of choice without preference must be held to apply to the human sphere alone, and not to the divine sphere. Random selection is not an option for God.

101. The significance of this discussion does not hinge on the issue of God's existence. Its bearing is entirely hypothetical: if there were a God along the traditional lines, how would he function?

102. In the "Introduction" to the *Analogy*, Bishop Butler writes: "Probable evidence, in its very nature, affords but an imperfect kind of information; and is to be considered as relative only to beings of limited capacities. For nothing which is the possible object of knowledge, whether past, present, or future, can be probable to an infinite intelligence; since it cannot be discerned absolutely as it is in itself, certainly true or certainly false. But to us, probability is the very guide of life."

Only man's ignorance permits him to resolve questions of choice without preference behind the veil of chance.

Once we allow (against Leibniz) the possibility that strictly indifferent choices can arise for the supreme being, we must, I think, be prepared to grant the right to Ghazâlî, against the Arabic Aristotelians. For here a solution is possible only in terms of an inscrutable will, capable of effecting out of its own resources differentiations in the absence of any relevant difference.[103] In this regard, it is clear, we must consequently renounce the possibility of human rationalization of divine acts. The problem of choice without preference was a shrewdly selected example in support of the position maintained by the Islamic theologians in their dispute with the philosophers: this problem does illustrate effectively the thesis of Arabic Scholasticism that choices made by the divine intellect may ultimately prove inscrutable in human terms of reference.[104, 105]

103. Ghazâli makes the point (S. van den Burgh, trans., *The Incoherence of the Incoherence*, vol. 1, pp. 18–19) that it is senseless to speak of God making choices by chance, for instead of saying, "God chose to do so-and-so in a chance manner," one might instead just as well say, "So-and-so happened by chance."

104. Jonathan Edwards offers the following remarks: "If, in the instance of the two spheres, perfectly alike, it be supposed possible that God might have made them in a contrary position: that which is made at the right hand, being made at the left: then I ask, whether it is not evidently equally possible, if God had made but one of them, and that in the place of the right-hand globe, that he might have made that numerically different from what it is, and numerically different from what he did make it; though perfectly alike, and in the same place . . . ? Namely, whether he might not have made it numerically the same with that which he has now made at the left hand, and so have left that which is now created at the right hand, in a state of non-existence? And if so, whether it would not have been possible to have made one in that place, perfectly like these, and yet numerically different from both? And let it be considered, whether from this notion of a numerical difference in bodies, perfectly alike. . . . it will not follow, that there is an infinite number of numerically different possible bodies, perfectly alike, among which God chooses, by a self-determining power, when he sets about to make bodies" (*A Careful and Strict Enquiry into the Modern Prevailing Notions of That Freedom of Will which Is Supposed to Be Essential to Moral Agency, Virtue and Vice, Reward and Punishment, Praise and Blame* [Boston, 1754], pt. 2, sect. 12, subsect. 1; quoted from A. N. Prior, *Past, Present and Future* [Oxford, U.K. Clarendon Press, 1967], pp. 141–42.)

105. This essay is a somewhat expanded version of an article originally published in *Kantstudien* 51 (1959–1960): 142–75.

Chapter 2

NICHOLAS OF CUSA ON THE KORAN
A Fifteenth-Century Encounter with Islam

1. BACKGROUND

The year 1964 saw the five-hundredth anniversary of the death of Nicholas of Cusa—equally well known under the Latinized name of Cusanus—commemorated throughout centers of learning in the West. The attention of many minds focused once more upon the work of this great Catholic thinker who stood on the threshold of that crucial juncture of the Renaissance, separating the medievals from the moderns. Scholar, philosopher, theologian, cardinal, church official, and personal friend to a pope, Nicholas embodied a truly remarkable versatility of capabilities and achievements. On the sky map of philosophy, his star has gleamed brightly century after century.

Perhaps the best way to commemorate an important thinker lies in taking serious account of his work rather than in simply praising it. And since one cannot, within the limit of a single essay, take into serious account the vast output of such a multifaceted and productive scholar, it becomes necessary to confine oneself to some particular part of his work. Accordingly, the present discussion will deal with Nicholas of Cusa's treatise on the Koran, seeing that this treatise is both of considerable interest in itself and also throws an instructive light upon Nicholas's tenor of thought.

To appreciate the significance of Nicholas of Cusa's work on the Koran, one should begin by looking briefly at the historical background of the thinking about Islam in the realm of Latin Christianity. This historical course of development may be divided into three (somewhat overlapping) phases.

The first period runs from around 1100 to somewhat after 1250. This period saw a great deal of interest in Islam within Latin Christendom. Many Christian scholars occupied themselves with Arabic works in science and philosophy, and the period was one of active translation of philosophical, scientific, and even theological works from Arabic.

It was during this period that Peter the Venerable, abbot of Cluny (d. 1156), an able and farsighted scholar and friend of the eminent philosopher Bernard of Clairvaux, sponsored a Latin translation of the Koran. This translation was prepared around 1141–1143 by collaboration between a Spaniard, Hermannus Dalmata, and an Englishman, Robertus Angligena, "Robert the Englishman," also known as Robertus Retenensis. This version, which "abounds in inaccuracies and misunderstandings, and was inspired by hostile intention,"[1] was destined to become the form in which the Koran was known in Latin Christendom. Numerous manuscript copies were made in medieval times, and four centuries later it was published by Theodor Bibliander of Zürich.

During this first period, then, an active and intelligent, albeit disapproving, interest in matters relating to Islam was manifest among European men of learning.

The second period runs from roughly 1250 to around 1400. During this period, with the gradual collapse of the Crusades—and the increasing stridency of the Church in keeping crusading fervor aglow in the face of mounting difficulties—a shrill, almost hysterical, tone comes into the discussion. One instance, among many, is the *Gesta imperatorum et pontificium* by Thomas of Tuscany (d. 1278). According to Thomas, Muhammad is a thief, a murderer, a beast in human form, a magician, the firstborn and emissary of Satan himself.[2]

The third period runs from about 1400 to around 1500. With the ending of the Crusades and the waning of the crusading spirit—and the concomitant concentration upon domestic issues and difficulties—European interest in Islam went into a state of suspension. It was well on the way to atrophy when a development of political history occurred which is of great significance as background for Nicholas's treatise. But during the first half of the fifteenth century, the eyes of thinking European Christians turned once again to the East, focusing upon Constantinople. That great city had slipped by gradual stages into the state of an isolated enclave existing as a beleaguered Christian island within the hostile surrounding sea of the Ottoman Turks. This situation led, on the one hand, to an interest in a possible reconciliation between the Church of Rome and that of the East, a circumstance that took Nicholas himself on a mission to Constantinople in the late 1440s. On the other

---

1. A. J. Arberry, *The Koran Interpreted* (New York: Macmillan, 1955), p. 7.

2. Nikolaus von Cues, *Sichtung des Alkorans*, trans. Paul Naumann (Leipzig: F Meunier, 1943); *Schriften des Nikolaus von Cues*, ed. Ernst Hoffman, vols. 6 and 7), p. 26 of "Preface."

hand, the Turkish threat to Constantinople rearoused the European interest in Islam that had become dormant since the fervor of the Crusades. And the fall of the city in 1453 saw a revival in the Christian polemic against Islam.

Thus, Nicholas of Cusa's treatise on the Koran was part of the reawakening of European concern about Islam that arose in the face of the imminent and ultimately actual fall of Constantinople to the Turks.

2. NICHOLAS'S SOURCES

What were Nicholas of Cusa's sources of information about Islam? We are in the fortunate position of being able to answer this question with great accuracy. For not only did Nicholas, as a good scholar, cite the sources for his work, but he also left his books to the library of the hospital that was endowed by him at Cusa. Here the very books used by him are preserved and his annotations of them can be inspected by interested students.

For the Koran, as he himself tells us in the preface of his book, Nicholas used the already-mentioned translation sponsored by Peter the Venerable in the twelfth century. This translation was unquestionably a mixed asset, for although it did make it possible to have at least some firsthand contact with the Koran, its errors and inaccuracies were so numerous and so significant that they rendered the original quite unrecognizable.

Apart from this deficient translation of the Koran itself, Nicholas's most important—and actually more helpful—source was the treatise entitled *Propugnaculum fidei* by the Florentine Dominican Ricoldus of Monte Crucis (written ca. 1310; printed Venice, 1609).[3] Ricoldus had traveled extensively in the East, and had lived for some years in Baghdad. He knew Arabic and in his book cites the Koran in accurate translations of his own. He is reasonably well informed about Islam, and evinces a more factually accurate understanding of Islam than virtually any other medieval writer on the topic. It was in large part from this distinctly superior source that Nicholas's understanding of the nature and teachings of Islam were derived; indeed, his own work draws upon that of Ricoldus at virtually every important point.

Let us now turn from its sources to the work itself.

3. See further J. S. Sweetman, *Islam and Chistian Theology*, part 2, vol. 1, pp. 116, 160.

3. THE LEADING IDEA

In 1461–1462, a period during which he held important offices in Rome under the aegis of his friend Pope Pius II, Nicholas of Cusa wrote his *Cribratio Alchorani* (Sifting of the Koran).[4] He had been equipped for this task by some personal experience of Islam derived from a visit to Constantinople in 1437–1438, in connection with a mission working in the interests of unity between the Eastern and Western churches. (It might be noted parenthetically that, in consequence of this mission, Nicholas himself participated in the negotiations at the Council of Florence in 1438 that resulted in an abortive agreement for such a union.)

Over and above this brief occasion for firsthand contact, Nicholas was widely read in the ramified literature on Islamic matters available in Latin. No contemporary European theologian could match his knowledge of the Latin literature relating to Islamic philosophy and religion.

The guiding idea of Nicholas's *Cribratio Alchorani* is a shrewd and an interesting one. It is definitely not, as the majority of its medieval predecessors were, a blanket denunciation, but a careful attempt to sift out the Christian and the non-Christian elements of the Koran. (This objective is made explicit in the very title of the treatise itself: *cribrare* = to sift out.) Rather than reject the Koran en bloc, Nicholas wants to distinguish between a Muhammad who has listened to the voice of the God who enters into the hearts of all men, and a Muhammad who advances ideas and objectives of his own.

Notwithstanding its greater discrimination, Nicholas's *Sifting of the Koran* is avowedly a work of Christian polemic against Islam. Conforming to the tradition derived from St. John of Damascus in the eighth century, who classes Islam as a Christian heresy, Nicholas regards Muhammad as having started from a Christian position under the influence of Christian (Nestorian) teachers, and then departing from it at first partly under the corrupting influence of Jews, and partly to render the message more readily audible to the heathen Arabs. Then, ultimately, Muhammad made increasingly radical departures in order to exploit his growing following as an instrument of personal power.

Inherent in this view is a possibility that greatly intrigued Nicholas and some of his friends. If Islam is a corrupted version of Christianity so that Christianity is the starting point of Islam—the purified proto-Islam

4. Nicholas of Cusa's *Cribratio Alchorani* is now readily accessible in a German translation by Paul Naumann (see note 2); my discussion owes much to Naumann's informative introduction. Mention must also be made of Nicholas's tract *On Peace Among the Religious* (*De pace seu concordantia fidei*), translated by Klaus Berger (*Vom Frieden Zwischen den Religionen* [Frankfurt: Insel Verlag, 2002]).

of a corrupted Koranic Islam—then a Muslim "return" to the Church becomes a thing conceivable. This train of thought provides the background for that very curious document of church history, the letter of 1461/1462 of Pope Pius II to Sultan Muhammad II calling upon the sultan to accept Christianity and to become the successor of the Byzantine emperors as temporal head of the Christian Orient.[5] This letter, to which the sultan did not even deign to make a reply, for a brief time aroused the imagination of Europe by the dazzling prospect of a religious triumph as compensatory climax to a long course of military catastrophe in the East.

4. NICHOLAS'S VIEW OF THE KORAN

Nicholas of Cusa's conception of the Koran is, as already indicated, unique in its radical departure from the standard strain of Christian polemic against Islam. His view is as follows:

Muhammad's basic impulse was good—his eye was upon the path to God revealed to men imperfectly by Moses and fully by Christ, and he sought to guide the heathen Arabs to this path and make it easy for them. The Muslim well arose from a sound spring, even though heretical Christians and corrupting Jews poisoned it, and the self-interest that made Muhammad into a tool of the devil ultimately perverted it.

Not only was Muhammad's starting intention valid, but the work he produced, the Koran, is of genuine religious merit. It contains much that is sound and incorporates a great deal of truth. It is a work heavily influenced by the Old and New Testaments, whose reflected light illuminates it at many points. (The extent to which this view requires sympathetic interpretation is evidenced by the fact that the Koran contains but one direct quotation from the Scriptures: Koran 21:105, which quotes Ps. 37:29.) Of course it goes amiss at numerous and crucial junctures, and of course it contains nothing of merit over and above what is to be found in the Gospels. *Si quid pulchri, veri et clari in Alcoran reperitur, necesse est, quod sit radius lucidissimi Evangelii* (*Cribratio,* 1.6).

How did Nicholas explain his view that Muhammad, having caught many glimpses of Christian truths, went fundamentally astray? How did he account for the departures of the Koran from the New Testament? Here Nicholas has ready a threefold answer: (1) misunderstandings due to the impeding machinations of Nestorians and of Jews who influenced Muhammad, (2) deliberate didactic departures to adapt the message to the primitive and pagan Arabs, and (3) deliberate falsifications

5. See P. Naumann, trans., Nikolaus von Cues, *Sichtung des Alkorans*, pp. 11–12; cf. Sweetman, *Islam and Christian Theology*, p. 161, n. 3.

to serve the self-interest of the Prophet and/or the political advantage of his following.

The greater part of Nicholas of Cusa's discussion is thus devoted to a detailed critique of the departures of the Koran from Christian teachings and the deployment of a Christian polemic—in its fundamentals along the usual lines—against the teachings of Islam, dwelling largely upon an apology for those Christian teachings which, like the doctrine of the Trinity, had formed foci of Islamic attacks on Christianity.

On Nicholas's view of the matter, the Koran is thus a mixture in which the sound grains of truth are intermingled with the chaff of falsity. The correct Christian approach to the bible of Islam cannot be a complete condemnation, but should be a carefully discriminative sifting *(cribratio)* of truth from error.

This attitude infuses and shapes the whole strategy of Nicholas's polemic against Islam. It is entirely *internal,* taking its stand upon the Koran itself and that book's own acknowledgment of the truth of the Gospels. As Nicholas saw the matter, the Koran, in its recognition of the Bible and in the acceptance of the biblical view of Jesus' message and role, condemns itself out of its own mouth at all points of conflict. In particular, his polemic against Islam dwelt upon those matters in which the declarations of the Koran appeared to him as self-contradictory. (One example is Chapter 9 of Book 3, devoted to the thesis "that Muhammad wrote of Christ sometimes as god and man both, sometimes only as man, and sometimes as god in the singular, sometimes in the plural.")

This point of view also provides the rationale that brought Nicholas to that favorite concept of our own day: the idea of a dialogue. Writing to his friend John of Segovia, he welcomed the idea of a conference with the Muslims: *Non est dubium medio principium temporalium quos Teucri sacerdotibus praeferunt, ad colloquia posse perveniri, et ex illis furor mitigabitur, et veritas se ipsam ostendet cum profectu fidei nostrae.* In this hopeful view of the constructive value of a "dialogue" *(colloquium)*—that this would mitigate the furor of disputation and prove useful for religion—Nicholas of Cusa is perhaps more a child of our time than of his own.

5. SOME BLIND SPOTS IN NICHOLAS'S VIEW OF THE KORAN

It is, however, only just to say that—despite the fact that his judgment of the Koran was unusually favorable for his place and time—Nicholas's view of the Bible of Islam was subject to certain sharp limitations, perhaps even deserving the name of blind spots.

Of these, the first and most obvious relates to the literary quality of the Koran. The Bible of Islam is a work whose beauty of language was from the first accepted by Muslims as a proof of divine inspiration. This element was, of course, wholly lost on Nicholas, for whom the Koran (seen only in dry-as-dust translations) might as well have been a dissertation of Scholastic theology.

A more crucial point is bound up with this first blind spot. Nicholas is able to see merit in the Koran only at those points at which it agrees with the Gospels. He is flatly unwilling to grant that there may be some special merit of insight or inspiration in the scripturally nonredundant parts of the Koran—not, to be sure, as regards its declarations on matters of faith and doctrine, but in its essentially secular ordinances, for example, those regarding the reformation of the social or communal affairs of the Arabs.

Moreover, in his eagerness to use the Koran itself as an instrument of his cause, Nicholas is occasionally led to do (no doubt unwittingly) violence to the text in order to bend it to his objectives. Consider, for example, the following Koranic passage, cited in the translation of A. J. Arberry: (Sūrah 4, "Women," verses 167–70):

People of the Book, go not beyond the bounds in your religion, and say not as to God but the truth. The Messiah, Jesus son of Mary, was only the Messenger of God and His word that He committed to Mary, and a Spirit sent by Him. So believe in God and his Messengers. Say not, "Three." Refrain; better is it for you. God is only One God, Glory be to Him. Say not that He should have a son! To Him belongs all that is in the heavens and in the earth; God suffices for a guardian. The Messiah will not disdain to be a servant of God, nor will the angels who are near stationed to Him.[6]

This is an obvious piece of anti-Christian, anti-Trinitarian polemic. But Nicholas cites only a part of the text in isolation from its context: "Jesus son of Mary is God's messenger" (*Cribratio*, 1.12). Taken thus, out of context and in deceptive translation, Nicholas uses this passage as a proof text to show that the Koran itself countenances a Trinitarian position, and acknowledges the divinity of Jesus.

Needless to say, however, there should be no astonishment regarding the fact that the merits that Nicholas can find in the Koran extend over a limited area. The noteworthy thing is that there is any such area at all.

---

6. The best English translation of the Koran is that of A. J. Arberry, *The Koran Interpreted*, 2 vols. (New York: Macmillan, 1955). Arberry's "Preface" provides much interesting information about the transmission of the Koran to Europe.

6. THE RATIONALE OF NICHOLAS'S TREATISE

The unique character of Nicholas's treatise as a Christian evaluation of the Koran that is prepared to find in it good points as well as bad derives not from his sources—how could it?—but from his own brain. It developed against the backdrop of his thinking about the nature of religion as such.

Nicholas's attitude toward the nature and diversity of religions is set forth in his important treatise *De pace seu concordantia fidei* (On peace or concord in religion).[7] Here Nicholas expounds a view of religions that, while not (of course) overtly relativistic, nevertheless emanates a certain aura of relativism. The basic concept developed here may be indicated by the analogy of mountain climbing. The mountaintop represents the summit of genuine religious knowledge, and the different paths leading up to the same summit—some rendering its attainment easy of access, others rocky, difficult, and full of pitfalls—represent diverse religions. The analogy—here used only for explanatory purposes, it being nowhere explicit in Nicholas's writings—illustrates graphically the tenor of his thought about religious diversity within Christianity itself. For he views this diversity as perfectly legitimate—if not as regards the fundamentals of doctrine, then at any rate as regards rite: *una religio in rituum varietate*. The positivity of Nicholas's approach to the Koran must be judged—and can only be understood—within this background context of the generously open tendency of his religious philosophy. The comprehensive philosophical perspective he brought to the particular case made it possible for Nicholas to see gleams of the light of Truth where eyes of narrower vision saw only the handiwork of the devil.

7. CONCLUSION

We live in an era that, whatever may be its shortcomings in other respects, is a time of increased mutual sympathy and understanding among diverse religious groups.[8] In a domain once ruled by bitter theological warfare, we can occasionally hear the beating of the wings of the dove of peace. The idea of Christianity's reconciliation with Islam may even nowadays seem remote, but it cannot today be dismissed as an utter absurdity. The thesis of St. John of Damascus that Islam is but a

7. See further R. Klibansky and H. Bascour, *Nicolai de Cusa de Pace Fidei*, Supp. 3 of *Mediaeval and Renaissance Studies*, the Warburg Institute, University of London, 1956.

8. [Footnote added in 2003] This overoptimistic assessment was written in 1964, and the unhappy fact is that much turbulent water has flowed since then under the bridge that separates Christianity and Islam.

Christian heresy provides the continuing basis for a possible reconciliation, at any rate on the Christian side of the divide. Nicholas of Cusa realized, more clearly than any other theologian of his day, the implications, both theological and practical, of such a position. One cannot but honor him both as having a mind of great penetration and as being a man of goodwill, whose sympathetic vision was able to discern some good where his compatriots saw nothing except the unmixed blackness of wicked error.[9]

9. This chapter is a lightly redacted version of an essay that was originally published in *The Muslim World* 55 (1965): 195–202. It grew out of a public lecture delivered at the Cusanus Commemoration Conference held at the University of Rochester on November 6, 1964.

Chapter 3

ON LEARNED IGNORANCE AND THE LIMITS OF KNOWLEDGE

1. KNOWLEDGE ABOUT IGNORANCE

We are well advised to follow the counsel of Nicholas of Cusa and endeavor to be knowledgeable about our own ignorance. For in endeavoring to get a firm grasp on the human situation, one of the most problem-strewn regions of inquiry relates to this issue of the limitations of our knowledge. It is next to impossible to fathom the depth of our ignorance and get a clear fix on it. After all, whatever people can know, they can also be ignorant about—perhaps with a handful of Cartesian exceptions such as the fact that they themselves exist and can think.

There is, of course, no difficulty about my knowing that there are *some* facts that I do not know. And there is certainly no difficulty of principle in *your* knowing in detail what some of these facts are. But my knowing that there is a *particular* fact which, as such, is unknown to me is impracticable for me. For there is a crucial difference between the indefinite "I know that there is some fact that I do not know" and the specific "Such and such is a fact of which I know that I do not know it." The first is unproblematic but the second is not, since to know of something that it is a fact I must know it as such, so that we have what is effectively a contradiction in terms. I can know about my factual ignorance only at the level of generalized indefiniteness, but cannot know it in concrete detail. I can coherently hold that $2 + 2 = 4$ is a *claim* (or a *supposed* fact) that I do not know to be the case, but I cannot meaningfully hold it to be an *actual* fact that I do not know to be the case. For to acknowledge a fact as fact is to assert knowledge of it.[1]

---

1. Factual knowledge is the central factor here. Performative knowledge is something else again—one can certainly know that there are various specific things we cannot do. Again, I can know of my ignorance of a certain *range* of facts (the geography of Nepal, the dreams of Julius Caesar, what it is that yon Urdu speaker is saying), but the specifics of such ignorance are bound to elude me.

The reality of it is that even knowledge about the *extent* of my igno-rance is unavailable to me. For what is at issue with extent is the ratio of the manifold of what I do know to the manifold of what I do not know. And it is impossible in the nature of things for me to determine the lat-ter with exactitude. After all, the actual situation is not that of a cross-word puzzle—or that of geographic exploration—where the size of the terra incognita can be somehow measured a priori, in advance of the details that are going to be filled in. We can form no sensible advance estimate of the imponderable domain of what can be known but is not. (We can specify various questions that we cannot answer, but we cannot specify any questions that have never occurred to us.) We cannot map the boundaries of our ignorance.

There are, of course, finite bodies of knowledge. There is only so much you can know about the content of Boston's 1995 telephone di-rectory, namely, the totality of what is on its pages. But this sort of thing can transpire only in very special circumstances and never with respect to fields or areas of knowledge such as medicine or physics that deal with the products of nature rather than with human artifice since fur-ther discovery is always in prospect here.

2. SCIENTIFIC PROGRESS: DIFFICULTIES IN PREDICTING FUTURE KNOWLEDGE

Our ignorance here and now is indicated in a particularly vivid way in relation to future knowledge.[2] The splendid dictum that "the past is a different country—they do things differently there" has much to be said for it. For the progressive and developmental nature of knowledge means that knowledge of the future is substantially unavailable to the investigators of the present. The prospect of present knowledge about future discoveries is deeply problematic because the future of knowl-edge is inherently impredictable. If the substance of future discoveries were available here and now, then these discoveries themselves would be made here and now and would not—contrary to hypothesis—consti-tute future discoveries. The details of the cognitive future are hidden in an impenetrable fog.

And this is nowhere more decidedly the case than with respect to nat-ural science. Making scientifically responsible predictions about the fu-

2. As the medievals saw it, even an omniscient God has problems where knowledge of the future is concerned. The literature of this subject is vast, but a good entry is provided by Calvin Normore, "Future Contingency," in Norman Kretzmann et al., eds., *The Cam-bridge History of Later Medieval Philosophy* (Cambridge, U.K.: Cambridge University Press, 1983), pp. 358–82.

ture of science itself is an impracticable project. All that we know is that it will be different from the existing situation in important but unforeseeable ways. The best that we can do in matters of science and technology forecasting is to look toward those developments that are "in the pipeline." Here the reasonable extrapolation of the character, orientation, and direction of the current state of the art is a powerful forecasting tool on the positive side of the issue. But even this conservative approach has its problems. For since we cannot predict the answers to the presently open questions of natural science, we also cannot predict its future questions, which hinge upon those as yet unrealizable answers. The questions of the future are engendered by the answers to those we have on hand. Accordingly, we cannot predict science's future solutions to its problems because we cannot even predict in detail just what these problems will be.

We know—or at any rate we can safely predict—*that* future science will make major discoveries (both theoretical and observational) in the next century, but we cannot say *what* they are and *how* they will be made, since otherwise we could proceed to make them here and now. We could not possibly predict now the substantive content of our future discoveries—those that result from our future cognitive choices. For to do so would be to transform them into present discoveries which, by hypothesis, they just are not.[3] In the context of questions about matters of scientific importance, then, we must be prepared for surprises.

The inherent impredictability of future scientific developments—the fact that inferences from one state of science to another are impracticable—means that *present-day science cannot speak for future science.* Through-

---

3. As one commentator has wisely written: "But prediction in the field of pure science is another matter. The scientist sets forth over an unchartered sea and the scribe, left behind on the dock, is asked what he may find at the other side of the waters. If the scribe knew, the scientist would not have to make his voyage" (Anonymous, "The Future as Suggested by Developments of the Past Seventy-Five Years," *Scientific American* 123 [1920]: 321). The role of unforeseeable innovations in science forms a key part of Popper's case against the impredictability of man's social affairs—given that new science engenders new technologies, which in turn make for new modes of social organization; see K. R. Popper, *The Poverty of Historicism* (London: Routledge & Kegan Paul, 1957), p. vi and passim. The impredictability of revolutionary changes in science also figures centrally in W. B. Gallie's "The Limits of Prediction," in S. Körner, ed., *Observation and Interpretation* (New York: Academic Press, 1957). Gallie's argumentation is weakened, however, by a failure to distinguish between the generic fact of future discovery in a certain domain and its specific nature. See also Peter Urbach, "Is Any of Popper's Arguments against Historicism Valid?" (*British Journal for the Philosophy of Science* 29 [1978]: 117–30; see esp. pp. 128–29), whose deliberations seem (to this writer) to skirt the key issues. A judicious and sympathetic treatment is given in Alex Rosenberg, "Scientific Innovation and the Limits of Social Scientific Prediction," *Synthese* 97 (1993): 161–81. On the present issue Rosenberg cites the instructive anecdote of the musician who answered the question: "Where is jazz heading," with the response: "If I knew that, I'd be there already" (p. 167).

out the domain of innovation in science, technology, and the arts we find processes of creative innovation whose products defy all prospects of predictability. The key fact in this connection is that of the fundamental epistemological law that the cognitive resources of an inferior (lower) state of the art cannot afford the means for foreseeing the operations of a superior (higher) one.

Illustrations of this situation abound in historical experience. If there was one thing of which the science of the first half of the seventeenth century was unalloyedly confident, it was that natural processes are based on contact and interaction, and that there can be no such thing as action at a distance. Newtonian gravitation burst upon this scene like a bombshell. Newton's supporters simply stonewalled. Roger Cotes explicitly denied that there was a problem, arguing (in his preface to the second edition of Newton's *Principia*) that nature was *generally* unintelligible, so that the unintelligibility of forces acting without contact was nothing specifically worrisome. However unpalatable Cotes's position may seem to us as a precept for science—after all, making nature's workings understandable is one of the aims of the enterprise—there is something to be said for it, albeit not as science but as metascience. For we cannot hold the science of tomorrow bound to the doctrines and dogmas of the science of today. The fact that science faces the ongoing prospect of a change of mind means that its cognitive future is inaccessible to even the ablest of present-day workers. After Pasteur had shown that bacteria could come only from preexisting bacteria, Darwin wrote that "it is mere rubbish thinking of the origin of life; one might as well think of the origin of matter."[4] One might indeed!

3. QUESTION PROPAGATION

Cognitive progress is commonly thought of in terms of the discovery of new facts—new information about things. But the situation is more complicated because not only *knowledge* but also *questions* must come into consideration. For progress on the side of *questions* is a crucial mode of cognitive progress, correlative with—and every bit as important as—progress on the side of *information*, of course. The questions opened up for our consideration are as crucial and definitive a facet of a body of knowledge as are the theses that it endorses. And frequently the questions of the future are engendered by the answers that the future will give to currently unanswered questions. Accordingly, we can-

4. Quoted in Philip Handler, ed., *Biology and the Future of Man* (Oxford, U.K.: Clarendon Press, 1970), p. 165.

not predict science's solutions to its problems because we cannot even predict in detail just what these problems will be.

Change in knowledge carries change in questions in its wake, so the state of questioning this changes no less drastically than the state of knowledge. Any alterations in the membership of our body of knowledge will afford new presuppositions for further questions that were not available before. The question solved in one era could well not even arise in another—for example, Aristotle could not have wondered whether plutonium is radioactive. And it is not just that he did not know what the correct answer to the question happens to be: the very question not only *did* not occur to him, but actually *could* not have occurred to him because the cognitive framework of the then-existing state of knowledge did not afford the conceptual instruments with which alone this question can be posed.

Moreover, questions can even disappear altogether from the agenda of cognitive concern. The reality of it is that we can discover:

1. New (i.e., *different*) answers to old questions.
2. New questions.
3. The impropriety or illegitimacy of our old questions, in that they were based on erroneous or untenable presuppositions—that is, once-purported "facts" that are no longer viewed as acceptable.

With type 1 we uncover an error of commission by discovering that a wrong answer has been given in our previous question-answering endeavors. With type 2 we discover that there are certain questions that have not heretofore been posed at all: we uncover an error of omission in our former question-asking endeavors. Finally, with type 3 we find that one has asked the wrong question altogether: we uncover an "error of understanding" in the context of our former question-asking endeavors. Thus if we abandon the luminiferous aether as a vehicle for electromagnetic radiation, then we lose at one stroke the whole host of questions about its composition, structure, mode of operation, origin, and so on. For such improper questions rest on incorrect presuppositions (and are thus generally bound up with type 1 discoveries).

The second of these types of question-oriented discovery represents a characteristic phenomenon. As further lines of questioning unfold, our old answers can come to be seen as untenable and in need of correction or replacement. The course of change with respect to questions is no less dramatic than that of cognitive change itself, seeing that the questions we pose at any juncture will have to be based on the presuppositions of the existing stage of the art. And it lies in the nature of this developmental process that our knowledge is incomplete at any stage—irrespective of what the date on the calendar may happen to be.

The phenomenon of the ever-continuing "birth" of new questions was first emphasized by Immanuel Kant, who described it in terms of a continually evolving cycle of questions and answers:

Who can satisfy himself with mere empirical knowledge in all the cosmological questions of the duration and of the magnitude of the world, of freedom or of natural necessity, since *every answer given on principles of experience begets a fresh question, which likewise requires its answer* and thereby clearly shows the insufficiency of all physical modes of explanation to satisfy reason.[5]

The line of thought set out in the italicized passage suggests the following *Principle of Question Propagation (Kant's Principle):* "The solution of any factual (scientific) question gives rise to yet further unsolved questions." This principle of question proliferation in empirical inquiry indicates a fact of importance for the theory of scientific progress. One need not claim longevity—let alone immortality—for any of the *current* problems to assure that there will be problems ten or one hundred generations hence. (As immortal individuals are not needed to assure the immortality of the race, so immortal problems are not needed to assure the immortality of problems.)

4. INCOMPLETENESS

Could we ever bring our scientific understanding of the world's ways to a state of completeness? This issue dissolves into a plurality of questions:

A. Could we ever be in a position to claim that we can predict everything that will or will not occur? (Predictive completion)

B. Could we ever be in a position to claim that we know all the laws of nature? (Nomic completion)

C. Could we ever be in a position to claim that we can explain everything that occurs? (Explanatory completion)

D. Could we ever be in a position to answer all our scientific questions? (Erotetic completion)

Let us consider in turn these different modes of potential scientific completeness:

5. Immanuel Kant, *Prolegomena to Any Future Metaphysic* (1783), sect. 57.

A. Predictive Completeness

The idea of predictive completeness calls for being able to predict everything that occurs in nature. It represents a forlorn hope. For predictors—who are, after all, themselves part of the world—are of necessity bound to fail even in merely self-predictive matters. Thus consider confronting a predictor with the problem posed by the question:

P_1: When you answer this question, will the answer be negative?

This is a question which—for reasons of general principle—no predictor can ever answer satisfactorily. For consider the available possibilities:

	Actually	
Answer given	*correct answer?*	*Agreement?*
YES	NO	NO
NO	YES	NO
CAN'T SAY	NO	NO

On this question, there just is no way in which a predictor's response could possibly agree with the actual facts of the matter. Even the seemingly plausible response "I can't say" automatically constitutes a self-falsifying answer, since in giving this answer the predictor would automatically make "No" into the response called for by the proprieties of the situation.

Nevertheless, there actually is a fact of the matter here. The problem poses a perfectly meaningful question to which *another* predictor could give a putatively correct answer—namely, by saying: "No—that predictor cannot answer this question at all; the question will condemn a predictor to baffled silence." So while the question posed in P_1 will be irresolvable by a *particular* predictor, it could—in theory—be answered by *other* predictors and is accordingly not predictively intractable flat-out.

There are, however, other questions that do indeed represent predictive *insolubilia* of a more drastic sort. One of them is:

P_2: What is an example of a predictive question that no predictor will ever state?

No doubt there are such items. But in answering *this* question the predictor would have to stake a claim of the form: "Q is an example of a predictive question that no predictor will ever state." And in the very making of this claim the predictor would falsify it. It is thus automatically impossible to effect a satisfactory resolution. However, the question is neither meaningless nor irresolvable. Its definitive presupposition, "There is a predictive question that no predictor will ever consider," is beyond doubt true. What we thus have in P_2 is an example of an in-principle solvable—and thus "meaningful"—predictive question that, as a matter of necessity in the logical scheme of things, no predictor can ever resolve satisfactorily. No predictor can manage it—nor can the megapredictive project at issue with science-at-large. Predictive completeness is just not in prospect.

B. Nomic Completeness

Let us now turn from events to laws. What of completeness in point of discovering nature's laws?

Here too the outlook is not propitious. After all, even a system that is finitely complex both in its physical makeup and in its functional laws might nevertheless be infinitely complex in the phenomena that it manifests over time. For the operations of a structurally and lawfully finite system can yet exhibit an infinite intricacy in *productive complexity*, manifesting this limitless diversity in the working out of its processes rather than as regards its spatiostructural composition or the nomic comportment of its basic components. Even if the number of constituents of nature were small, there will be endless ways in which they can be combined to yield an emergently ever more complex lawful order. Think here of the examples of letters, syllables, words, sentences, paragraphs, books, genres (novels, reference books, etc.), libraries, and library systems. Even a finite nature can, like a typewriter with a limited and operationally simple keyboard, yield an endlessly varied text with unending strata of lawful order—even though they would not exist without them. And those higher level laws need not be derivable from lower level ones. For nature can produce a steady stream of new products—"new" not necessarily in kind but in their functional interrelationships and thus in their theoretical implications.

And there is no need to assume a ceiling to such a sequence of levels of integrative complexity of phenomenal diversity. The different levels each exhibit an order of their own. The phenomena we attain in the n-th level can have features whose investigation takes us to the $n + 1$ level. As the course of cosmic evolution proceeds from physics to chemistry to biology and beyond, new phenomena and new laws arise at every further level of integrative order. The diverse facets of nature can generate conceptually new strata of operations that yield a potentially unending sequence of domain levels, each giving rise to its own characteristic principles of organization, themselves quite unpredictable from the standpoint of the other levels. In this way, even a relatively simple world as regards its basic operations can come to have an effectively infinite cognitive depth, once the notion of a natural phenomenon is broadened to include not just the processes themselves and the products they produce but also the relationships among them.

Take, for example, some repeatedly exemplified physical feature and then contemplate the sequence of os and 1s obtained according to the rule that the i-th entry in the sequence is 1 if this feature is exemplified on occasion number i, and o if not. Whenever two such feature-concepts, say C and C', generate such sequences in the manner of

$C:$ 01001 10100 . . .
$C':$ 1001011010 . . . ,

then we can introduce the corresponding matching sequence for C and C', 0010010001 . . . , which is such that its i-th position is 1 if the two base sequences agree at their respective i-th positions, and o if they disagree. Such matching sequences will have a life of their own. For example, even if two base sequences are random, their matching sequences need not be—for example, when those base sequences simply exchange os and 1s. (Even totally random phenomena can be related by orderly laws of coordination.)

And so our knowledge of nature's workings can in principle be endlessly enhanced and deepened by contemplating an unending proliferation of phenomenal levels that exhibit emergently novel sorts of lawful order.

C. Explanatory Completeness

Could we manage to *explain everything* that occurs in nature? Clearly not. For one thing, since nothing in nature is self-explanatory, we could not explain our explanations through to the bitter end. Moreover, certain occurrences are—to all present appearances—going to be unexplainable in principle in a stochastic universe: for example, why a certain atom of an unstable transuranic element decayed at the exact time it did.

The best that science can do—and the most we can ever reasonably ask of it—is to be able to explain everything that is explicable. And just here—on this issue of what is explicable—science itself must by our source of information. It alone can be allowed to determine the legitimacy of explanatory questions. And here the *present* state of the art in science can never be accepted as altogether definitive. To determine that science can indeed resolve every appropriate explanatory question we would first have to assume a completed and perfected science to rule on this issue of appropriateness. And this consideration alone renders the idea of explanatory completeness deeply problematic if not altogether unrealizable.

D. *Erotetic Completeness*

Could we ever possibly achieve erotetic completeness, the condition of being able to resolve, in principle, all of our (legitimately posable) questions about the world? Could we ever actually find ourselves in this happy position?[6]

In theory, yes. A body of science certainly could be such as to provide answers to all those questions it allows to arise. But just how meaningful would this mode of completeness be?

It is sobering to realize that the erotetic completeness of a state of science does not necessarily betoken its comprehensiveness or sufficiency. It might reflect the paucity of the range of questions we are prepared to contemplate—a deficiency of imagination, so to speak. When the range of our knowledge is sufficiently restricted, then its question-resolving completeness will merely reflect this impoverishment rather than its intrinsic adequacy. Conceivably, if improbably, science might reach a purely fortuitous equilibrium between problems and solutions. It could eventually be "completed" in the narrow erotetic sense—providing an answer to every question one can pose in the then-existing (albeit possibly still imperfect) state of knowledge—without thereby being completed in the larger sense of answering the questions that would arise if only one could probe nature just a bit more deeply. And so our corpus of scientific knowledge could be erotetically complete and yet fundamentally inadequate. Thus, even if realized, this erotetic mode of completeness would not be particularly meaningful. (To be sure, this discussion proceeds at the level of supposition contrary to fact. The exfoliation of new questions from old in the course of scientific inquiry that is at issue in Kant's Principle of Question Propagation spells the infeasibility of ever attaining completeness in question resolution.)

Lessons

Theorists from time to time indulge in eschatological conjecture by telling us that the scientific venture is approaching its end.[7] And it is, of course, entirely *conceivable* that natural science will come to a stop, and

---

6. Note that this is independent of the question "Would we ever want to do so?" Would we ever really want to answer all those predictive questions about ourselves and our environment, or are we more comfortable in the condition in which "ignorance is bliss"?

7. This sentiment was abroad among physicists of the fin-de-siècle era of 1890–1900;

will do so not in consequence of a cessation of intelligent life but in C. S. Peirce's more interesting sense of a completion of the project: of eventually reaching a condition after which even indefinitely ongoing inquiry will not—and indeed in the very nature of things *cannot*—produce any significant change, because inquiry has come to "the end of the road." The situation would be analogous to that envisaged in the apocryphal story in vogue during the middle 1800s regarding the commissioner of the U.S. Patents Office who resigned his post because there was nothing left to invent.[8]

Such a development is in theory possible. But the fact is that we can never determine that it is actual. For there is no practicable way in which the claim that science has achieved temporal finality can be validated. The question "Is the current state of science, *S*, final and altogether fixed?" is one for which we can never legitimate an affirmative answer since the prospect of future changes of *S* can never be precluded. The evidential realities of our epistemic situation are such that we cannot plausibly move beyond it. A prevailing state of scientific knowledge cannot establish its own permanence. For taking this posture embeds *finality* in *completeness*, and in doing so jumps from the frying pan into the fire.

We can never ascertain that science has attained the w-condition of final completion, since from our point of view the possibility of further change lying "just around the corner" can never be ruled out finally and decisively. The reality of natural science is such that our knowledge of nature must ever be presumed to be incomplete.

And so we have no alternative but to proceed on the assumption that the era of cognitive innovation is not over—that *future* science can and will prove to be *different* science and that the pool of potential discovery is in principle bottomless.

5. RELATING KNOWLEDGE TO IGNORANCE

The fact that we can never resolve all of our questions decisively means that we must come to terms with the unavoidability of ignorance. Just how serious a liability does this constitute?

Although ignorance lies at the core of the present discussion, this should not be seen as an invitation to radical skepticism. After all, even

---

see Lawrence Badash, "The Completeness of Nineteenth-Century Science," *Isis* 63 (1972): 48–58. And such sentiments are coming back into fashion today; see S. W. Hawking, "Is the End in Sight for Theoretical Physics?," *Physics Bulletin* 32 (1981): 15–17.

8. See Eber Jeffrey, "Nothing Left to Invent," *Journal of the Patent Office Society* 22 (July 1940): 479–81.

in cognitive matters we can—strange to say—manage to extract truth from error. Accordingly, one fundamental feature of inquiry is represented by the following:

Thesis 1: *Insofar as our thinking is vague, truth is accessible even in the face of error.*

Consider the situation where you correctly accept *P*-or-*Q*. But—so let it be supposed—the truth of this disjunction roots entirely in that of *P*, while *Q* is quite false. However, you accept *P*-or-*Q* only because you are mistakenly convinced of the truth of *Q;* it so happens that *P* is something you actually disbelieve. Yet despite your error, your belief is entirely true.[9] Consider a concrete instance. You believe that Smith bought some furniture because he bought a table. However, it was, in fact, a chair that he bought, something you would flatly reject. Nevertheless, your belief that he bought some furniture is unquestionably correct. The error in which you are involved, although real, is not so grave as to undo the truth of your belief.

Ignorance is reflected in an inability to answer questions appropriately. But one has to be careful in this regard. Answering a question informatively is not just a matter of offering a *correct* answer but also a matter of offering an *exact* answer.

Thus consider the question "What is the population of Shanghai?" If I respond "More than ten and less than ten billion," I have provided a *correct* answer, but one that is not particularly helpful. This example illustrates a more far-reaching point.

Thesis 2: *There is in general an inverse relationship between the precision or definiteness of a judgment and its security: detail and reliability—infiniteness and probability—stand in a competing interconnection.*

Increased confidence in the correctness of our estimates can always be purchased at the price of decreased accuracy. We estimate the height of the tree at *around* 25 feet. We are *quite sure* that the tree is 25 ± 5 feet high. We are *virtually certain* that its height is 25 ± 10 feet. But we can be *completely and absolutely sure* that its height is between 1 inch and 100 yards. Of this we can be "completely sure" in the sense that we are "absolutely certain," "certain beyond the shadow of a doubt," "as certain as we can be of anything in the world," "so sure that we would be willing to stake our life on it," and the like. For any sort of estimate whatsoever there is always a characteristic trade-off relationship between the evidential *security* of the estimate, on the one hand (as determinable on the basis of its probability or degree of acceptability), and, on the other

9. Examples of this sort indicate why philosophers are unwilling to identify *knowledge* with *true belief.*

hand, its contentual *definitiveness* by way of exactness, detail, precision, and the like. A *complementarity* relationship of sorts thus obtains here as between definiteness and security.

This line of thought points toward the instructive lesson that insofar as our ignorance of relevant matters leads us to be vague in our judgments, we may well manage to enhance our quota of available information. The fact of the matter is that we have:

Thesis 3: *By constraining us to make vaguer judgments, ignorance enhances our access to correct information (albeit at the cost of less detail and precision).*

Thus if I have forgotten that Seattle is in Washington State, then if "forced to guess" where it is I might well erroneously locate it in Oregon. Nevertheless, my vague judgment that "Seattle is located in the northwestern United States" is quite correct. This state of affairs means that when the truth of our claims is critical we generally "play it safe" and make our commitments less definite and detailed.

Consider, for example, so simple and colloquial a piece of factual reportage as "The servant declared that he could no longer do his master's bidding." This statement is pervaded by a magisterial vagueness. It conveys very little about what went on in the exchange between servant and master. We are told virtually nothing about what either of them actually said. What the object of their discussion was, what form of words they used, the manner of their discourse (Did the master order or request? Was the servant speaking from rueful incapacity or from belligerent defiance?)—all these are questions we cannot begin to answer. Even the relationship at issue, whether owner/slave or employer/employee, is left in total obscurity. In sum, there is a vast range of indeterminacy here—a great multitude of very different scenarios would fit perfectly well to the description of events which that individual statement puts before us. And this vagueness clearly provides a protective shell to guard that statement against a charge of falsity. Irrespective of how matters might actually stand within a vast range of alternative circumstances and conditions, a vague statement remains secure, its truth unaffected by which possibility is realized. And in practical matters in particular, such rough guidance is often altogether enough. We do not need to know the likelihood of rain to three decimal places to make it sensible for us to take an umbrella with us when we go out.

Other cognate considerations also condition the pursuit of truth in inquiry. When we are dealing with *assured* truths, additional information cannot unravel or destabilize what we have. Since the-truth-as-a-whole must be consistent, truths have to be compatible with one another and new truths cannot come into logical conflict with old ones. Actual truths, once we have them, are money in the bank. But *likely* truths—plausible or probable truths—are something else again. Consider the case of the "Lottery Paradox." A million tickets are out there. It is highly likely that No. 1 will not be drawn. And the same with No. 2—and with No. 3, and so on. And yet by the time we have conceived this process of 1,000,000—always ongoing while we merely obtain with what had gone before—we know we have falsehood on our hands.

In theory, our putative truths are generally vulnerable. New plausible or probable truths can destabilize old ones. Additional evidence can unravel old conclusions. P can be probable relative to Q and yet improbable relative to $Q + R$. Inductive conclusions are never money in the bank. When what we accept is inductively derived from probabilities and plausibilities, it is vulnerable to unraveling. It is an ever-present prospect that we will have to revisit and reassess them in the light of new information.

This line of thought has important implications for the applicative bearing of knowledge. For the reality of it is that to act with more and better information is not necessarily to act more effectively. One of the deepest ironies of the epistemic realm is represented by:

Thesis 4: *It would be an error to think that a conclusion based on fuller information is necessarily an improvement, presenting us with a result that cannot be false if its "inferior" predecessor was already true.*

Consider the following example, based on the question "What will John do to occupy himself on the trip?" Suppose that we require an answer to this question. But suppose further that the following data becomes successively available:

1. He loves doing crosswords.
2. He loves reading mysteries even more.
3. He didn't take any books along.

It is clear that we are led to-and-fro. Initially (at stage 1 of information access) we incline to the answer that he will be working crosswords. At the next stage, when item 2 arrives, we change our mind and incline to the answer that he will be reading. At stage 3 we abandon this idea and go back to our initial view. And, of course, a subsequent stage, say one where we have

4. One of this fellow passengers lends him a book

can nevertheless reverse the situation and return matters to step 2. And who knows what step 5 will bring? The crucial point is that additional information need not serve to improve matters by bringing us closer to the truth: more information can just as well prove misleading as informing.

6. LESSONS: LEARNED IGNORANCE

And so we return to the point made at the very outset: the ironic, though in some ways fortunate, fact is that one of the things about which we are most decidedly ignorant is our ignorance itself. The doctrine of learned ignorance—*docta ignorantia* as its originator Nicholas of Cusa had it—involves being learned *about* our ignorance through securing a well-informed view about the prospects and shortcomings of our knowledge. It requires no small sagacity to form a reasonably realistic appreciation of the extent and nature of one's own ignorance—and to know what to do about it.

In the end, it is clear that the sensible management of ignorance calls for proceeding in the realm of practical considerations exactly because the knowledge required for theoretical adequacy in matters of larger significance is—all too often—not at our disposal. And yet we nevertheless have no rational alternative but to proceed, here as elsewhere, subject to the basic pragmatic principle of accepting the best that we can do as good enough—while nevertheless recognizing its potential imperfection.[10]

10. This chapter is a revised and expanded version of a paper of the same title that appeared in the *Southern Journal of Philosophy* 37 (1999): 479–93. Some considerations relevant to its deliberations are presented in the author's *The Limits of Science* (Pittsburgh: University of Pittsburgh Press, 1999).

Chapter 4

UNANSWERABLE QUESTIONS AND *INSOLUBILIA*

1. PROPOSITIONAL VERSUS EROTETIC IGNORANCE

The scope and limits of our knowledge is an issue that has been on the agenda of human concern since classical antiquity, and it is clearly an issue in which we have a significant stake. For insofar as there are such limits, our hopes of making the realm of fact intelligible to us can only be realized to an extent that is imperfect and incomplete.

Personal ignorance is a matter of the shortfall of a particular individual's knowledge. It has two principal versions, the propositional and the erotetic.

A person's *propositional ignorance* is a matter of failing to realize that some fact or other is the case. This involves two elements: the existence of a certain fact (e.g., that Shakespeare wrote *Hamlet*) and a failure on the individual's part to know this fact.

Since *Homo sapiens* is a cognitively limited and imperfect being, there are, of course, many facts that any one of us does not know. The world's complexity provides for innumerable instances, and indeed we can find a good many of them in the restricted confines between the covers of an encyclopedia.

But while daily experience brings to my view many facts that I *did not* know, I cannot possibly give an example of a fact that I *do not* know. For when claiming something to be a fact I cannot coherently go on to claim that I do not know it. No doubt, *you* can unproblematically give examples of particular facts that I do not know, but I myself cannot manage to do it.

To deal with one's own case, one must look to ignorance of another sort, ignorance that is not *propositional* but *erotetic*.

Erotetic ignorance is a matter of an inability to answer questions. This is, in effect, *adverbial* ignorance, consisting in an inability to answer questions inquiring as to who, why, when, where, whence, whither, how, and so on. Thus *X* is ignorant with respect to the question "Who killed Cock Robin?" if there is indeed someone—namely Sparrow—who did this, and *X* does not know *that* Sparrow killed Cock Robin. In just this way, erotetic ignorance carries propositional ignorance on its back: it always involves propositional ignorance of some fact. To be ignorant with regard to a question is to fail to know what the (correct) answer to it is. Accordingly, from the logical point of view, erotetic ignorance is a generalization of propositional ignorance. With erotetic ignorance the knower at issue simply does not know that such-and-such a proposition correctly answers the question at hand. That is, there is no proposition such that the knower knows it to be correct, and moreover knows it to be an answer to the question.

However—and this is the important point—people can be adequately informed about their erotetic ignorance. *X* can realize perfectly well that he does not know who killed Cock Robin. What he cannot know is that his defect of knowledge consists in not realizing that it is in fact Sparrow who killed Cock Robin. To realize this he would have to know something which, by hypothesis, he does not.

In regard to erotetic ignorance a few distinctions must be carefully heeded. One of these is that between *a possible* answer (which may or may not be correct) and *the correct* answer. Consider: "What is the sum of 2 + 2?" There are lots of *possible* responses—answers, if you will—among them "13." It is just that this is not *the answer*, that is, the correct one. If little Johnny offers this response, he has indeed given *an* answer, but it happens to be one that is incorrect. He has not given us *the answer*. Ignorance is a matter of inability to give not *an* answer—that is, a mere reply—but *the* answer to the question at hand, one that is correct.

A second significant distinction is that between *ignorance* and *misinformation*. The person who simply does not know the answer to some question is ignorant in this regard. The person who *thinks* he knows the answer but is wrong about it is not just ignorant but misinformed. The error here is not just one of omission but one of commission.

2. CONTINGENT AND NECESSARY PROPOSITIONAL IGNORANCE

There are, clearly, more facts—say, about numbers, or about the world—that I can come to know. So there are some facts that I will never learn. But, of course, my ignorance of many of these facts is shallow and contingent, relating to facts that I could learn—that is, would come to know if I took the appropriate steps. But are there also facts that I could not possibly come to know, facts that are beyond my cognitive reach?

Let *f* be one of these facts which—for contingent reasons—I will never come to know. Then "*f* is a fact that Rescher will never come to know" is true. It represents a genuine fact. Is this a fact that I could ever come to know? Clearly not, seeing that "Rescher knows that *f* is a fact that Rescher will never come to know" is self-contradictory. This is something I cannot possibly know, albeit the impossibility here is contingently based and is consequently a hypothetical (rather than an absolute) impossibility. And the ignorance at issue, while indeed necessary, is so by a hypothetical rather than by an absolute (categorical) necessity.

One must distinguish between *shallow* ignorance, a matter of what someone *does* not know, and *deep* ignorance, a matter of what someone *cannot* know. Merely shallow ignorance is contingent and relates to facts that one could possibly know but does not. Thus while I do not know the present number of office buildings in Shanghai, this is something I could, in principle, find out about. Such facts are within learning range, so to speak. But deep ignorance is something more fundamental and relates to matters outside our cognitive range.

3. CONTINGENT VERSUS NECESSARY EROTETIC IGNORANCE

There are such things as paradoxical questions—questions that just do not admit of a true answer. Consider, for example, the question: "When you respond to this question, will the answer be negative?" Consider the situation of Display 1. The inability to answer such a question correctly cannot, of course, be counted as ignorance: after all, the question has no correct answer.[1] This sort of thing will not concern us here. Our interest in ignorance relates to questions that have answers that remain unknown.

Given the cognitive situation of *Homo sapiens*, there are many questions that none of us is able to answer simply due to lack of information

DISPLAY 1. Response to the Question: "When you respond to this question, will the answer be negative?"

Answer given	Truth status of this answer
YES	FALSE
NO	FALSE

1. The question is not in principle improper. In particular it does not violate the distinction between object and metalanguage but deals with an issue of the relationship between the two.

("Just what did Julius Caesar eat for breakfast on that fatal Ides of March?"). Such questions indicate our merely shallow ignorance. But there are also questions that none of us can possibly manage to answer for reasons of logico-conceptual impossibility:

- What is an example of an integer nobody will ever specifically mention?
- What idea has never occurred to anybody?

Some extramundane intelligence might be able to answer these questions correctly, but we humans certainly cannot manage it.

4. GENERAL NECESSARY IGNORANCE

General erotetic ignorance relates to questions no one is able to answer. This will, of course, occur contingently whenever there is some piece of information that people-in-general lack. We have already seen various instances of this (e.g., Caesar's breakfast). The more interesting situation is that of those cases where no one can possibly answer the question at hand.

As noted above, there are matters of which individuals are ignorant: propositions whose truth status a given individual cannot determine. But it can also be established in general that if X is ignorant about the truth status of some proposition p and Y is ignorant about the truth status of some proposition q, then there will be a proposition that combines p and q about whose truth status both are alike ignorant.

The crux here is that when the truth status of p is unknown to X and that of q unknown to Y, then the *conjunction* of p or not-p (whichever is true) with q or not-q (whichever is true) will be a true proposition unknown to both X and Y alike, irrespective of what else it is that they do or do not know. But this means that in a (finite) society of individuals each of whom is ignorant of some fact or other, there will be a megafact about which *all* of them are ignorant. And there will thus be a universal puzzle-question that no one can actually answer.

This being so, the question yet remains: Is there such a thing as generally necessary erotetic ignorance, questions that no one can *possibly* answer?

5. UNANSWERABLE QUESTIONS

In inquiring into this problem area, we are not interested in questions whose unanswerability resides merely in the contingent fact that certain information is not in practice accessible—for example, "Did

Julius Caesar hear a dog bark on his thirtieth birthday?" There is no possible way in which we can secure the needed information here-and-now (time travel is still impracticable). But, of course, such questions are not inherently unanswerable and it is unanswerability as a matter of principle that will concern us here.[2]

If such questions can indeed be adduced, then, while one cannot identify an *unknown* truth, one would be able to identify cases of *unspecifiable* truth, propositions such that either p_0 or not-p_0 must be true and yet nevertheless there is no prospect of determining which it is. Here we can localize truth by emplacing it within a limited range (one here consisting of p_0 and $\sim p_0$) but cannot pinpoint it within this range of alternatives. One member of the assertion/denial pair will unquestionably prove to be true, but we cannot possibly say which it is: the specifics of the matters are unknowable.

There are two principal sorts of unanswerable questions: those that are *locally* irresolvable, and those that are so *globally*. Locally unanswerable questions are those that a particular individual or group is unable to answer. An instance of such a question is: "What is an example of a fact of which you are altogether ignorant?" Clearly you cannot possibly manage to answer this, because whatever instance you adduce as such a fact must be something you know or believe to be such (i.e., a fact), so that you cannot possibly be altogether ignorant of it. Yet, on the other hand, it is clear that *somebody else* could readily be in the position to answer the question. Again, consider such questions as:

• What is an example of a problem that will never be considered by any human being?
• What is an example of an idea that will never occur to any human being?

There are sound reasons of general principle (the potential infinitude of problems and ideas; the inherent finitude of human intelligence) to hold that the items at issue in these questions (problems that will never be considered; ideas that will never occur) do actually exist. And it seems altogether plausible to think that other (nonhuman) hypothetically envisionable intelligences could well answer these questions correctly. But it is equally clear that we humans could never provide the requisite answers.

And looking beyond this we can also contemplate the prospect of

2. Nor will we be concerned here with the issue of indemonstrable truths and unanswerable questions in pure mathematics. Our concern is only with *factual* truths, and the issue of truth in such formal disciplines as mathematics or logic will be left aside.

globally intractable questions such that nobody (among finite intelligences, at least) can possibly be in a position to answer them (in the strict sense described at the outset). These questions have an appropriate answer but for reasons of general principle no one—no finite intelligence, at least—can possibly be in a position to provide it.

An example of such globally unanswerable questions can be provided by nontrivial but yet inherently uninstantiable predicates along the lines of

- "What idea is there that has never occurred to anybody?"
- "What occurrence is there that no one ever mentions?"

There undoubtedly are such items, but, of course, they cannot be instantiated, so that questions that ask for examples here are inherently unanswerable.[3] With such answer-possessing but unanswerable questions it accordingly must transpire that the answer that, abstractly speaking, has to be there is one that cannot possibly be specified by way of particularized identification.

6. INTRACTABLE QUESTIONS ABOUT THE COGNITIVE FUTURE AND SURD GENERALITIES

As already noted, we can move from the by-X unanswerability of: "What is an example of truth that you, X, do not know to be so?," to the universally insoluble: "What is an example of a truth that no one whatsoever knows to be so?" For in a finite society of imperfect knowers, the existence of such a truth is guaranteed by the considerations mooted above. But while we must suppose reality's complexity to be such that there are unknowable facts, we nevertheless cannot provide any specific examples of them. For, as already observed, the specification of unknowable facts is totally infeasible since establishing factuality would automatically clash with unknowability. Knowledge being knowledge *of fact*, whatever instances of unknown truth that we can consider have to remain in the realm of conjecture rather than that of knowledge. Given that *knowledge* fails us here, the most and best we can do is to resort to guesswork. Accordingly, let us now explore the prospect of making an at least plausible conjecture at specifying an unknowable fact.

Some questions are unanswerable for essentially practical reasons: we lack any prospect of securing effective means for their resolution for reasons of contingent fact—the impractability of time travel, say, or of space travel across vast distances. But such contingently grounded igno-

---

3. This issue here is one of so-called vagrant predicates that have no known address.

rance is not as bad as it gets. For some questions are in principle irresolvable in that purely theoretical reasons (rather than mere pivotal limitations) preclude the possibility of securing the information required for their resolution. Nevertheless, there is—or may be—no sound reasons for dismissing such questions as meaningless because a hypothetical being can be imagined by whom such a question can in theory be resolved. But given the inevitabilities of *our* relation as time-bound and finite intelligences, the question may be such that any prospect of resolution is precluded on grounds of general principle.

Are there any such meaningful yet intractable questions?

Our best strategy here is to consider the situation of natural science, focusing specifically on the problem of our knowledge of the scientific future. Clearly, to identify an insoluble scientific problem, we would have to show that a certain inherently appropriate scientific question is nevertheless such that its resolution lies beyond every (possible or imaginable) state of future science. This is obviously a *very* tall order—particularly so in view of our inevitably deficient grasp of future science. After all, we cannot foresee what we cannot conceive. Our questions—let alone our answers—cannot outreach the limited horizons of our concepts. Having never contemplated electronic computing machines as such, the ancient Romans could also venture no predictions about their impact on the social and economic life of the twenty-first century. Clever though he unquestionably was, Aristotle could not have pondered the issues of quantum electrodynamics. The scientific questions of the future are—at least in part—bound to be conceptually inaccessible to the inquirers of the present. The question of just how the cognitive agenda of some future date will be constituted is clearly irresolvable for us now. Not only can we not anticipate future discoveries now, we cannot even prediscern the questions that will arise as time moves on and cognitive progress with it.[4]

Scientific inquiry is a venture in innovation. And in consequence it lies in the nature of things that present science can never speak decisively for future science, and present science cannot predict the specific discoveries of future inquiry. After all, our knowledge of the present cannot encompass that of the future—if we could know about those future discoveries now, they would not have to await the future. Accordingly, knowledge about what science will achieve overall—and thus just where it will be going in the long run—is beyond the reach of attainable knowledge at this or any other particular stage of the scientific "state of the art."

4. Of course, these questions already exist—what lies in the future is not their existence but their presence on the agenda of active concern.

Omar Khayyám lamented our human ignorance of what is to follow for us after this earthly life: "Into this Universe, and *Why* not knowing, . . . I know not Whither, willy-nilly blowing." But in this regard the human situation vis-à-vis the condition of the merely worldly future is not that all different from that of the afterlife. In particular, it is in principle infeasible for us to tell now not only how future science will answer present questions, but even what questions will figure on the question agenda of the future—let alone what answers they will engender. In this regard, as in others, it lies in the inevitable realities of our condition that the detailed nature of our ignorance is—for us at least—hidden away in an impenetrable fog of obscurity.

It is clear on this basis that the question *"Are there nondecidable scientific questions that scientific inquiry will never resolve—even were it to continue ad indefinitum?"*—the *Insolubilia* Question, as we may call it—is one that cannot possibly ever be settled in a decisive way. After all, how could we possibly establish that a question *Q* about some issue of fact will continue to be *raisable and unanswerable* in every future state of science, seeing that we cannot now circumscribe the changes that science might undergo in the future? Quite interestingly, this very question is self-instantiating: it is a question regarding an aspect of reality (of which, of course, science itself is a part) that scientific inquiry will never—at any specific state of the art—be in a position to settle decisively.[5]

The long and short of it is that the very impredictability of future knowledge renders the identification of *insolubilia* impracticable. (In this regard it is effectively a bit of good fortune that we are ignorant about the lineaments of our ignorance.[6]) We are cognitively myopic with respect to future knowledge, for were it not so, then present rather than future knowledge would—contrary to hypothesis—be stressed. And for this reason there are questions such as those instanced above that are inherently irresolvable.

But, of course, educated guesswork is something else again.

---

5. And this issue cannot be settled by supposing a mad scientist who explodes the superbomb that blows the Earth to smithereens and extinguishes all organic life as we know it. For the prospect cannot be precluded that intelligent life will evolve elsewhere. And even if we contemplate the prospect of a "big crunch" that is a reverse "big bang" and implodes our universe into an end, the project can never be precluded that at the other end of the big crunch, so to speak, another era of cosmic development awaits.

6. That contingent future developments are by nature cognitively intractable, even for God, was a prospect supported even by some of the Scholastics. On this issue, see Marilyn McCord Adams, *William Ockham*, vol. 2 (South Bend, Ind.: University of Notre Dame Press, 1987), chap. 27.

7. INTIMATIONS OF UNKNOWABLE TRUTH

The limits of knowledge acquisition pose particularly poignant issues. It is clear that the question

What's an example of a truth one cannot establish as such—a fact that we cannot come to know?

is one that leads ad absurdum. The quest for unknowable facts—the project seeking to identify them—is inherently quixotic and paradoxical because of the inherent conflict between the definitive features at issue: factuality and unknowability. Here we must abandon the demand for *knowledge* and settle for mere *conjecture*. But how far can we go in this direction?

To explore the prospect of identifying unknowable truth, let us consider once more the issue of future scientific knowledge—and specifically the already mooted issue of the historicity of knowledge. And in this light let us consider a thesis on the order of:

(T) As long as scientific inquiry continues in our universe, there will always be a time when some of the then-unresolved (but resolvable) questions on the scientific agenda of the day will be sufficiently difficult to remain unresolved for at least two years.

What is at issue here is clearly a matter of fact—one way or the other. But now let Q^* be the question: "Is T true or not?" It is clear that actually to answer this question Q^* one way or the other we would need to have cognitive access to the question agenda of all future times. By their very nature as such, the discoveries of the future are unavailable at present, and in consequence Q^* affords an example of an *insolubilium*—a specific and perfectly meaningful question that we shall always and ever be unable to resolve decisively—irrespective of what the date on the calendar happens to read.

But, nevertheless, the issue is certainly one that lies open to reasonable conjecture—something that is, of course, very far from achieving *knowledge*. And, viewed in this light, the thesis T is altogether plausible: it has all the earmarks of a likely truth.[7] And so it seems reasonable to hold that a conjecture of this sort is emblematic of the best and most that we can ever hope to do, given that actual knowledge in such a matter is clearly unattainable.

---

7. And, of course, there are many other plausible theses of this sort, such, for example, "As long as scientific inquiry continues in the universe, every scientific discovery will eventually be improved upon and refined."

8. IGNORANCE AND ERROR

How serious a matter in the cognitive scheme of things is mere igno-rance? In this regard it might seem on first thought that there is a pro-found difference between ignorance and error. For in relation to any particular truth T, it is clearly a very different matter to be merely obliv-ious to T's truth, on the one hand, and, on the other hand, mistakenly to see it as false by accepting not-T. But this consideration, although perfectly true, overlooks an important aspect of the matter.

The reality of it is that the manifold of truth overall forms a coherent and cohesive system. And in such a system the erasure of a single node leads to erroneous impressions overall in a way that leads from igno-rance to error. It you are unaware of that second "e" in "tweezer," you are going to spell the word incorrectly. If you do not know that John has joined the group, you are likely to misjudge the size of its membership. It you do not know that it is raining, you will form the wrong judgment about the state of the streets. Unknowing—mere ignorance—opens the doorway to error and means that in every domain of rational inquiry—philosophy included—we must be prepared not only for *additions* to our putative information, but for *corrections* as well. Our human intelligence is unquestionably a point of justifiable pride, but this must nevertheless be kept within reasonable bounds—if not by humility, then by realism.

Chapter 5

OMNISCIENCE AND OUR UNDERSTANDING OF GOD'S KNOWLEDGE

The limitations of human knowledge can be brought into vivid view by contrasting our situation with that of God. However, the present discussion does not propose to tangle with the atheist: the question of God's existence is irrelevant for its purposes. Our concern here will be strictly hypothetical, taking the form: *If* there is a God conceived of along the lines of traditional Christian theology, *then* how are we to understand what is at issue with God's knowledge? Accordingly, the focus of present deliberations is a conditionalized and conceptual question: How are we to conceive of God's knowledge—if he exists?

This issue of God's knowledge, of course, has many aspects and gives rise to very different questions. On the traditional approach to the matter, some of these have seemingly straightforward answers:

Q: *What does God know?* A: Everything! After all, he is supposed to be omniscient. Whatever the facts may be, God knows them.[1]

Q: *How does God come to know what he knows?* A: Learning is not really an issue with God. His knowledge is immediate and intuitive via an "intellectual vision." This view of the matter represents a position that, on the philosophical side, runs deep throughout Neoplatonism and invites further explanation and elaboration. But the net effect is straightforward: if something is the case, God directly and automatically knows it—no process of acquisition is involved. For unlike the case with ourselves, nothing *causes* or *produces* God's knowledge: it is immediate, direct, unmediated.

---

1. Some theologians deny that God knows the future contingencies that hinge on yet-unresolved free human choices, but reconcile this view with the principle under consideration by holding that while God does indeed know all facts, with future contingencies there just are (as yet) no facts of the matter. This issue poses complications that will not be pursued here.

A big problem nevertheless remains. *What form does God's knowledge take?* This question is going to be something of a stumbling block because the fact of it is that we can achieve no readily available answer here. As St. Thomas Aquinas cogently contended, the human understanding is fundamentally verbal—in regard to factual issues, with us *intelligere*, understanding, is always a *dicere*, a somehow verbalized affirmation. But such linguistic mediation is not required for God's understanding (*De veriate*, 4.2.5). The mechanics of divine knowledge must accordingly be something which, from our human point of view, is going to be decidedly problematic.

Various key aspects of God's knowledge are informatively discussed in Eleanore Stump's monumental *Aquinas*.[2] However, the presently operative problem—"How is God's knowledge formulated? When the cat is on the mat, just how does God's knowledge of this fact find expression in his mind?"—is something left untouched in this discussion as in others. To be sure, as already indicated, when something is so, then, according to Aquinas, God "sees" it by an intellectual vision. But it is not the cat's presence on the mat that is then in the mind of God, but rather *an apprehension of the fact that the cat is on the mat.* And the puzzle is how we are to conceive of this apprehension. There is, to be sure, the option of saying that we don't and we can't—that this is just one of those mysteries whose resolution rests with God himself. But that is rather unhelpful, and certainly did not satisfy Aquinas himself. Yet the analogy of vision, on which he placed great weight in his epistemology of divine knowledge, left matters in an unsatisfactory condition here— as well as elsewhere (as Stump indicates).

The limits of logic are absolute and hold for God as well as for his creatures. And so even as God can do only what is doable for a being of his nature (and thus, for example, cannot annihilate himself), so he can only know what is knowable for a being of his nature (which means that—perhaps—he cannot have knowledge of particulars or—possibly—of future contingencies, and conceivably he could have difficulty with nonexistents as well). But none of this affects our present problem of the modus operandi of God's knowledge with respect to those things that he indeed knows.

How does God get to know about us? Our actions do not *affect* the mind of God because they do not *effect* changes in it. Rather, his knowledge of our doings is not experiential but a priori, inhering in the fact that he is the author of our existence. (Of course, the fact that he is our creator does not make him responsible for our actions, any more than

2. Eleanor Stump, *Aquinas* (London: Routledge, 2003).

the parent of a child is responsible for his or her actions.) But still there are difficulties. For it would certainly seem that a God emplaced outside the physical framework of space-time causality would be at a stultifying disadvantage as regards knowledge of his creatures because while he would unquestionably know the whole theoretical/causal story of *how pain occurs* but, yet for lack of actual experience, he could not have access to the phenomenological story of what *pain feels like*. (From the theoretician's point of view, this could be one of the prime facets of the rationale for the Incarnation of the second person of the Trinity.)

Except for utter skeptics, who ex officio deny all human knowledge whatsoever, people can certainly say a good deal about what God knows, since any knowable fact is thereby known to an omniscient being. And this will doubtless include abstract facts of possibility and necessity. But while God's knowledge of what is necessary and what is possible can proceed abstractly from concepts alone (even as will be the case with us), nevertheless his knowledge of concrete actuality must be different since, unlike our knowledge, it will be somehow "intuitive" rather than sensuously mediated.[3] And this will have to be so since God as creator can proceed (antecedently, as it were) to *envision* his creation while we must proceed (consequently) to *perceive* it. But, of course, the detail of the matter—the *how* of it, so to speak—lies beyond our grasp. There is no gainsaying the position of Aquinas on this point: the modus operandi of an "intellectual vision" is bound to be beyond our ken. While we can demonstrate *that* God, regarded through the tradition's eyes, has understanding (since understanding is pure perfection), we really cannot grasp the *how* mode of this understanding so as to say *what* it is like (*De potentia Dei*, 8.1.12). For God's knowledge of things is direct, unmediated, and intuitive while ours is causally produced and materially mediated.

So in the end we had best grasp the nettle of inapprehension here. For it is clear that God's thought must proceed on a basis very different from ours, limited beings that we are. Philosophers sometimes speak of a "God's eye view" of things. But whatever this may be, we imperfect humans cannot manage to see matters with God's eyes. Our thought about things is mediated by language and the instrumentalities of symbolic representation, while God's thought is presumably nothing like that. Speculation about the language of God is an ill-directed endeavor.

Of course, we humans can only learn about the world by *interacting*

---

3. On these issues, see John F. Boler, "Instructive and Abstractive Cognition," in Norman Kretzman, ed., *The Cambridge History of Later Medieval Philosophy* (Cambridge, U.K.: Cambridge University Press, 1998), pp. 460–78, esp. pp. 465–69.

with it. Our knowledge of concrete things and occurrences is invariably channeled through experiential encounters conditioned by the circumstances of space, time, and physical causality, since our only access to facts about the world is though the window afforded us by the senses. But God's knowledge about the world has to be something quite different, something that roots in immediate intuition. After all, he does not *encounter* the world but *makes* it.

Since the world is the product of God's free creation decisions, and since, clearly, God "knows what he is doing," his knowledge of contingent fact is a straightforward aspect of his self-knowledge. As St. Thomas puts it:

God himself is, through his essence, the cause of being of other things. And so, since he has the fullest possible cognition of his essence, we must hold that he has cognition of other things as well. (*Summa contra gentiles,* 1.49.412)

And so, human concepts, based as they are on a level of understanding conformed to our cognitive capacities and our experience, are simply inadequate to represent the realities of the situation of a divine being. More generally, our concepts cannot properly—and thus correctly— represent God himself. And this goes specifically and particularly for God's mental (cognitive) operations as well. (All this was clearly explained and expounded in detail by St. Thomas Aquinas.)

Accordingly, the medieval philosopher-theologians sensibly held that in our deliberations regarding God's thoughts and his mode of understanding we are restricted to negativities. We can say a good deal negatively about what does *not* hold for God's thought, but little if anything about what holds positively of it. What we principally know relates to the things that, thanks to its perfection, it does not, will not, and cannot do.

And there is much to be said for this view. These milestones along the *via negativa* of our access to God's knowledge include the facts that it is:

—not sensorily mediated
—not incomplete, imprecise, inaccurate, vague
—not representatively mediated (and so not symbolic)
—not discursive (but direct, immediate, intentive)
—not erroneous or incorrect
—not involved in impossibilities (and thus not encompassing with matters that cannot possibly be known, such as things that are not matters of actual fact)
—not formed in terms of the inadequate conceptions of cognitively imperfect beings such as ourselves

—not developed from a perspective based in the orders of space and time.[4]

But, of course, all of this involves matters on the negative side of the ledger. As St. Thomas insisted, the positivities of God's knowledge lie beyond our grasp. The long and short of it is that we cannot possibly know what the terms of reference are that he employs in thinking about things.[5]

Clearly the thoughts of God cannot be made intelligible to the mind of man to any great extent. "They know not the thoughts of the Lord" (Micah, 4:12). "For as the heavens are higher than the earth, so are my ways higher than your ways, and my thoughts than your thoughts" (Isaiah, 5:9). The power of the human mind is as nothing in comparison with that of God: "The foolishness of God is wiser than [the wisdom of] men" (1 Corinthians, 1:25). Clearly, whatever truths we actually *know* an omniscient God knows as well, and indeed he knows that and how we know it. But while we know *that* he knows it, we cannot adequately answer the question of just exactly *how* he does so.

For us, the pervasive aura of negativity that prevails here has ominous implications. Philosopher-theologians have long been preoccupied with the problem of how cognitively feeble man can possibly understand the ideas and thought processes of a cognitively infinite deity. And the sensible response here lies in the suggestion that this can at best and at most be accomplished by us through the use of analogies.

But, of course, matters are bound to stand quite differently with the inverse question of how God is to understand us. In addressing this issue, it just will not do to invoke the mechanism of analogy as an instrumentality of God's cerebrations. For an all-powerful mind has no business transacting its conceptual affairs by the use of mere analogies, seeing that all analogies are by nature incomplete and imperfect. God's own understanding must be such as to have no use—and no need—for mere analogies.

Nor is the matter of God's knowledge of the world resolved by the consideration that he made it. For insofar as the it is material in nature, there arises the puzzle of how a being whose own nature and mental ex-

---

4. See A. N. Prior, "The Formalities of Omniscience," *Philosophy* 37 (1962): 114–29; reprinted in Prior, *Papers on Time and Tense* (Oxford, U.K.: Clarendon Press, 1968).

5. Speaking of the fundamental or "primitive" ideas in whose terms God's conception of the world is framed, G. W. Leibniz wrote (A VI, UA, 530 [C. 514]): "Non videtur satis in potestate humana esse Analysis aonceptuum, ut scilicet passimus pervenire ad notiones primitivas, seu ad ea quae per se concipiuntur" (An analysis of the concepts enabling one to arrive at the primitive [divine] notions, through which things themselves are [actually] conceived does not seem to be within human power).

perience is purely spiritual can possess the concepts requisite for an adequate grasp of such a material realm. How can a pure spirit proceeding without sensory interaction manage to comprehend the machinations of matter? How can a cognitively unlimited being manage to enter into the thoughts of a limited, imperfect, finite mind whose ideas are confused and whose beliefs are erroneous? How can a being functioning entirely outside the physical framework of space, time, and nature's causality get a mental grip on our confusion, ignorance, uncertainty, and the like? All this is something that is pretty well bound to confound us.

Many of our concepts are vague or confused. (How many rocks does it take to make a "heap"? What differentiates a "boat" from a "ship"?) But if *our* thinking is muddled, how can a God who is himself incapable of muddled thinking possibly understand it? Can he know what we are thinking when we think confusedly? Can the idea of "a good many" or "very few" have any meaning for a being who always knows exactly how many and for whom every idea is clear? No doubt he can know *that* I'm confusing *X* with *Y*. But can he know what's going on when I do this and comprehend the confusedness of my thought? After all, to respond to analogy once more, while a teetotaler can see the effects of inebriation, how—without the experience of drinking—can God possibly grasp not just what being drunk *is* but what being drunk *is like*.

To be sure, when *we* address the question "How does God conceive our thoughts?," this effectively comes down to "How are we to conceive of his doing so?" For in posing the former question we cannot manage to do so without in effect addressing the latter one. And so, with us the issue of God's modus operandi in understanding our human thoughts ironically—but inexorably—returns to the previous matter of *our* knowledge of God's thoughts. In consequence, analogies (however unsatisfying) will inevitably have to come into it—though they will be *our* analogies and not God's. And here perhaps the most useful analogy is that of the situation of a less powerful but yet finite mind as compared to a more powerful one.

A fundamental law of epistemology is at issue here, to wit, that *a mind of lesser power is for this very reason unable to understand adequately the workings of a mind of greater power*. To be sure, the weaker mind can doubtless realize *that* the stronger mind can solve problems it itself cannot. But it cannot understand *how* it is able to do so. An intellect that can only just manage to do well at tic-tac-toe cannot possibly comprehend the ways of someone who is an expert at chess.

Consider in this light the vast disparity of computational power between a mathematical tyro like most of us and a mathematical prodigy like Ramanujan. Not only cannot our tyro answer the number-theoretic question that such a genius resolves in the blink of an eye, but the tyro cannot even begin to understand the processes and procedures that the Indian genius employs. As far as the tyro is concerned, it is all sheer wizardry. No doubt once an answer is given he can check its correctness. But actually finding the answer is something which that lesser intellect cannot manage—the how of the business lies beyond its grasp. And, for much the same sort of reason, a mind of lesser power cannot discover what the question-resolving limits of a mind of greater power are. It can never say with warranted assurance where the limits of question-resolving power lie. (In some instances it may be able to say what's in and what's out, but it can never map the dividing boundary.)

It is not simply that a more powerful mind will know more facts than a less powerful one, but that its conceptual machinery is ampler in encompassing ideas and issues that lie altogether outside the conceptual horizon of its less powerful compeers.

Of course, a lesser intellect can know various things about what questions a more powerful intelligence can answer and may even come to be informed about what those answers are. (After all, even someone who has no clue about how to extract the square root of a number will generally be able to check that another's answer affords a correct solution.) But what an ineptling cannot do is to perform that feat of discovery on his own. The weaker intellect can certainly know *that* the stronger can accomplish something and yet will be unable to form even crudely any correct conception as to *how*.

It is instructive in this regard to contemplate an analogy. We—and indeed any other type of inquiring being—must in forming our scientific view of the world work with the resources at our cognitive disposal. And three prime considerations are paramount here:

• *Computing power* in relation to the mechanism of calculation and inference at one's disposal
• *Descriptive power* in relation to the sensors for detecting the phenomena and the instrumentalities of measuring the parameters of nature
• *Conceptual power* in relation to the sophistication of the available machinery for conceptualization and theoretical systematization

And the last of these interpretative powers is critical. For mental capability is preeminently of conceptualization and its lack means an inability to understand concepts and issues—and not just ignorance regarding the truth or falsity of various (understood) propositions.

Consider an illustration. The overall state-of-the-art of science at a time t will depend critically on the power of the available resources in these regards. And nothing is clearer than that the state of science in the fifteenth century was vastly inferior in comparison to that of the twentieth century. And it is also clear that increased cognitive power in these regards transforms the intellectual situation of science. Consider the perspective of a science of the distance future, say, of the year 3000. There is ample reason of general principle to think that the natural science of this later era will differ from ours to an extent substantially less than that of which our science of the present day differs from that of the year 1700. It is critical here that scientific progress is not just a matter of a crossword puzzle–like filling in of blanks in a fixed and unchanging framework. It is a matter of transforming the conceptual landscape in such a way that the new situation cannot ever be understood from the conceptual vantage point of an earlier, less sophisticated state of the art.

Now insofar as the relation of a lesser toward a higher intelligence is substantially analogous to the relation between an earlier state of science and a later state, some instructive lessons emerge. It is not that Aristotle could not have comprehended quantum theory—he was a very smart fellow and could certainly have learned. But what he could not have done is to formulate quantum theory within his own conceptual framework, his own familiar terms of reference. The very ideas at issue lay outside of the conceptual horizon of Aristotle's science, and like present-day students he would have had to master them from the ground up. Just this sort of thing is at issue with the relation of a less powerful intelligence to a more powerful one. It has been said insightfully that, from the vantage point of a less-developed technology, another, substantially advanced technology is indistinguishable from magic. And exactly the same holds for a more advanced *conceptual* (rather than physical) technology.

It is instructive to contemplate in this light the hopeless difficulties encountered nowadays in the popularization of physics—of trying to characterize the implications of quantum theory and relativity theory for cosmology into the subscientific language of everyday life. A classic obiter dictum of Niels Bohr is relevant: "We must be clear that, when it comes to atoms, language can be used only as in poetry." When physicists discuss the composition, structure, and comportment of the universe in everyday language, they proceed by putting scare quotes around every other word because no term continues to function in anything like its ordinary sense. After all, there is in principle no end to the extent to which—on the indications of contemporary physics—the world could manage to be bizarre. (E.g., who knows but that our entire physical universe is but a subatomic particle of some unimaginably greater megauniverse?) Medieval theologians insisted that our descriptive predications with respect to God are always merely analogical. Modern scientists have taken this doctrine over and apply it lock, stock, and barrel to physical nature.

But, of course, the step from present-day science to future science is bound to be vastly less than that from present-day science to the ideal and perfected science that functions (so we may suppose) in the definitive thought of an omniscient intellect. If we are destined to incomprehension vis-à-vis the unpredictable science of the distant future, we are, a fortiori, so destined vis-à-vis the perfected knowledge of an omniscient being. We simply have to acknowledge that the ways and means of God's knowledge are literally incomprehensible to us. We just cannot expect to get a grasp on his thinking. And for this reason, the problem of our knowledge about God's knowledge has a relatively simple solution— one that (as we have seen) cannot but proceed in the negative. There is effectively nothing we can hope to achieve here. We can only realize this in a dim, imperfect, inadequate, and essentially negative and thereby indefinite way. For—to reemphasize—the crux of it is that a mind of lesser power cannot get an adequate grip on that of a greater power.

Accordingly, the salient lesson of these deliberations is that those biblical texts that were quoted above have the essentials of the matter right: If the aim of a "cognitive theodicy" indeed is "to render the mind of God intelligible to the mind of man," than there is no sensible alternative to seeing this project as a lost cause, destined to futility because of the fundamental principles that characterize the conceptual realities of the situation. For, in the final analysis, the inadequacy of our understanding of God's knowledge does not lie solely in considerations of theology, but has its roots in the fundamental principles of the theory of knowledge.

Chapter 6

ISSUES OF INFINITE REGRESS

1. VICIOUS REGRESS

Prominent in the argumentation of Aquinas's "Five Ways" for demonstrating the existence of God is a rejection of the possibility of an infinite regress—be it of movers, of causes, or of necessities engendered through the necessity of another. Moreover, as St. Thomas saw it, the universe has to issue from the creative nature of God without any causal "act of creation" on his part. For the creative act of a perfectly rational agent would require an additional act of deliberation, and this in turn would require a determinative act of its own, and so on ad infinitum. Any such an infinite regress of reasoning is impossible, as St. Thomas saw it.

But just what is it that renders unending regression self-defeatingly vicious? And is this ground of infeasibility—such as it is—actually operative in the instances addressed by St. Thomas?

The philosophical dismissal of infinite regresses is as old as the paradoxes of Zeno (b. ca. 485 B.C.) and the refutatory regresses of Plato (b. ca. 428 B.C.).[1] Aristotle too regarded infinite regress as impracticable in various contexts of discussion,[2] and recourse to the idea as an instrument of refutation served as a standard procedure with the ancient Skeptics.[3] And the medieval Schoolmen took the same line. As they saw it in the wake of this tradition, an infinitely iterative process of unending antecedence is bound to be vicious (or vitiating) because its nontermination would prevent realization of the end product that is putatively at issue.[4] Thus the idea that a witness is only to be deemed reliable

---

1. On Zeno, see the author's *Paradoxes* (Chicago: Open Court, 2001). Plato invokes the futility of infinite regress in several contexts, for example, with the explanatory regress of definitions (*Cratylus*, 421d9), the functional regress of "for the sake of" purposes (*Lyses*, 219e5), and—most interestingly—as an objection to the theory of ideas (*Parmenides*, 130–132).

2. See the list of references appended below, esp. the monograph by Herbert Stekla.

3. See Sextus Empiricus, *Pyrrhôneiôn Hypotypôseôn* (I.xv and II.iii).

4. The Scholastics generally spoke of a *progressus in infinitum.* The expressions *regressus*

when there are other reliable witnesses who can attest to his reliability must be abandoned on grounds of regressive viciousness. Again, a regress of demonstrations would be unavailing that did not somehow terminate in unexplained explainers as per the axioms of Euclidean geometry. If before asserting something we had to assert that we were asserting it, nothing would ever get asserted. And an infinite definitional regress is self-defeatingly vicious, seeing that the fixation of meaning at issue in definitions is unachievable in situations that require further definition of the terms being employed—continuing on without end.

All in all, then, the philosophical tradition saw infinite regresses as automatically vicious. But there is in fact reason to think that the matter is not quite so straightforward.

2. HARMLESS REGRESS: STRUCTURAL REGRESSION

To begin with, it deserves note that in the domains of physical nature and of mathematical structure regression can in theory go on and on endlessly without problem. For consider the availability of an infinite "regress of integers," as with:

. . . $-4, -3, -2, -1, 0$

Clearly, there is no limit to numerical regressiveness here. Moreover, a further pathway to regressive harmlessness is the prospect of convergence thanks to an endless diminution, as with:

. . . $\frac{1}{16}, \frac{1}{8}, \frac{1}{4}, \frac{1}{2}, 1$

Here the convergence of the regress atones for the limitation of finitude.

These, to be sure, are mathematical examples. But in physics we can also manage to have an unending regression of states within the physically structured manifold of space, time, and causality. Here too regress can encounter the same two avenues to harmlessness: feasible infinitude and finitizing convergence. Thus, in the case of physical causality, the regress will be harmless if past time is infinite, or again if the operation of earlier causes can be squeezed into an endlessly smaller timespan so that convergence can result. For the purposes of illustration, consider the Zeno-derived paradox of motion discussed by Aristotle at *Physics* 239b9–19. It involves the following line of thought:

---

in infinitum arose in German neo-Scholasiticism via the *Metaphysica* of Baumgarten, whose usage was adopted by Immanuel Kant.

An object can never move from one position to another. For if it starts at A and is to move to B, then it will have to reach the halfway point between these, say B_1. But to reach this point it will first have to reach the halfway point to it, namely, B_2. And so on. Since there are *always* prior movements to be accomplished—and indeed even an infinity of them—the object will never be able to get a motion under way at all. Hence all objects are immovable and motion is impossible.

The previous deliberations have already indicated how it is that the regress at issue here is not vicious but harmless, being rooted in a series that is convergent.

Moreover, in the causal commerce of things, a result R can causally require the requisite R_1, which in turn can causally require the requisite R_2, and so on. Such an ontological regress of causally connected prerequisites can in principle go on ad indefinitum, since here too there can be convergence. For an infinite causal regress can be at work even in a world whose history is finite in time, as is illustrated by a linear time manifold that is "open to the left" as per

If the cause of the situation at any juncture is inherent in the situation halfway between it and that missing starting point, than an infinite number of causes can be fitted comfortably into a finite timespan. And since causation is in principle infinitely compressible (unlike any cognition-involving process), there is no reason why a universe that has a finite past cannot accommodate infinite causal regresses. In theory, every event can have a cause as per the Principle of Causality. There is nothing insuperably problematic here: the crux is an extratemporal inauguration-juncture that is not itself part of the temporal manifold. In such a setting every (temporal) event can have an antecedent cause, ad infinitum, and there is accordingly nothing impossible or impractical about an infinite causal regress.

To be sure, medieval theologians—following the lead of the Church Fathers—sought to prove the existence of God from the impossibility of an infinite regress of causes.[5] Thus Thomas Aquinas denied the possibility that one could "go on to infinity with efficient causes, for in an ordinal series the first is the cause of the intermediate and the intermediate the cause of the last" and "if there were not a first among efficient causes. . . . there would be no intermediate causes nor an ultimate effect."[6]

5. And not Christian theologians alone. This also was the view of the Islamic philosopher-theologian al-Ghazâlî. See Taneli Kukkonen, "Possible Worlds in the *Tahâfut al-tahâfut:* Averroes on Plenitude and Possibility," *Journal of the History of Philosophy* 38 (2000): 329–47; see esp. p. 345.

6. St. Thomas Aquinas, *Summa theologica,* Ia, 2, 3; cf. *Summa contra gentiles,* I, 13; *Compendium theologiae,* I, 3; and *Commentary on the Metaphysics,* II, 3, 303.

And Scotus too argues (via five distinct arguments) that an infinite se-ries of antecedent causes is impossible.[7] And just this is what the present perspective renders problematic.

What this array of examples of harmless regression suggests is that re-gressive viciousness is not something automatic. For the real problem resides not in endless regression as such, but rather in envisioning the accomplishment of an infinite task.

Thus, for example, the matter would be quite different with explana-tory grounds in the sense of reasons for being *(rationes essendi)*.[8] For while the reasons *we can give* are always finite, the reasons *that these are* need not be. After all, it is perfectly conceivable that the manifold of fact constitutes a dense field in that not only is every fact explicable but every one is actually explained by some others. It is just that we cogni-tive agents could not possible map out such a field. Indeed, we could not even trace out the explanation of one single given fact all the way down. (But, of course, this incapacity of ours with respect to explaining does not go to show that such explanations are nonexistent.)

What these deliberations indicate is that positional regression in some structured domain can be quite harmless, but that performatory regression—requiring for some end the completion of an infinite num-ber of presupposed tasks—is for this very reason vicious. Let us examine this situation more closely.

3. THE LOGIC OF THE SITUATION

Basic to this discussion is the underlying idea of a regressive relation subject to the definition that:

The relation R is regressive over a set S if it establishes a serial order through af-fording an irreflexive, asymmetrical, and transitive relation that assigns to each S-item one or more other S-items as its predecessors (or antecedents).

On the basis of this definition, a relation R can be characterized as vi-ciously regressive if

---

7. *Opus oxoniensis*, 40–42, in *Philosophical Works*, ed. Allan B. Wolter (London: Nelson, 1962).

8. For instructive discussions of the views of Aquinas and Scotus regarding infinite causal regress in the context of the Cosmological Argument for God's existence, see William L. Rowe, *The Cosmological Argument* (Princeton, N.J.: Princeton University Press, 1975), and William Lane Craig, *The Cosmological Argument from Plato to Leibniz* (London: Macmillan, 1980). And see also Patterson Brown, "Infinite Causal Regression," *Philosophi-cal Review* 75 (1966): 510–25.

1. R is a regressive relation (over the set S) in the sense just defined.

2. R represents a condition of sine qua non requiredness: that is, an item would not exist as an *S*-member of relevant items if all of its *R*-antecedents did not exist.

3. In the nature of the case, no *S*-member can possibly have an infinite number of *R*-antecedents.

The viciousness at issue here lies in the fact that 1–3 are collectively inconsistent: when conjoined they engender a logical contradiction.[9] In a situation where 1–3 are claimed an error of some sort must have crept in: one of those three conditions simply has to fail.

And so when the items that are connected by a supposed regress relation do not constitute a clearly defined group, then viciousness is removed from the scene. The situation is not clear-cut enough to make for contradiction. Nor is there now any need to look for a regress stopper. The idea of seeking out a starting point—a first (or indeed any other superlative)—is useless with respect to a group whose boundaries are not decisively and decidedly delineated.[10]

Thus three strong universal generalizations will have to obtain for various regressiveness to result, namely,

1′. The relation R is defined *for every member* of *S*.
2′. *No member of S* would exist were it not that . . .
3′. *No member of S* can possibly . . .

All of these universalistic conditions on the *S*-series must hold if the inconsistency at issue with viciousness is to be engendered. Throughout, a lapse from universatility would break the chain of inconsistency.

There are, however, two decidedly different sorts of regressive relations *R:* the equivalent and the diminishing. Thus a regress of steps is diminishing when all members of the series are significantly smaller in magnitude than their predecessors. With steps there can generally be smaller and larger. And this holds even for cognitive regresses. Thus a regress of explanation can be diminishing, with earlier steps being somewhat less adequately explanatory than later ones. Again, consider the regress of ideas at issue with the thesis "Every idea emerges out of previous ideas" or the regress of theories at issue with "Every theory is the emendation of an earlier one." As we move backward in such a regress, the earlier members become so diminutive (have so little

9. The flaw at issue with vicious regressiveness is thus not an independently self-sustaining fallacy of some sort, but something that comes to light through reductio ad absurdum. On this point, see Clark 1988, p. 378.

10. On these issues, see the author's *Philosophical Standardism* (Pittsburgh: University of Pittsburgh Press, 1994).

ideation or theorizing about them) that we can scarce tell whether an idea or a theory is at issue at all. The regress peters out into an imperceptible minuteness, much like the images in two facing mirrors. Such diminution to a subliminal obscurity creates a regress ad indefinitum rather than ad infinitum, and such regression need not be logically incoherent, seeing that conditions 1–3 are now not cosatisfied.

With unending regresses we must take the idea of endlessness seriously. A nonequivalently diminishing regress that fades away by receding into a fog of impermeable obscurity—the ancestry of a human, for example, as it loses its way along the evolutionary corridor of prehistoric time—is indefinite rather than infinite, and thereby avoids the theoretical problems that could otherwise arise. In specific, when a regression has a *sine qua minus* rather than a *sine qua non* character, viciousness fails to materialize because regression peters out into harmless nothingness.

With equivalent, that is to say, nonterminating regresses, the situation is quite different. For instance, a regress of definitions will be equivalent: definition does not admit of degrees. And when the performance of a task of some sort requires (ad indefinitum) the prior performance of the same sort, and this sort of task, as actual performance, is not endlessly compressible—and so cannot be performed in a timespan of arbitrary minuteness—then this task is impossible on grounds of vicious circularity. On this basis, Gilbert Ryle in *The Concept of Mind* objects quite rightly to the "intellectualist legend" that every intelligent mental operation is itself the product of an intelligent mental operation. This sort of thing would, of course, be vicious. Accordingly, it was shrewd of the sagacious Leibniz not to argue for the necessity of a first cause on the ground of the infeasibility of an infinite regress of causes, but rather to argue against the infinite regression of causal explanations.[11]

4. HARMFUL REGRESSION: INCOMPRESSIBLE ACTIONS

As the preceding considerations indicate, viciousness does not lie in regressiveness as such, but in the *nature* of the regress. An infinite regress of stages within a larger structure is feasible, an infinite regress of actions within a larger process is not, since actions always require some finite timespan for their performance.[12]

11. "On the Radical Origination of Things" (1697), in L. E. Loemker, ed., *G. W. Leibniz: Philosophical Papers and Letters* (Dordrecht: Reidel, 1969), pp. 486–91.
12. This significant point is stressed in Dingler 1930, p. 578.

With structures as such there is upon the scene no such thing as a *performative* precondition. For example, in going from point o to point 1 you must cross the halfway point ½.

o   ½   1

This does not in fact engender an impossibility because reaching points is the sort of thing that is accomplished in an infinitesimal timespan. The process at issue is infinitely compressible. And this is practicable because what is at issue is a series of *stages* and not of *performances*. For while you have to *reach* ½ and *cross* ½, these are mere stages and not performances, results you neither intend nor try to do. For "reaching" and "crossing" are accomplishment verbs that involve no conscious mental process, whereas anything that involves intention and trying will be quite different in this regard.[13] Reachings and crossings can be infinite in nature but intendings and tryings—and performances in general— cannot. The infinitism of physical structure does not recur at the level of mental performance. And so while structurally geared processes can come to terms with infinite complexity, mentally geared performances cannot, seeing that they lack the requisite time divisibility.[14]

The viciousness of regress in matters of performance can be explained as follows: humans are finite creatures. Anything they willingly do, be it physical or cognitive, has the aspect of a synoptically finite process that has a beginning, a middle, and an end. Accordingly, a *sine qua non* regress within the realm of deliberate human production—be it cognitive or physical—must ultimately terminate simply because it cannot go on indefinitely thanks to an insufficiency of time for accomplishing the task at issue. We can make the components of a machine or a building or a cake, and then make the components of these components, but this productive regress must terminate at some point in ingredients that are natural and unmade by human artifice. And this is just as true where cognitive products rather than those of physical artifice are at issue. Here too a productive regress must ultimately terminate in

---

13. That processes involving conscious human thought cannot be infinitely regressive has been stressed by various writers. See, e.g., Sanford 1984, p. 105; see also Thomson 1954–1955.

14. This serves to explain the phenomenon (remarked upon by Clark 1988, p. 1) that vicious regresses figure prominently in philosophy but not in mathematics and physics. For intervals of numbers, time, and space are infinitely divisible into others but actions are not. On the other hand, regress dismissal does (or can) figure in biology. The finite history of the Earth means that the thesis "Humans can only spring from humans" must be rejected on grounds of regressive viciousness. The idea of an origin of species can thus be filled out with an essentially a priori validation.

something that is provided by nature rather than produced by us. In the final analysis, the requisites at which a productive regress in the cognitive domain terminates—alike in matters of definition, explanation, interpretation, and cognition—will have to be items that are not themselves products of our own productive processes. Whenever productive regresses are matters of deliberate performance they must have a stop.

The difference between structural and performatory regression is crucial here, seeing that the former is generally innocuous but the latter vicious. Thus consider: it is a precondition for a proposition's truth that all its preconditions are satisfied. So let

$T(p)$ abbreviate "p is true."
$P(p)$ abbreviate "All of p's preconditions are satisfied."

We now have

p if $T(p)$ if $P(p)$

And we now embark on an infinite regress, seeing that p requires $T(p)$, which requires $P(p)$, which requires $P(T[p])$, which requires $P(P[p])$, and so fourth. But of course "precondition" here means *logical* precondition and not *procedural* precondition. (It is clearly not the case that to assert p we must somehow first independently establish that p is true.) We are dealing here with a family of theses interrelated in logical "space," and not with a set of *performatory* prerequisites. And this is not only important but also fortunate, seeing that if the latter were indeed at issue, the regress would indeed be vicious.

The key role of the performatory aspect can be seen as follows. Consider the following theses:

• A number (n) is an integer if one can specify another larger integer $(n + 1)$ that is its immediate successor.
• A proposition (p) is a truth iff one can specify some other "stronger" truth $(p + r)$ that entails it.

These perspectives are rendered innocuous and true by the consideration that

• A number (n) is an integer if there is another, larger integer $(n + 1)$ that is its immediate successor.
• A proposition (p) is a truth if there is another, "stronger" truth $(p + r)$ that entails it.

Both of these generalizations are unproblematically true in virtue of the structure (be it mathematical or logical) of the overall manifold of integers or truths, respectively.

However, the following specifications would at once issue in a vicious circularity:

- A number *(n)* is an integer if one has specified another, larger integer $(n + 1)$ that is its immediate successor.
- A proposition *(p)* is a truth if one has specified another, "stronger" truth $(p + r)$ that entails it.

For here the shift from structure to performance, from *can be specified* to *has been specified*, is fatal. For it imposes on the realization at issue (of a number or of a truth) the unrealizable prerequisite burden of accomplishing an infinitude of tasks.

And so it transpires in general that if a time-incompressable task is such that its accomplishment requires a prior accomplishment of exactly the same sort, then this task is impossible on grounds of vicious circularity. Thus consider the following theses:

- To define a term, some of the terms employed in this definition must first be defined.
- To prove a fact, some of the facts deployed in its proof must first be proven.
- To explain an idea, some of the ideas needed for its explanation must first be explained.
- To manufacture an item, some of its components must first be manufactured.
- To make a plan, one must first plan out the process of doing do.
- To decide an issue, one must first decide to decide it.
- To desire something, one must first fix upon something for whose sake this is being desired.

All of these specifications lead to an in principle vicious regress.

It was in just this vein that Aristotle wrote:

There is some end to the things we do which we desire for its own sake and we do not choose everything for the sake of something else. For then the process would go on to infinity so that our desire would be empty and vain. (*Nicomachean Ethics*, 1.2; 1094a 18–22; cf. *Metaphysics*, Alpha 2; 994a 1–9)

In all such cases the accomplishment of a result requires the prior accomplishment of exactly the same sort of thing by a process that is time-incompressible. All such tasks are impossible because they call for a prior sense of identical steps whose performance cannot be realized in an infinitesimal amount of time. And all such specifications can be ruled out on grounds of vicious circularity. For cognition-involving processes—such as defining, proving, and the like—just do not work like this. Here regression runs into the stone wall of inescapable finitude.

In specific, with respect to explanation, it should be noted that in accounting for facts through their explanatory subsumption under general principles, we embark on a process which, as Herbert Spencer has argued, must inevitably have a stop:

Can we go on forever explaining classes of facts by including them in larger classes. . . . The supposition that the process is unlimited, were any one absurd enough to espouse it, would still imply that an ultimate explanation could not be reached. . . . Manifestly, as the *most* general cognition at which we arrive cannot be reduced to a *more* general one, it cannot be understood. Of necessity, therefore, explanation must eventually bring us down to the inexplicable. The deepest truth which we can get at must be unaccountable.[15]

Cognitive accomplishments—acts of awareness, recognition, realization, or states of mind such as worriment or rejoicing—are never instantaneous. And human consciousness is not so much a continuous stream as a chain of interlocked units of discrete jumps and starts—units whose temporal duration may be brief but never infinitesimal. And whenever regressive steps cannot be compressed below some finite timespan, however minuscule—which is certainly the case with cognitive acts of comprehension—then a correlative temporal regress will be vicious when unending. Here we arrive at the conclusion that cognitively homogeneous (i.e., like-presupposing) cognitive actions are impracticable because—unlike some mathematical and physical processes—their reduction in size cannot continue ad infinitum.

A further vivid illustration of the difficulty is afforded by the so-called Third Man Argument against the theory of ideas addressed in Plato's *Parmenides*. The theory at issue holds in effect that:

To be in a position to claim that two items A and B are alike in some respect R requires a mediating item, X_R, distinct from both A and B, such that both of them resemble X_R in the relevant respect R.

This formula straightaway engenders the complication of an incompletable infinite regress.

Yet another good illustration of the impracticability of infinite cognitive regresses is provided by etymology, the explanation of word meanings in terms of changes in the meanings established in an earlier stage of word-usage customs. Here we cannot proceed ad infinitum because the establishment of a particular word-usage custom is something that

15. Herbert Spencer, *First Principles*, 5th ed. (London: Appleton, 1885), pp. 62–63.

requires a substantial period of time and cannot be compressed into a diminutively small-time interval.

Again consider the example afforded those probability epistemologists such as J. M. Keynes who hold (1) that we are never entitled to make categorical judgments but only judgments of probability, and yet (2) that as regards probability assessments we can only evaluate conditional probabilities because absolute evaluations of probability are impracticable. Here too we are embarked on an infinite cognitive regress, being put in the position that we can only evaluate p's probability relative to q but yet cannot determine q's probability as such but only its probability relative to q_1, whose own probability in turn we can only evaluate relative to q_2, and so on. In consequence, we are launched upon an infinite cognitive regress whose viciousness invalidates the whole enterprise.

The pivotal issue is the same throughout such examples. For while structural regresses in any spacelike setting are potentially harmless on grounds of nonterminating divisibility, the situation is radically altered when we turn to action performance of any sort. For actions—of *any* description, be it physical or cognitive—are never infinitely compressible within time.

5. THE REGRESS OF REASONS

In recent years a teacup storm has broken out in the philosophical literature regarding the viciousness of an infinite regress of reasons.[16] Unfortunately, the achievement of clarity has been impeded here by the failure to draw the crucially needed distinction between

1. the (normative) reasons *that there are*, abstractly speaking, for a person's doing something—that is, available facts which, purely understood, would lead a rational person to take this course, and

2. the de facto reasons that actually actuate a person's doing something—that is, the actual considerations by which the agent is moved to do this thing.

And so (at least) two sorts of "reasons" come on the scene with respect to an agent's acts: the good reasons that (abstractly speaking) there are

16. See Peter Klein, "Foundationalism and the Infinite Regress of Reasons," *Philosophy and Phenomenological Research* 58 (1998): 919–25, and "Human Knowledge and the Infinite Regress of Reasons," *Philosophical Perspectives* 13 (1999): 297–325; Carl Gillett, "Infinitism *Redux?*: A Response to Klein," *Philosophy and Phenomenological Research* 66 (2000): 709–17; and Peter Klein, "When Infinite Regresses Are Not Vicious," *Philosophy and Phenomenological Research* 66 (2000): 710–29.

for his performing that act, and by contrast, the actually operative reasons that actuated him in his considerations and deliberations. The logical geography of fact is a diversely connected structural network. Nothing prevents the first sort of reasons—the *normative* reasons—from forming part of an infinite manifold in which regression ad infinitum is innocuously possible. But, of course, the second sort of reasons—those that in actual fact figure explicitly in course of consideration and deliberation—cannot regress unendingly. These performatory processes must be finite and their regress must terminate so that here infinite regress is inacceptable on grounds of viciousness.

6. EXPLANATORY REGRESSION

The critical difference between a physical and a cognitive regress can be instanced via the mythical Hindu cosmology that envisions the Earth's position in the cosmic void in terms of its being emplaced on the back of an elephant that stands on the back of a tortoise that stands on the back of an alligator that . . . . (Perhaps from there on it is a matter of "alligators all the way down.") It is conceivable that the *structure* of the cosmos could be like that. But this would still afford no *explanation* of the Earth's seemingly stable position in the cosmos. For a cognitive regress—unlike a physical one—is vitiated if it cannot be brought to a satisfactory termination. So while there is nothing inherently impracticable about an alligator-on-alligator-and so on *cosmology*, an alligator-on-alligator-and so on *explanation* of the Earth's stability is impracticable.

Just what is one to make of the infeasibility of regressiveness with respect specifically to *explanation*? When we explain one fact by means of others and these in turn by means of still others, where does it all end? Over the years, different philosophers have construed the idea of explanation stoppers in somewhat different ways:

- propositions that are self-certifyingly necessary (Spinoza)
- propositions that are explicitly analytic (Leibniz)
- propositions that are necessary a priori (Kant)
- propositions whose denials are inconceivable (Herbert Spencer)
- propositions that are (self-)evident (Roderick Chisholm)

But throughout this tradition people saw the explanatory regress as coming to a halt in a category of "ultimate" propositions that themselves need no further explanation—a rock bottom of self-validating propositions that contain their explaining reasons within themselves—their own substantive nature. The problem, however, is finding something that will do the job. This quest encounters serious difficulty. To the extent that our beliefs are self-validating, they are bound to be either trivial ("Knives have blades") or subjective ("That object looks like an apple to me"). And in neither case will they be sufficiently informative to evidentiate any significant substantive conclusion. We are caught in a bind: to whatever extent beliefs are self-validating they are informatively too empty to evidentiate anything objective, and to whatever extent they provide useful evidentiation they are too substantively laden to be self-validating.

Such difficulties of self-evidentiation suggest shifting to a rather different line of approach—one that is distinctly pragmatic in its orientation and thereby seeks to achieve explanatory adequacy without requiring a rock bottom of explanation-stopping self-evidencers. For one can avoid an endless explanatory regress—not through reaching a rock bottom of adamantine necessity, but simply by going back *only as far as is contextually appropriate* within a particular domain of deliberation. Here there is no infinite regress at all, but simply a petering out, not because the process of regression has hit a roadblock but because the process has gone on as long as need be—there is neither need nor point to continuing the process.

Our explanations, interpretations, evidentiations, and substantiations can always be extended. But when we carry out these processes adequately, then after a while "enough is enough." The process is ended not because it has to terminate as such, but simply because there is no point in going further. A point of sufficiency has been reached. The explanation is "sufficiently clear," the interpretation is "adequately cogent," the evidentiation is "sufficiently convincing." One can indeed go further, but the circumstance of diminishing returns indicates that there is no point in doing so. With these nonvicious cognitive regresses termination is not a matter of necessity but of sufficiency—of sensible practice rather of inexorable principle (as it is with *sine qua non* regresses). What counts is doing enough "for practical purposes."

The fact of it is that those "practical purposes" of the situation often bring a potentially infinite cognitive regress to an end fairly quickly. For example, you are thinking of reading a certain book or seeing a certain film. This being so, you would be well advised to look up some reviews. And when you have them at hand you would even be well advised to seek out some reviews of the work of those reviewers. And when you find these you might even want to go to the length of seeking out reviews of the work of the relevant reviewers of reviewers. But while this process can in theory be extended indefinitely, you would in practice be foolish—as well as unreasonable—to fail to call it a day at this stage. In such a process, the thread of relevancy soon peters out.

And so, regressive viciousness in explanation can be averted not by a recourse to self-validating basics of some sort, but rather by the consideration that the practical needs of the situation rather than considerations of general principles serve to resolve our problems here. (Just how such a program can be made to work out in detail is a long story that need not preoccupy us further here.[17])

We are here brought to one of the key ideas of the philosophy of Kant. As he saw it, it lies in the nature of rationality to stake a demand for the completion of the regressive series of reasons. Theoretical reason, that is to say, ideally wants everything demonstrated, and in these demonstrative matters "[theoretical] reason demands completeness on the side of conditions."[18] But at the same time—and this is to Kant's mind the irony of it—reason acknowledges that a finite creature cannot accomplish this task: regressive completing is beyond its capacity. Accordingly, our knowledge cannot be validated demonstratively "all the way through" (so to speak) and its substantiation must always ultimately come to a stop in a nondemonstrative resource, namely, experience. (Here Kant was in agreement with Aristotle.) For finite creatures, cognitive validation is thus achieved not when *everything* has been done to achieve the deductive regress ideally necessary to rational systematization, but when *enough* has been done for the purposes at hand. Since we cannot achieve *totality*, we must settle for *sufficiency*, and this is ultimately a practical rather then a purely theoretical matter. Thus, for Kant, the ultimate fruit of the unrealizability of an infinite regress in cognitive matters is the crucial lesson that the prioritizing of practical over theoretical reason is an inescapable aspect of the human condition.

To be sure, the situation can also be regarded in a rather non-Kantian way by simply rejecting the idea that "reason demands demonstrative completeness." The approach now at issue would propose to see it as outright unreasonable to demand something that is not to be had. Contrary to Kant, reason would then be regarded in a more modest light, subject to the idea that even theoretical reason can recognize and acknowledge its unavoidable limitations and settle in cognitive matters for cogent substantiation rather than always and everywhere requiring categorical demonstration. And so, in the end, what matters for rational substantiation is not theoretical completeness but pragmatic sufficiency.

---

17. For details, see the author's *Epistomology* (New York: State University of New York Press, 2003), chap. 5.

18. *Critique of Pure Reason*, A409.

7. BACK TO ST. THOMAS

The salient lesson of the present deliberations is that regression is not automatically vicious. For a regressive process that merely displays the unending complexity of a structure (say, in arithmetic or in the case of a physical manifold on the order of space-time causality) can prove to be perfectly innocuous. However, a regressive process that looks to uniformity in the performance of such actions that as, by nature, are not time compressible must for this very reason prove vicious. An unending regress of causes is conceivable, an unending regress of causal explanations is not—at least as long as those explanations are to be intelligible to us humans.

What matters crucially for regressive viciousness is not merely the existence of an infinite antecedence of prior steps but

   1. That these steps do—or are supposed to—represent indispensable *sine qua non* preconditions for reaching the prevailing position, and

   2. That the time-incompressibility of their accomplishment renders their realization impossible in principle.

And so when St. Thomas maintained that an infinite regress of causes is impossible he treads on problematic ground.

All the same, it appears that St. Thomas's basic position makes good sense even in the face of the additional complications introduced in our present analysis of infinite regress. For while an infinitely powerful intelligent being could doubtless institute an infinitely complex universe within which an infinite regression of movers, causes, and grounds would be operative, nevertheless such a world could not be domesticated to the inherent requirements for intelligibility imposed by the limitations of finite intelligences whose intellectual processes must proceed discretely in time. After all, an infinite regress of humanly accessible *causal explanations* is impossible—but this is due to the time-incompressibility of explanations as a valid process, and not to the inherent impossibility of an infinitude of temporal processes as such. So as long as the possibilities at issue are our human possibilities, the regressive situation envisioned in the "Five Ways" will have to prevail. A world that is user-friendly to finite intelligence must be such as to avert the need for explanatory regression.[19]

---

19. When Leibniz later viewed the situation from the standpoint of God, he abandoned the idea that an infinite regress is necessarily vicious and came to regard infinitude as a characteristic hallmark of divine workmanship. See the present author's account in "Leibniz on God's Free Will and the World's Contingency," *Studia Leibnitiana* 34 (2004): 208–20.

REFERENCES

Albert, Hans. *Traktat über Kritische Vernunft.* Tübingen, Germany: J. C. B. Mohr, 1968 (2nd ed. 1991). See esp. pp. 13–15.
Aquinas, St. Thomas. *Summa theologica.*
Aristotle. *Physics* 239b9–19; *Metaphysics,* Gamma 4, 1066a8ff.; *Posterior Analytics,* A3, 72b5ff.
Bendiek, J. "Regressus/Progressus in infinitum." *Historisches Wörterbuch der Philosophie* 8 (1992): 487–89.
Black, O. "Infinite Regress of Justification." *International Philosophical Quarterly* 28 (1988): 421–37.
Clark, Romane. "Vicious Infinite Regress Arguments." In J. E. Tomberlin, ed., *Philosophical Perspectives,* 369–80. Atascadero, Calif.: Ridgeview Press, 1988.
Craig, William Lane. *The Cosmological Argument from Plato to Leibniz.* London: Macmillan, 1980.
Dingler, Hugo. "Zum Problem des *regressus in infinitum.*" In F. J. Von Rintelen, ed., *Philosophia Perennis,* 571–86. Regensburg, Germany: J. Habbel, 1930.
Fumerton, R. *Metaepistemology and Skepticism.* Boston: Rowman & Littlefield, 1995.
———. "Replies to My Three Critics." *Philosophy and Phenomenological Research* 58 (1998): 927–37.
Geach, Peter. *Truth, Love and Immortality: An Introduction to McTaggart's Philosophy.* Berkeley and Los Angeles: University of California Press, 1979.
Kant, Immanuel. *Critique of Pure Reason,* A512–B545.
Klein, Peter. "Foundationalism and the Infinite Regress of Reasons." *Philosophy and Phenomenological Research* 58 (1998): 919–25.
———. "Human Knowledge and the Infinite Regress of Reason." *Philosophical Perspectives* 13 (1999): 58–79.
———. "When Infinite Regresses Are *Not* Vicious." *Philosophy and Phenomenological Research* 66 (2003): 718–29.
MacKay, A. F. "Impossibility and Infinity." *Ethics* 90 (1980): 367–81.
Mellor, D. H. *Real Time.* Cambridge, U.K.: Cambridge University Press, 1981.
Moser, Paul. "Whither Infinite Regresses of Justification?" *Southern Journal of Philosophy* 23 (1985): 65–74.
Oakley, I. T. "An Argument for Skepticism Concerning Justified Beliefs." *American Philosophical Quarterly* 13 (1976): 221–28.
Passmore, John. *Philosophical Reasoning.* 2nd ed. London: Duckworth, 1970.
Post, J. "Infinite Regresses of Justification and Explanation." *Philosophical Studies* 38 (1980): 31–52.
Riley, J. "Arrow's Paradox and Infinite-Regress Arguments." *Ethics* 92 (1982): 670–72.
Rowe, William L. *The Cosmological Argument.* Princeton, N.J.: Princeton University Press, 1975.
———. "Cosmological Arguments." In Philip Quinn and Charles Taliaferro, eds., *Companion to the Philosophy of Religion,* 114–22. Oxford, U.K.: Basil Blackwell, 1997.
Ryle, Gilbert. *The Concept of Mind.* London: Routledge, 1949.
Sanford, D. H. "Infinity and Vagueness." *Philosophical Review* 84 (1975): 520–35.
———. "Infinite Regress Arguments." In J. H. Fetzer, ed., *Principles of Philosophical Reasoning,* 93–117. Totowa, N.J.: Rowman & Allanheld, 1984.

Sosa, Ernest. "The Raft and the Pyramid: Coherence versus Foundationalism in the Theory of Knowledge." *Midwest Studies in Philosophy* 5 (1980): 3–25.
Stekla, Herbert. *Der regressus ad infinitum bei Aristoteles.* Meisenheim am Glan, Germany: Hain, 1970.
Thomson, James. "Tasks and Supertasks." *Analysis* 15 (1954–1955): 1–13. Reprinted in W. C. Salmon, ed., *Zeno's Paradox,* 89–102. Indianapolis and New York: Bobbs Merrill, 1970.

Chapter 7

BEING QUA BEING

1. INTRODUCTION

This discussion will trace out a definite story line. Initially it seeks (in sections 2–3) to clarify the idea of "an actually existing thing" along lines that combine classical philosophical approaches with contemporary analytical perspectives. It then seeks (in sections 4–5) to show how the resulting conception of such actually existing objects involves identifiability and intelligibility in a way that endows this idea with a mind-coordinated and idealistic aspect in a manner reminiscent of medieval conceptualism. Finally, the ensuing discussion (sections 6–7) elucidates the sharp contrast between actual existence and merely mind-projected possibilities. Overall, this discussion stresses the fact that the concept of existence so functions as to demand that the manifold of existing things must form a conceptually integrated and systemic whole. In this way, discussion tries to show how a proper understanding of existence that is faithful to the mainstream of philosophical tradition must negotiate its way between both idealistic and realistic approaches.

2. DEFINING "EXISTENCE"

Existence spreads its arms wide to embrace a great many things. But what can be said about reality at large—about existence in general? Is existence even definable? Can we devise a definition to capture the claim that something "is" or "exists"?

What is a definition anyway? What is needed to *define* a term? On historical principles, the idea at issue is that a "definition" must provide two things. It must *specify* the meaning of the term at issue in such a way as to distinguish it from anything else, and it must *clarify* the meaning by making it more clear, more cognitively accessible than it was to begin with! Thus Dr. Johnson's notorious "definition" of *net* as a "reticulated texture with large interstices" fails decidedly in the second respect. A proper "definition" must elucidate matters; it must not explain a term by means of expression that is comparatively more obscure.

On this basis, it seems plausible to say that *existence* is an indefinable term. There is nothing we can do to restate the meaning of is/exists in terms of reference clearer and more accessible than those of the expression itself.

But how can one come to grips with a term that is indefinable? The answer is that its meaning must be abstracted from its use. It has to be learned by experience that manages to draw lessons from the observation of practice in a way that is characteristic of intelligent beings. The situation that obtains here is analogous to that of a skill that is learned by practice/doing rather than by learning and following the instructions of some set of rules.

3. CHARACTERIZING "EXISTENCE"

But even though we may not be able to define *is/exists/has being*—to restate its meaning in simpler, more accessible terms—there are various explanatorily helpful generalizations that we can make about it. For even when a term is not *definable*, it may be *characterizable* in terms of various generalizations that can properly be made about it.

The first and foremost thing that can be said about existence is that "to be is to be an item, to be a unit of some sort, however complex." In other words, to claim that something exists is to claim it to be a unit. Integrity and identity are required for unity. A unit can, of course, be complicated in its natural structure and have many facets, parts, and components. But these must be integrated into one whole. It is accordingly seems in order to stand committed to the principle:

$$x \text{ exists} \rightarrow x \text{ is a unit}$$

For genuine things (of whatever sort they be) must admit of counting, something that is clearly impossible in the absence of identifiable units. An item is thus a *particular*—something that is distinct from everything else.

Of course, something can be a unit in some respect and not in others. The Italy of his day, so Bismark said, was not a nation but a geographic region. It was, that is to say, not a political but a geographic unit. But that, of course, is enough for *existence*, seeing that to exist is to be a unit *of some sort*. An internally complex and disaggregated whole can certainty exist (e.g., the group of wives of Henry VIII). But insofar as what is at issue here happens to be a complex (or composite or group), it is *one* complex (or composite group) irrespective of the number of its components. No doubt unity is a flexible idea, but then, of course, so is existence.

On the other hand, the reverse does not seem to be the case. The Easter Bunny is a unit, no doubt. But it simply does not exist. The Scholastic dictum that being and unity convert *(ens et unum convertuntur)* does not seem to get it right. Only a real item that figures in some actually realized domain can qualify as an existent.

4. DETERMINING EXISTENCE: PHYSICAL EXISTENCE AS PARADIGMATIC

Given the diversity of this idea's applications, existence is best seen as a feature rather than as a descriptive property. And while the idea is not readily definable, there are some rather evident standards for its determination. Paradigmatic illustrations of existing items are afforded by concrete physical objects (e.g., trees, rocks, dogs) and concrete physical processes (e.g., magnetic storms, heat waves). Then, additionally, there will, of course, also exist whatever items are required adequately to describe, classify, or explain the things that exist—the things, processes, or features that function in an adequate account of existence. We thus arrive at an essentially "recursive" characterization of existence running essentially as follows:

1. Concrete physical objects or processes exist.
2. Whatever items (things, features, processes) are needed for an adequate causal or explanatory account of the origins, nature, or operations of something existing—its properties, its features, and its modes of functioning—will also exist.

To exist is accordingly to have some role in the world's structural or processual makeup. It is to play a substantive role in the explanatory scheme of things. On this basis the crux for existence can be a matter of conception rather than perception in specific.

This characterization of existence accordingly also links the concept with the issue of causality. This linkage is bound up with the traditional idea that only *real* causes can have *real* effects—that whatever is at issue with the causal origins of something existing will itself thereby be real, and more generally that whatever constitutes an element in the explanation of something real must for this reason also exist. And, of course, anything that can be successfully indicated ostensively in the public domain—this pen, that page, yon thunderbolt, that color—is going to be real in virtue of this fact.

Physical (spatiotemporal) existence thus provides the paradigmatic exemplification of existents. Physical existence has two definitive features: it is locatable in space-time, and it forms part of the world's causal commerce. Whatever has being of this sort is on this account a component or a facet of the physical world's manifold of space-time causality. And in virtue of this, any element of physical existence is, in principle, accessible to experience. That is, it must, by its nature, be able, in principle, to figure in the experience of some sort of creature or other—not necessarily ourselves, but some theoretically and naturally possible sort of creature. And, conversely, anything that figures in the experience of a sentient being—be it actual or possible—is actually existent as such. To be sure, the item at issue may be an illusion, like the pink elephant seen "the morning after." But what is an illusion here is that pink elephant and not the experience itself—the phenomenal elephant sighting—which is as such (i.e., as a phenomenon) as real as could be.

5. IS "EXISTENCE" UNIVOCAL?

Given that the idea of existence resists definition, it is not surprising that there is no genus of which all existents are species. The idea is "transcategorematic" and is effectively applicable in every descriptive category of things.

The question of whether existence/being is univocal or not—whether existence is strictly one sort of thing or whether an inherent diversity splits it into different types or modes as regards the meaning of what is at issue—is a question that was debated extensively among the Schoolmen. Duns Scotus (ca. 1266–1308) was one of the most decided univocalists. One of his key arguments was a reductio ad absurdum that ran essentially as follows: If *being* were an equivocal term admitting a plurality of versions—so that being-1 were altogether different from being-2 in meaning—then we would not be able to say whether or not an object has being without fixing whether it is being-1 or being-2 that is at issue, which (so Scotus argued) may fail to be the case. But this view of the matter appears to be deeply problematic. For there seems to be nothing of which one could meaningfully say that it had being without an at least tacit indication of the sort of being involved—for example, whether it is being-as-a-physical-object or being-as-a-number that is at issue.[1]

Scotus's argumentation was apparently based on a line of thought that runs somewhat as follows: Suppose that *being* were an equivocal term admitting of two altogether different specific senses, say being-1 and being-2. Still, nothing could prevent us from amalgamating the two

1. See Peter King, "Scotus on Metaphysics," in Thomas Williams, ed., *The Cambridge Companion to Duns Scotus* (Cambridge, U.K.: Cambridge University Press, 2003), pp. 15–68; see esp. p. 18.

terms into a generic single unit via the definition that x has being *simpliciter* if x either has being-1 or x has being-2. On this basis, so it would seem, there automatically results a unified sense of being that is univocal and applies equally and alike to beings-1 and beings-2. But such a stratagem will not actually do the job because it is deeply problematic. For disjunction effects a merely formal and not a conceptually coherent unification. One can certainly propose the definition

Tirgret = tiger or egret

But this definition fails its intended purpose: it does not manage to introduce a conceptually unified and coherent mode of animal designation into the sphere of our considerations. It is based upon a linkage that is nominal rather than natural—in name only rather than in function. And to all visible appearances the same is true of the very artificial unification that the present approach envisions.

Scotus also introduced a further argument for the univocality of being that runs roughly as follows[2]: Existence must be universal and manage to characterize—uniformly and equally—innumerable fundamentally different sorts of things. For it characterizes all concrete substances that are revealed by our senses. And the only factor that all such things have in common is the fact that they exist. Existence must therefore apply universally across the board to all of the concrete substances that figure in our thought and discourse.

However, this argumentation has its problems. For the fact of it is that there are many other factors that all the substances that figure in our deliberations have in common. They all possess various features: they are all items that we can identify; they are all objects that figure in our deliberations; and so on. That commonality betokens existence is a very problematic idea.

Consider the "existence" of such things as physical objects, physical processes, natural dispositions, trends and tendencies, natural laws, states of affairs, properties and qualities of physical objects, or numbers. With some of these it may seem more proper to say that they function or obtain or are operative, but the point is that they all do or can have a reality of sorts even though different sorts of locutions are sometimes used to indicate this. All of them, that is, are viable units of some sort.[3]

It thus seems reasonable to say that different types of things "exist" in different ways or modes in such a deep-rooted way that different senses of the term are at issue—that the existence of numbers, for example, is

---

2. Ibid.
3. Physical objects exist (or not), states of affairs obtain (or not), solutions to problems are available (or not), etc.

something rather different from the existence of trees. To say both "exist," while in a way true, manages to mask a conceptual distinction by a terminological uniformity. Existence is not a concept that has an essentialistic common core: it diversifies into very different modalities and modes of being that are at best related in something of the "family resemblance" manner. Different sorts of things have such "existence" as they do in very different sorts of ways.[4]

6. THE PASSIVE/IDEALISTIC ASPECT OF "EXISTENCE"

How does existence look from the angle of mind? How does actual being relate to the reach of mind in the context of perception, understanding, and the grasp of intelligence in general? How do matters of epistemology (i.e., of understanding and knowledge) bear upon matters of ontology (i.e., of being and existence)?

Bishop Berkeley maintained that

• To be is to be conceived.

But unless one is, like the good bishop, prepared to press God into service as a philosophical resource, it would be more strictly correct merely to say:

• To be is to be conceivable.

Along these lines, compare and contrast the theses that:

• To be is to be

—identifiable (recall Quine's dictum: "No entity without identity")
—describable
—classifiable/categorizable
—experienceable

Observe that all of these purportedly essential characteristics of existing things have certain features in common:

• They are passive rather than active. That is, they relate to what can be done with or to existing things, rather than to what such things themselves do.

• They are mentalistic in nature, and relate to things that only mind-equipped beings can possibly do.

4. To say this is not, of course, to gainsay that various appropriate generalizations can be made—after all, no matter how loose-jointed that "family resemblance" may be, all members of a family can be human.

It warrants note in this regard that anything characterizable as an activity cannot possibly be common to *all* existents—of whatever sort. For there clearly are some existents—for instance, abstract ones like numbers—that never change at all. Changeability may well be a universal characteristic of concrete *physical* existents, but not one of existents in general. Only passive features—and cognitively geared ones at that—can plausibly be held to be universal among existents. What is common to *all* existents is not a matter of what they themselves *do* but rather of what *can be done* with them by intelligent beings engaged in apprehension and inquiry.

In the final analysis, it makes no sense to ascribe existence to that which—even in principle and in theory—lies outside the potential reach of mind. Whatever plays a role in the realm of the real is bound to be such that some possible (inarguable, conceivable) intelligence can come to grips with it.

7. ABSTRACT VERSUS CONCRETE "EXISTENCE" *(Dasein)*

Neither is all existence physical, nor yet is all physical existence concrete. For something is concrete only if it both (1) has what Kant called *Dasein*, that is, presence in the world and thereby spatiotemporal location, and moreover also (2) does this uniquely—that is, by way of being a definite particular item not admitting of multiple instantiations, realizations, exemplifications.[5] An example of physical-existence-in-the-world that is *not* concrete is afforded by the laws of nature (e.g., the Law of Gravitation). And *facts* afford another example. Such things, however, are not concrete. For concrete physical existence is spatiotemporally localized—unlike the nonlocalizably diffused realities such as a probability distribution.

Again, certain mental events and occurrences, though realized in time, fail to have spatial location. One's brain has physical location, but one's ideas do not. And one's worries and headaches, while perfectly real, are not concrete because they lack a position in space. Such items have being (existence) but not spatially a localizable being-in-the-world *(Dasein)*. They are real without being concrete. The fact remains, however, that real physical *objects* are invariably concrete.[6]

In overview, existents over and above those that are concrete can be classified as follows:

5. Use of the German word *Dasein* ("being there") for concrete existence goes back at least to Kant. See Rudolf Eisler's *Kant Lexikon* (Hildesheim, Germany: G. Olms, 1989).

6. On the concreteness of the real, see Charles Hartshorne, *Anselm's Discovery* (La Salle, Ill.: Open Court, 1965), pp. 189–92.

• Those that are neither spatially not temporally located (the number 2).

• Those that are located temporally but not spatially (headaches, thoughts, Caesar's birthday).

All such items have an identity but are not concrete. Concreteness is only achieved through spatiotemporal localization. However, not only physical *objects* can have concreteness but also *states of affairs* as well. The cat's presences on the mat from 2:00–4:00 P.M. this afternoon is a concrete state of affairs.

8. THE COMPLEXITY OF CONCRETE EXISTENCE

While abstract objects will unquestionably have existence in their own way and manner, nevertheless, the *paradigmatic* existents are the concretely real things of this world. And this reality is endlessly complex in its details. As we standardly think about particulars within the conceptual framework of our factual deliberation and discourse, *any* real concrete particular has more features and facets than it will ever actually manifest in experience. For every objective property of a real thing has consequences of a dispositional character, and these are never completely surveyable because their dispositions inevitably have endowed them with an infinitistic aspect that cannot be comprehended within experience.[7] This desk, for example, has a limitless manifold of phenomenal features of the type "having a certain appearance from a particular point of view." It is perfectly clear that most of these will never be actualized. Moreover, a thing *is* what it *does:* entity and operation are coordinated correlates—a good Kantian point. And this consideration that real things must exhibit lawful comportment in behavior means that the finitude of experience precludes any prospect of the *exhaustive* manifestation of the descriptive facets of any actual existents.[8]

7. To be sure, various *abstract* things, such as colors or numbers, will not have dispositional properties. For example, being divisible by four is not a *disposition* of sixteen. Plato got the matter right in Book 7 of the *Republic:* in the realm of mathematical abstracta there are not genuine *processes*—and process is a requisite of dispositions. Of course, there may be dispositional truths in which numbers (or colors, etc.) figure that do not issue in any dispositional properties of these numbers (or colors, etc.) themselves—a truth, for example, such as my predilection for odd numbers. But if a truth (or supposed truth) does no more than to convey how someone *thinks* about a thing, then it does not indicate any property of the thing itself. (Fictional things, however, *can* have suppositional dispositions: Sherlock Holmes was addicted to cocaine, for example.)

8. This aspect of objectivity was justly stressed in the "Second Analogy" of Kant's

All concrete things not only have more properties than they ever *will* overtly manifest, but they have more properties than they ever *can* possibly actually manifest. This is so because the dispositional properties of things always involve what might be characterized as *mutually preemptive* conditions of realization. This lump of sugar, for example, has the dispositional property of reacting in a particular way if subjected to a temperature of 10,000°C and of reacting in a certain way if placed for one hundred hours in a large, turbulent body of water. But if either of these conditions is ever realized, it will destroy the lump of sugar as a lump of sugar, and thus block the prospect of *its* ever bringing the other property to manifestation. The severally and separately *possible* realization of various dispositions may fail to be mutually *compossible*, and so the dispositional properties of a real thing cannot ever be manifested completely—not just in practice, but in principle. Our objective claims about real things always commit us to more than we can actually ever determine about them. Our information about things is always simply the visible part of the iceberg.

The existence of this latent (hidden, occult) sector is a crucial feature of our conception of a real thing. Neither in fact nor in thought can we ever simply put it away. To say of this apple that its only features are those it actually manifests is to run afoul of our conception of an apple. To deny—or even merely to refuse to be committed to the claim—that it *would* manifest certain particular features *if* appropriate conditions came about (e.g., that it would have such-and-such a taste if eaten) is to be driven to withdrawing the claim that it is an apple. The latent, implicit ramifications of our objective factual claims about something real is potentially endless, and such judgments are thus "nonterminating" in C. I. Lewis's sense.[9] The totality of facts about a thing—about any real thing whatever—is in principle inexhaustible and the complexity of real things is in consequence descriptively unfathomable. Endlessly many true descriptive remarks can be made about any particular actual concrete object. For example, take a stone. Consider its physical features: its shape, its surface texture, its chemistry, and so on. And then consider its causal background: its subsequent genesis and history. Then consider the multitude of functional aspects reflected in its uses by the stonemason, or the architect, or the landscape decorator, or whomever. There is, after all, no end to the perspectives of considera-

---

Critique of Pure Reason, although his discussion rests on ideas already contemplated by Leibniz. See G. W. Leibniz, *Philosophische Schriften*, ed. C. I. Gerhardt, vol. 7 (Berlin: Weidmann, 1890), pp. 319ff.

9. See C. I. Lewis, *An Analysis of Knowledge and Valuation* (La Salle, Ill.: Open Court, 1962), pp. 180–81.

tion that we can bring to bear on things. The botanist, herbiculturist, landscape gardener, farmer, painter, and real estate appraiser will operate from different cognitive "points of view" in describing one selfsame vegetable garden. And there is in principle no theoretical limit to the lines of consideration available to provide descriptive perspectives upon a thing.

Our characterization of real things can accordingly become more *extensive* without thereby becoming more *complete*. New descriptive features can and do ongoingly come into view with the progress of knowledge. (Caesar not only did not know, but in the then prevailing state of knowledge could not have known, that his sword contained tungsten.) Real things are—and by their very nature must be—such that their actual nature outruns any particular description of it that we might venture. From this angle, too, it is clear that the realm of reality-appertaining fact inevitably outruns the reach of our descriptive information-at-hand.[10]

It follows from such considerations that we can never justifiably claim to be in a position to articulate "the whole truth" about a real concrete object. The domain of thing-characterizing fact inevitably transcends the limits of our capacity to *express* it, and a fortiori those of our capacity to canvas it completely. In the description of concrete particulars we are caught up in an inexhaustible detail: the cardinal feature of reality is its inherent complexity. There are always bound to be more descriptive facts about actual things than we are able to capture with our linguistic machinery: the real encompasses more than we can manage to say about it—now or ever. The position of St. Thomas Aquinas was right on target in this regard, for as he saw it no concrete entity can possibly be described completely. The very idea of a complete description of such an entity is in principle impracticable.

After all, the truth regarding any particular actual existent runs off into endlessly proliferating detail. No matter how much is told us, we can ask for yet more pertinent information and in principle expect a sensible and informative answer. It is a crucial facet of our epistemic stance toward the real world that there is always more to be known than what we now explicitly have. Every part and parcel of reality has features

10. The reference to *us* is crucial here. Duns Scotus rejected Aquinas's fundamental contention that concrete entities do not admit of descriptive completeness. To be sure, object description is not a finite process—and for this reason we humans could never manage to realize it. But God can do so. He can achieve what Leibniz was later to call the *complete individual concept* of a concrete particular. But, of course, what is possible for an omnipotent and omniscient God is not within our limited reach. Dealing concretely with nonexistents and *irrealia* is effectively beyond us.

lying beyond our present cognitive reach—at *any* "present" whatsoever.

Consider an example. On a map of the United States, Chicago is but a dot. But when we go to a map of Illinois it begins to take on more detail, and on a map of Cook County it presents a substantial and characteristic shape. Yet the line does not end there. We could, in theory, go on to map it block by block, house by house, room by room, dish by pitcher, molecule by molecule. And with increasing detail new and different features constantly emerge. Where does the process stop? Not with atoms, certainly—for the impenetrable and unchanging atoms of the ancient Greeks have become increasingly dematerialized and ethereal, in the light of modern physics even composed of ongoingly smaller processes. As we increase the power of our particle accelerators, our view of the makeup of the physical world becomes not only ever different but also ever stranger. There is, as best we can tell, no limit to the world's ever-increasing complexity that comes to view with our ever-increasing grasp of its detail. To all visible appearances the realm of fact and reality is endlessly layered: no matter how far our descriptive characterizations go, there is always more to be said. In this setting, exhaustiveness and completion are simply not realistic prospects.[11]

9. IRREALITY AND CHAOS

All determinalism is negation, so Spinoza urged, insisting that in specifying what something is we thereby distinguish it from that which it is not. In this light it is both constructive and instructive to contrast existents with nonexistents.

How do actual existents compare with what is at issue with merely speculative possibilities regarding things that are not? The things that are and the features and relationships they exhibit constitute the manifold of fact and define the lineaments of truth. But what happens when we suppose what might have been and insert falsehoods among truths?

From the cognitive point of view, there is good reason to think that the move from existence to unrealized possibility is a plunge into chaos.

---

11. To be sure, someone might maintain that while it is always possible to say more about an existing thing, that nevertheless a Law of Diminishing Returns becomes operative so that whatever new and additional material comes to view will after a certain point make only trivial additions to what has gone before, thus filling in increasingly small-scale details that leave the previously established "big picture" substantially intact. There are, however, cogent reasons why this line of thought does not succeed in the present context. For details, see the author's *The Limits of Science* (Pittsburgh: University of Pittsburgh Press, 1999). On the other hand, the circumstance that there is always more that *can be* said does not contravene the fact that in the context of a particular question or issue one can readily reach the point where nothing further *needs to be* said.

A *chaotic condition,* as natural scientists nowadays use this term, obtains when we have a situation that is tenable or viable in certain circumstances but where a change in these circumstances—even one that is extremely minute—will destabilize matters with imponderable consequences, producing results that cannot be foreseen in informative detail. When a precarious condition exists, even a small change in the prevailing circumstances can produce results that are at once large and unpredictable.

Historians and students of human affairs generally regard the state of public affairs as representing a chaotic condition of this sort. Who can say, they are wont to ask, what would have happened had Cleopatra's nose been longer—let alone if one of Hitler's failed assassins had succeeded or if President Kennedy's successful assassin had failed. The result of changes in the historical course of things cannot be assessed with any reliability. Historians—and diplomats as well—are reluctant to enter into what-if speculation because the firm ground not just of reality but of realism is then apt to dissolve beneath their feet.

And much the same case holds among present practitioners of astrophysics and cosmology. Given the structure of fundamental physical law as we have it, they see the universe as existing early on in a highly precarious position with respect to the value of the fundamental physical constants. They view the universe as incredibly fine-tuned, arguing that if its fundamental forces (gravitation, nuclear binding force, etc.) were even the least bit different, a universe of stable objects could never have developed.[12] But exactly what sorts of conditions would have resulted if the universe had to evolve under different conditions (i.e., different laws and operating principles) is a matter of risky speculation that permits no confident resolution on the basis of our knowledge about how matters stand.

To leave reality behind is thus to open the door to chaos. Every false supposition, every hypothetical change in the physical makeup of the real—however small—sets in motion a vast cascade of further such changes either in regard to the world's furnishings or in the laws of nature. For as we conjure with those pebbles, what about the structure of the envisioning electromagnetic, thermal, and gravitational fields? Just how are these to be preserved after the removal and/or shift of the pebbles? How is matter to be readjusted to preserve consistency here? Or are we to do so by changing the fundamental laws of physics?

And what is true at the physical level holds at the ontological level as well. For it is readily seen that we cannot make hypothetical alterations

12. See Martin Rees, *Just Six Numbers* (New York: Basic Books, 2000).

in the makeup of the real without thereby setting out on a course that raises an unending series of questions. And not only do *content redistributions* raise problems but so do even mere *content erasures*, mere cancellations, because reality being as it is they require redistributions to follow in their wake. If by hypothesis we zap that book on the self out of existence, then what is it that supports the others? Just exactly when and how did it disappear? And if it just vanished a moment ago, then what of the law of the conservation of matter? And whence the material that is now in that book-denuded space? Once more we embark upon an endless journey.

Reality as such is something definite. And when one thing changes in the real world (e.g., when someone new enters the room) a definite course of coordinated change is set in motion. The problem with *hypothetical* changes in the structure of the real is that this offers reality an open-ended series of possible alternatives and that the responsive re-design of reality projects a series of in-principle possibilities so vast and diversified that concretization becomes impracticable.

Thus suppose that we contemplate only a very small alteration in the descriptive composition of the real—say, by adding one pebble to the river bank. But which pebble? Where are we to get it and what are we to put in its place? And where are we to put the air or the water that this new pebble displaces? And when we put that material in a new spot, just how are we to make room for it? And how are we to make room to the so-displaced material? Moreover, the region within six inches of the new pebble used to hold N pebbles. It now holds $N+1$ pebbles. Of which region are we to say that it holds $N-1$ pebbles? If it is that region yonder, then how did the pebble get here from there? By a miraculous instantaneous transport? By a little boy picking it up and throwing it? But then, which little boy? And how did he get there? And if he threw it, then what happened to the air that his throw displaced that would otherwise have gone undisturbed? Here problems arise without end. To project hypotheses that carry us into "other possible worlds" is to enter a realm pervaded by regions of impenetrable darkness.

And there is good reason for this situation.

10. REALITY AND ORDER: THE SYSTEMIC UNITY OF THE REAL

The manifold of reality is an interwoven fabric where the severing of any thread unravels the whole—with results and consequences that are virtually impossible to discern in advance.

And this situation obtains at the deeper level of logical general principles. For the fact is that the interlinkage of our beliefs about the real is such that belief-contravening suppositions always function within a wider setting of accepted beliefs $B_1, B_2, \ldots, B_n$ of such a sort that when one of them, for simplicity say B_1, is abandoned owing to a hypothetical endorsement of its negation, nevertheless the resulting group $\sim B_1, B_2, \ldots, B_n$ still remains collectively inconsistent. And the reason for this lies in the logical principle of *the systemic integrity of fact.* For suppose that we accept B_1. Then let B_2 be some other claim that we flatly reject—one that is such that we accept $\sim B_2$. Initially, however, since we accepted B_1, we will certainly also have accepted B_1 or B_2. But now consider the group of accepted theses: B_1, B_1 or B_2, $\sim B_2$. When we drop B_1 here and insert $\sim B_1$ in its place, we obtain $\sim B_1$, B_1 or B_2, $\sim B_2$. And this group is still inconsistent. The structure of fact is an intricately woven fabric. One cannot sever one part of it without unraveling other parts of the real. Facts engender a *dense* structure, as the mathematicians use this term. Every determinable fact is so drastically hemmed in by others that even when we erase it, it can always be restored on the basis of what remains. The fabric of fact is woven tight. Facts are so closely intermeshed with each other as to form a connected network. Any change anywhere has reverberations everywhere. And this condition of things is old news. Already in his influential *Treatise on Obligations*[13] the medieval Scholastic philosopher Walter Burley (ca. 1275–ca. 1345) laid down the rule: *When a false contingent proposition is posited, one can prove any false proposition that is compatible with it.* His reasoning was as follows. Let the facts be that:

(P) You are not in Rome.
(Q) You are not a bishop.

And now, of course, also:

(R) You are not in Rome or you are a bishop. *(P* or not-*Q)*

All of these, so we suppose, are true. Let us now posit by way of a (false) supposition that:

Not-*(P)* You are in Rome.

Obviously *(P)* must now be abandoned—"by hypothesis." But nevertheless from *(R)* and not-*(P)* we obtain:

You are a bishop. (Not-*Q*)

13. Translated in part in N. Kretzman and E. Stump, *The Cambridge Translation of Medieval Philosophical Texts*, Vol. 1: *Logic and Philosophy of Language* (Cambridge, U.K.: Cambridge University Press, 1988), pp. 389–412.

And in view of thesis *(Q)* this is, of course, false. We have thus obtained not-*Q* where *Q* is *an arbitrary true proposition.*

It is clear that this situation obtains in general. For let *p* and *q* be any two (arbitrary but nonequivalent) facts. Then all of the following facts will also of course obtain: ~(~*p*), *p* + *q*, *p* v *q*, *p* v ~*q* v *r*, ~*p* v *q*, ~(~*p* + *q*), and so on. Let us focus upon just three of these available facts:

1. *p*
2. *q*
3. ~(~*p* + *q*) or equivalently *p* v ~*q*

Now let it be that you are going to suppose not-*p*. Then, of course, you must remove 1 from the list of accepted facts and substitute:

1´. ~*p*

But there is now no stopping. For together with 3 this new item at once yields ~*q*, contrary to 2. Thus that supposition of ours that runs contrary to accepted fact (viz., not-*p*) has the direct consequence that *any other arbitrary contingent truth must also be abandoned.* This circumstance is one of the salient aspects of the aforementioned systemic integrity of fact.

And on this basis Burley's Principle has far-reaching implications. Inserting the false among the true creates chaos. As far as the logic of the situation is concerned, you cannot change anything in the domain of fact without endangering everything. The domain of fact has a systemic integrity that one disturbs at one's own cognitive peril: a change at any point has further reverberations elsewhere.

We thus have little alternative but to acknowledge the systemic integrity of the real. As Burley's reasoning makes manifest, the realm of truth and fact as such is so dense as to exclude any prospect of "extraneous" additions from the realm of falsity.

Reality, to reemphasize, is a manifest, interconnected whole. As regards its *causal* structure, it is an ordered series of dominos where any one that falls brings down others further along the line. And much the same holds as regards its *logical* structure: any hypothetical change involves an endless (and systemically imponderable) series of further modifications. Once you embark on a reality-modifying assumption, then as far as pure logic is concerned all bets are off. At the level of abstract logic, the introduction of belief-contravening hypotheses puts everything at risk: little if anything is safe any more. To maintain consistency you must revamp the entire fabric of fact, which is to say that you confront a task of Sisyphean proportions. (This is something that people who make glib use of the idea of other possible worlds all too easily forget.) Reality has a grip upon us that it will never entirely relax: it is something too complex to be remade more than fragmentally by our thought, which can effectively come to terms only with piecemeal changes *in* reality, but not with comprehensive changes *of* reality.

11. REAL EXISTENCE VERSUS FICTION

In contrasting reality with fiction, the first thing to note is that the bottomless descriptive depth of the real inherent in its unending detail. Fictions, unlike real things, are descriptively limited because there are no (item-specific) facts of the matter about fictional items over and above what is overtly or implicitly said about them in their formative suppositions. Accordingly, fictional, unrealized possibilities will differ from actual realities in this respect, that with fictions, the course of meaningful questioning must come to a stop. Did Sancho Panza trim his mustache short? And just how much of it had turned gray? Seeing that Cervantes did not tell us, there is no way of securing an answer. Fiction has finite cognitive depth: the quest for detail comes to an end of the line.

The world of fiction has informative limits in a way that the real world does not. With concrete reality, once the resources of ostension (of pointing and other modes of self-correlative locating) are available, we can speak simply of that dog (pointing) or "the only globe in this room" and manage to identify an object unambiguously with a bare minimum of descriptive elaboration. Only when dealing with nonexistents—objects beyond the reach of ostension—are we thrown entirely upon descriptive resources all by themselves.

In clarifying the difference at issue it is useful to distinguish between two types of information about a thing, namely, what is *generic* and what is not. Generic information involves those features of the thing that it has in common with everything else of its kind or type. Now a key fact about *fictional* particulars is that there is only so much one can ever manage to say about them. Thus there are decided limits to what we can assert nongenerically about Don Quijote: namely, just as much as Cervantes told us. A point will always be reached with regard to fictional individuals when one cannot say anything characteristically new about them—presenting nongeneric information that is not inferentially implicit in what has already been said. And this informational finitude of a fictional object's cognitive depth means that where such objects are at issue the presentation of ampliatively novel nongeneric information must in the very nature of the case come to a stop. With *real* things, on the other hand, there is no reason of principle why this process need ever terminate.

Again, real things always have potentialities—and counterfactual potentialities at that (e.g., His neighbor would certainly have recognized Smith if he had not been wearing that false mustache). But counterfactual reasoning about fictional objects is something else again—something far more problematic save in the generic case. Who (possibly excepting Cervantes) can say what Don Quijote would have thought of those windmills if he had not mistaken them for giants. Fiction can only present incomplete alternatives *within* reality because its very finitude prevents it from presenting a comprehensive alternative *to* reality.

And so while fact may or may not be *stranger* than fiction, it will always be more *complex.* And the reason for this is straightforward. Fictions are creatures of thought, and the capacity for the management of complexity in thought that we finite creatures possess is limited. Nature is vastly more complex then our brain—if only because we ourselves are merely a minor constituent of nature itself. The states of affairs that our minds can envision are vastly fewer and simpler than those that nature can present. (To give just one rather obvious example, we cannot even begin to conceive the facts and phenomena that will figure on the agenda of the science of the future.)

The cognitive depth of fiction is always finite because fiction—unlike reality—is the finite product of a finite mind. It relates to a realm whose constituent detail is the limited creation of a limited intellect. And unlike the real world, the realm of fiction is accordingly bounded by the limits of explicitly available thought and language. Because of this, one is bound to reach the end of its road with a finite number of steps. But reality just is not like that. It is like an unendingly layered onion; in theory, and presumably in practice as well, one can always peel off further layers of detail without ever reaching an end. Thus reality has more complications, more unanticipatable twists and turns, than fiction ever could have. It can surprise and astound us in ways more profound than fiction ever could. Reality is to fiction somewhat as chess is to tic-tac-toe—but a great deal more so. Fiction just cannot achieve the complexity-indicative detail needed to realize the complexity dovetailed and integrated systematicity that does—and must—characterize the manifold of the real.

All in all, then, the fact remains that while a great deal can be said about the conceptual structure of being at a considerable level of generality, nevertheless, it really does not make all that much sense to look for or to expect a univocal *definition* of existence. *Ontology*—the theory of existence—is not rendered an impracticable enterprise by the fact that its pivotal conception may not be definable in the classic sense of the term. For here, as elsewhere, the limits of definition fortunately do not constitute the limits of *elucidation.*

Chapter 8

NONEXISTENTS THEN AND NOW

1. PROBLEM: THE BEING OF NONEXISTENTS

In matters of irreality, medieval philosophers were not much concerned with fiction as such. The prime focus of their attention was theology, and their dealings with nonexistence related to the role of such items in relation to the thoughts of God rather than those of man. In this light, the medievals approached the issue of nonexistents on essentially the following basis:

God created the world about us. His choice to create this world was a free choice—had he wanted to do so, he could have created the world differently. The things that would have existed had he done this are, of course, nonexistent. And on this basis room must be made for such beings as a deliberative possibility because in order to make a rational choice God had to make comparisons. To assure the freedom of God's creative choice there have to be other possibilities, and to implement the idea of other possibilities it is necessary to postulate other possibles, that is, mere *possibilia*.

As the medievals saw it, in order to create his world in a manner that is wise and good, God had to compare his actual creation choices with their (inferior) alternatives. And so he therefore must, by way of contrast, contemplate nonexistence and nonexistents.[1]

But nonexistents are—so it would seem—in principle unknowable. The difficulty that arises here was contemplated by Moses Maimonides, whose position in this regard was summarized by Harry Austryn Wolfson as follows:

Knowledge of non-existent things . . . was objectionable to the medievals on two main grounds. First, it was not true knowledge, if by truth is meant correspondence of the idea in the mind to an object outside the mind. Second, in the

1. On medieval discussions of God's ideas of things merely possible and not actually created, see Marilyn McCord Adams, *William of Ockham*, vol. 2 (South Bend, Ind.: University of Notre Dame Press, 1987), chaps. 23–27.

event the non-existent object became existent, it would imply a change of the knower.[2] (Maimonides, *Or Adonai*, II, i, 2; *Milhamot Adonai*, III, ii, 6).

Given such problems, it should occasion no surprise that St. Thomas Aquinas grappled at some length with the issue of nonexistent possibles in the context of the question of God's knowledge of things that are not. A synopsis of Aquinas's general position is clearly conveyed in the following passage:

The relation of the divine knowledge to other things, therefore, will be such that it can be even of non-existing things. . . . Now, the artisan knows through his art even those things that have not yet been fashioned, since the forms of his art flow from his knowledge to external matter for the constitution of the artifacts. Hence, nothing forbids that there be in the knowledge of an artisan forms that have not yet come out of it. Thus, nothing forbids God to have knowledge of the things that are not. . . . Moreover, by that operation through which it knows what a thing is, even our intellect can know those things that do not actually exist. It can comprehend the essence of a lion or a horse even though all such animals were to be destroyed. But the divine intellect knows, in the manner of one knowing what a thing is, not only definitions but also enunciables as is clear from what we have said. Therefore, it can know even the things that are not. . . . But not all non-beings have the same relation to His knowledge. For those things that are not, nor will be, nor ever were, are known by God as possible to His power. Hence, God does not know them as in some way existing in themselves, but as existing only in the divine power.[3]

Thus Thomas's position is that God has full knowledge of nonexistents, since they correspond to concepts in his intellect, which comprehends all "enunciables." And indeed God must be able to grasp these, for several reasons: (1) because he otherwise would not be omniscient, (2) because his omnibenevolence requires comparative preferences, and (3) because his omnipotence would otherwise be impeded as well, since the full exercise of any power (including creative power) requires knowledge of the range of alternatives lieing "within one's power." That God can consider unrealized possibilities is thus inescapable. For him, knowledge of irrealia is simply an aspect of self-knowledge regarding his own power—of considering what he could create if he chose to do so.

But still, a theoretical difficulty remained. For, as already noted, truth or fact is, as the medievals saw it, a matter of correspondence with reality. And with nonexistents there just is no reality for truths about them to

2. Harry Austryn Wolfson, *The Philosophy of Spinoza*, vol. 2 (Cambridge, Mass.: Harvard University Press, 1934), p. 27.

3. *Summa contra gentiles*, translated by A. C. Pegis under the title *On the Truth of the Catholic Faith* (New York: Hanover House, 1955), chaps. 58–59; but see also the wider context of those passages.

correspond to since, by definition, nonexistents are not reals. And then, of course, fact and truth being absent, there is no prospect of any knowledge. Knowledge, after all, is a matter of knowledge *of truth*, and where there is no truth, no fact of the matter, there is nothing to be known.

Moreover, if there is to be a nonexistent *object*, then this would, as a proper object, have to be a unity, an *unum*. But medieval ontology correlated being and unity—*ens et unum cunvertuntur*—so that only an *ens*, an existent, can truly be an *unum*. After all, a nonexistent object must be a something-or-other—if it is to be an object, it must be a single unified item. As such it must represent a unit of being, so that it would appear that there can be no nonexistent objects. As Fredegisus of Tours (an Englishman who was a pupil of Alcuin and who died in 819) had written in his *Epistola de nihilo et tenebris*: "*Omnis significatio est quod est. 'Nihil' autem aliquid significat. Igitur 'nihil' ejus signification est quid est, id est rei existentis.*"[4]

To oppose such a position, Peter Abailard (d. 1142) had developed a rather sophisticated teaching regarding nonexistents.[5] He was primarily concerned with the question of how nonexistents can figure as subjects of true propositions (e.g., "Chimeras are imaginary animals"). But rather than establishing an ontology of nonexistents, he resolved this problem on strictly grammatical grounds. In the nominalistic manner of the Stoics, Abailard thinks that what is in question here is not an ontological category of quasi-things, but a purely linguistic resource. In this regard, such nonexistent unreals are, according to Abailard, to be distinguished from *fictive* things *(res ficta)* that—like winged horses—the mind concocts from its experiences of the real (and which he likens to mirror images in that they somehow reflect actually existing things).[6]

Aquinas, however, and most medievals with him, refused to equate nonexistents with mere fictions and so dismiss them as empty verbalisms. He—and they—sought for a via media, a middle way between

---

4. "The signification of anything is something that is. But 'nothing' signifies something. Therefore the signification of 'nothing' is something that is, i.e., an existing thing." See Migne, ed., *Patrologiae series Latina*, vol. 105, p. 751; quoted from S. van den Bergh, trans., *Averroes' Tahâfut al-Tahâfut*, vol. 2, p. 47, and n. 61.

5. Abailard's theory is described in detail in Martin M. Tweedale, "Abailard and Non-Things," *Journal of the History of Philosophy* 5 (1967): 329–42. My brief remarks here are based upon this valuable paper.

6. Many other medievals discussed problems in this general area. Particular importance attaches to the *quaestio* of Siger of Brabant: *utrum haec sit vera: Homo est animal nullo homine existente?* See Pierre Mandonnet, *Siger de Brabant et l'Averroisme latin au XIIe siècle*, pt. 2 (Fribourg: Libraire de l'Université, 1899), pp. 65–70. For further interesting details, see Albert Zimmerman, "Eine anonyme Quaestio: *Utrum haec sit cera: Homo est animal homine non existente*," *Archiv für Geschichte der Philosophie* 49 (1967): 183–200.

the unavailable realm of somehow existent inexistents and an ontologically void *flatus vocis* nominalism. And so they went on to hold that various nonexistents can have a foothold in reality through possessing a potential for existence, unlike various pure fictions. Nonentities can be seen as genuine *possibilia*. To be sure, this requires them to have an ontological grounding of sorts. From whence is it to come? The answer that was generally given is: from God. Just as they saw the actual things as created by God, so the medievals saw the possibility of things as divinely provided as well. They are part and parcel of God's consciousness of his own power, of his conditionalized self-awareness of what he can do if he so chooses.

With regard to nonexistents, the medieval mainstream thus sought to effect a compromise. On the one hand, their lack of reality, of actual existence, deprived nonentities of a self-sustaining ontological footing and made them into mind artifacts, *entia rationis*. On the other hand, their footing in the mind of God endowed them with a certain objectivity and quasi-reality that precluded them from being mere *flatus vocis* fictions, mere verbalisms that represent creatures of the human fancy. Accordingly, the "reality" of nonexistent *possibilia* lies in the role they actually play in the cognitive and productive powers of God.[7]

This opened up a line of reflection that was clearly set out by Leibniz, whose view of nonexistents was heavily influenced by the medievals and followed markedly in the footsteps of Aquinas and Scotus. The actuality of God and his thought is thus coordinate with the realm of that merely possible, with the result that, as Scotus held, "that some being *can* exist leads to the conclusion that God *must* exist."[8] For Leibniz, the very fact that there is a manifold of alternative possibilities constitutes the basis for an argument for the existence of God because God is required for there to be alternative possibilities at all: *Si nullum esset ens necessarium, nullum foret ens contigens.* Leibniz does not adopt Berkeley's maxim *To be is to be conceived* (by God) but espoused the far stronger Scotist idea that *To be possible is to be conceived* (by God). On this basis, Leibniz contemplates a proof of the existence of God on the on the grounds of his providing an indispensable basis for possibility. Leibniz thus supplemented the Cosmological Argument that God is needed for any-

---

7. For further consideration of the difficulties of the Schoolmen in coming to terms with a knowledge of nonexistents, see the discussion of Ockham and Scotus in John F. Boler, "Instructive and Abstractive Cognition," in Norman Kritzmann, ed., *The Cambridge History of Later Medieval Philosophy* (Cambridge, U.K.: Cambridge University Press, 1998), pp. 460–78; see esp. 469–70.
8. Calvin Normore, "Duns Scotus' Modal Theory," in Thomas Williams, ed., *The Cambridge Companion to Duns Scotus*, pp. 129–60; see esp. p. 151.

thing to *exist* by a Modal Argument to the effect that he is needed for anything to be possible.

So much for the earlier situation. But what of the moderns?

2. THE TRANSWORLD IDENTITY PROBLEM

The reality of it is that massive difficulties arise for the moderns in coming to terms with the idea of nonexistent possible objects in matters of semantics and metaphysics. To be sure, the metaphysics of possibility has been a growth industry in recent years. But various perplexities have arisen. In particular, their preoccupation with merely possible worlds and individuals has impelled recent theorists concerned with semantical and with metaphysical issues into an extensive debate about the problem of the "transworld identity" of individuals—the feasibility of encountering one selfsame individual in several distinct possible worlds.[9]

Two diametrically opposed positions have been staked out in these recent discussions regarding the prospect of having individuals recur across world boundaries. One school of thought sees individuals as world-bound, holding that no individual can ever be reidentified with any individual belonging to some different possible world. The basic argument here is that to be identified, individuals must have *all* of their features in common ("Leibniz's Law"), and no feature is more basic, more essential to an individual than that of being part of the world that contains it.

On the other side we find the theorists of world transcendence who hold that individuals can unproblematically be reidentified with others in other possible worlds because whenever an individual has any aspect of contingency about it, whenever events in its history could have eventuated in a way different from the actual, then there will be another realm of possibility, thereby another possible world, in which that selfsame individual actually finds itself in that alternative condition. Theorists of this school accordingly hold to a doctrine of world straddling by individuals on a basis rooted in their contingency.

Which side has it right? What is the sensible line to take on the issue of transworld individuation?

9. See the bibliography at the end of the article for some of the highlights of this literature.

3. TRANSWORLD IDENTITY DEMYSTIFIED

To clarify this issue, one does well to begin by asking how possible worlds could ever be arrived at by us—what sort of dealings we could ever possibly have with them.

Note to begin with that a merely possible world is never given. And it is not something we can possibly encounter in experience. The only world that confronts us in the actual course of things is the real world, this actual world of ours—the only world to which we gain entry effortlessly, totally free of charge. To move from it we must always *do* something, namely, to make a hypothesis—assumption, supposition, postulation, or the like. The route of hypotheses affords the only cognitive access way to the realm of nonexistent possibility. For unlike the real and actual world, possible worlds never come along of themselves and become accessible to us without our actually *doing* something, namely, making an assumption or supposition or suchlike. Any possible world with which *we* can possibly deal will have to be an object of *our* contrivance—of our making by means of some supposition or assumption.

But once one recognizes that this is so, the matter of transworld identity assumes a very different cast.

Consider the following challenge posed by R. M. Chisholm:

We will start by introducing alterations in Adam and Noah and then accommodate the rest of the world to what we have done. In [our world] . . . Adam lives for 930 years and Noah for 950. Then moving from one possible world to another [via successive one-year age transfers], but keeping our fingers, so to speak, on the same two entities, we arrive at a world in which Noah lives for 930 years and Adam for 950. In that world, therefore, Noah has the age that Adam has in this one, and Adam has the age that Noah has in this one; the Adam and Noah that we started with might thus be said to have exchanged their ages. Now let us continue on to still other possible worlds and allow them to exchange still other properties. We will thus imagine a possible world in which they have exchanged the first letters of their names, then one in which they have exchanged the second, then one in which they have exchanged the fourth, with the result that Adam in this new possible world will be called "Noah" and Noah "Adam." Proceeding in this way, we arrive finally at a possible world w^* which would seem to be exactly like our present world w, except for the fact that the Adam of w^* may be traced back to the Noah of w and the Noah of w^* may be traced back to the Adam of w. Should we say of the Adam of w^* that he is identical with the Noah of w and should we say of the Noah of w^* that he is identical to the Adam of w? . . . And how are we to decide?[10]

10. R. M. Chisholm, "Identity through Possible Worlds," *Nous* 1 (1967): 1–8; reprinted in Chisholm, *On Metaphysics* (Minneapolis: University of Minnesota Press, 1989), pp. 19–24, and in Kim and Sosa 1999, pp. 149–53; see esp. p. 150.

In fact, however, the answer here is simplicity itself. In such matters one achieves those unrealized possibilities as explicit suppositions—assumptions that something or other is so. And by hypothesis it is *to Adam* that we are assigning stepwise the properties of Noah and *to Noah* that we are assigning stepwise the properties of Adam. At each step of our assumptive proceedings the identity of the individual remains firmly fixed by the very hypothesis that we are making that it is *his* properties that are at issue—those of that very individual that we are altering.

In one relevant discussion Charles S. Chihara has put the problem as follows:

> What would it be for Bill Clinton to be in another possible world? After all, Bill Clinton need not have, there, the properties and features he possesses in the actual world. He need not be married, or over six feet tall, or President of the United States. He need not be living in the same country he does in the actual world; he could even be living on a different planet in a different solar system. He might even be living in a completely different time period from the one in which he actually lives. In that world, he need not be anything like he in fact is. Perhaps he might not even be male. Indeed, some have thought that he need not even be a human being (Lewis, 1986). But in that case, what would it mean to say that that strange thing in the other possible world *is* Bill Clinton?[11]

But what Chihara fails to acknowledge here is that once he has made Bill Clinton the focus of the discussion and then explicitly refers to *him* (via "he") in his modifactory hypotheses, he has forestalled any question about its being Bill Clinton that is at issue. The very hypotheses he puts before us fix the matter in this sense. Descriptive similarity or difference no longer has anything to do with it. An assumption on the order of "Suppose the Parthenon were the Eiffel Tower" may be crazy. But crazy or not, whatever "possible world" it carries us into will, come what may, by hypothesis be one in which the Parthenon *is* the Eiffel Tower. The question "Is it now true that: Parthenon = Eiffel Tower?" is now resolved and no longer controversial within the scope of this hypothesis. Further objection is futile. The details of how an item is introduced into the arena of discussion settles its identity once and for all.

The teacher asks little Johnny, "Suppose you had two apples and someone gave you two more. How many apples do you then have?" Little Johnny replies, "But I don't have two apples." Too bad, Johnny, you are missing the point of the exercise. And when Chihara worries about Bill Clinton's identity under those hypotheses of various Clinton modifications he too is missing the point. For with that hypothesis in place

11. Charles Chihara, *The Worlds of Possibility* (Oxford, U.K.: Clarendon Press, 1998); see p. 50.

there is no longer room for any worries about the identity of who is at issue. Thanks to the nature of the very hypothesis at issue, it will—and must—be Clinton himself. Clearly, in such cases, we are not led to unrealized individuals at all; we are dealing with hypothetical changes to perfectly real ones whose identity is firmly set in place by the substance of our own discussion.

But how else could those theorists have proceeded—how else could they have posed the problem of the identity of that hypothetically changed individual? Well, they couldn't have—or at least not coherently. If they tie the individual to a pure existing identity (say, via a proper name), then that settles the matter one way. If they refrain from identification and simply proceed descriptively by property indication, then there is no question of re-declarification. To pose their problem they need to have it both ways, and that just cannot be accomplished coherently.

Remember, we are not here talking about an actual change of an object's properties over a course of time but about a hypothetical change in its (actual) properties over a range of mere possibility. With all such suppositional alterations, identification lies in the nature of the hypothesis that we are projecting about individuals, and *not* in the properties that are being assigned to them. So when by assumption that individual is Adam, the question of his identity is no longer open. By the time that individual is characterized in that specified way (as "the Adam" of that world), it is too late to puzzle about his being identified with Adam. The damage—whatever it be—is done: that specified supposition has already settled the matter. If I project the hypothesis "Suppose that your cat had all the properties of this tree," it would (strange though it might be) be a cat—and specifically that one—which exhibits all those treelike properties exactly because this acceptance is fixed by the very hypothesis that is at issue. Even if we do not particularly like what is at issue in an assumption in making this assumption, we have no choice but to take on board whatever it is that it demands.

Again, David Lewis and Saul Kripke have debated the question of whether, had Hubert Humphrey won the presidential election of 1968, the Humphrey of the alternative world in which he is victorious would be the same individual who lost in this one. While Kripke sees that "alternative Humphrey" as being the same person as ours, Lewis sees him as merely a "counterpart" or "simulacrum" or some such. On this basis, Lewis presses his opposition to transworld identity via the following challenge:

[Transworld identity theorists are] insisting that, for instance it is [Hubert] Humphrey himself who might have existed under other conditions, who might have won the presidency, [etc.] . . . All that is uncontroversial. The controversial question is how he manages to have these model properties. The answer now mooted [i.e., favored by Lewis himself] is that he has them by being a shared part common to many worlds, and by having different properties relative to different worlds that he is a part of. Despite its lack of supporters, this answer deserves our attention . . . because it is agreeably simple.[12]

And indeed the situation here is simplicity itself: there is no need to bring nonexistent or parallel worlds into it. For here it is clearly to Humphrey himself that those modally variant properties are being attributed because our view of the contingency of such matters as election outcomes opens wide the door to the supposition (assumption, hypothesis) that Humphrey might have been elected in 1968 instead of Richard Nixon. Within the actual world Leibniz's principle holds: sameness of properties (across time) entails sureness of identity. But across different "possible worlds" all property-based bets about identity are off.

The real point in the Lewis example is that if it is indeed *Humphrey* whose suppositionally alternative fate is the entryway to that other world, then it is—by hypothesis—Humphrey who is at issue. Again the manner in which that world has been suppositionally generated already forecloses the issue of individual identity. And so when Lewis contemplates his variant Humphrey (the election victor, say, with six fingers on his left hand) he has already—like it or not—settled the question of identity in the very manner of making his supposition. In speaking of Humphrey and *his* fate in the election or of the fingers of *his* hand that anaphoric back-reference ties our suppositionally varied individual irremovably to the Hubert Humphrey we know and love.

Again, in a widely discussed paper, David Kaplan deliberated about "[the] doctrine that holds that it does make sense to ask—without reference to common attributes and behavior—whether *this* is the same individual in another possible world."[13] But, of course, if it indeed is the case that—as per the explicitly given formulation—it is *this* individual that is to be at issue, then clearly the issue of identity is *already* settled, irrespective of what worlds or what descriptions may be invoked.

The crux of the issue is a matter of the range of plausible suppositions—alternative possible-but-nonexistent *worlds* or *individuals* need never be brought into it. Modificatory hypotheses never transform an item into something else but only into an alternative of itself. They do

12. See David Lewis, in Jaegwon Kim and Ernest Sosa, eds., *Metaphysics* (Oxford, U.K.: Blackwell, 1999), pp. 157–58.
13. David Kaplan, "How to Russell or Frege-Church," *Journal of Philosophy* 77 (1975): 716–29; see esp. pp. 722–23.

not lead from reals to nonexistents: its identity shadows the thing wherever it goes.

The lesson of the preceding discussion of cross-world identity for individuals might seem to suggest that proper names are the crux, with named items such as Adam and Noah, Humphrey and Clinton, the Parthenon and the Eiffel Tower as determinative. And this impression is reinforced by Saul Kripke's thesis that names are "rigid designators" having a fixed object of reference across possible worlds. But the issue is broader. For the real crux is not *naming* but *referring* and specifically *identifying*. Thus the ostensive indication of "this desk" or "yon tree" are every bit as impervious to designation change in the wake of property-altering hypotheses as is Julius Caesar or Napoleon Bonaparte. When we make "this desk" the object of hypothetical changes that lead one into "another world," then it is this very desk that continues, *ex hypothesi*, to be at issue.

Whenever we contemplate an "alternative possible world" by saying that it realizes the possibility that some thing (or things) (Caesar, that cat on the mat, yon tree) somehow differ from the way *it* or *they* actually are, we immediately stipulate via the anaphoric back-reference if that *it* or *them* fixes the identity of what is at issue with something(s) among the actual formation of the world. No matter how large the difference being supposed, the very manner of the supposition effects a "transworld identification." By the very specification at issue, that supposition maintains a reference to the real-world item whose descriptive nature is being altered. For, in making a property-varying assumption about something, I clearly do not cease to tell about it—that selfsame item. If I assume that I *might* have acted otherwise in this world, then the suppositional I who *did* act differently in another possible world is clearly not somebody different. (If it had to be so, determinism would be a matter of logic, not of metaphysics.) In sum, Leibniz's Law that identity requires identical properties is not a categorically iron-clad principle of identity. It can be overridden by assumptions.

4. REFERENTIAL VERSUS DESCRIPTIVE CASES

Yet what if we proceed not referentially but purely and solely descriptively, so that—to all appearances—reidentificatory suppositions not come into it at all? What if the question is simply whether some individual X_1 of the merely possible world w_1 is or is not identical with X_2 of the merely possible world w_2? Now everything hinges on how these supposed individuals are specified. If the specification assumes their identity, then that's that—they are identical. If not, then they cannot and should not be identified. Thus assume that instead of saying "Suppose [a world in which] I were different only in being born three seconds earlier," one says: "Suppose [a world in which] there is an individual who is exactly like me except for being born three seconds earlier—and whatever else that readjustment may require in the interests of coherence." Then, clearly, we have not posed any issue of transworld identification, and there just is no question of reidentification here. For there is no reason whatsoever to think that a purely hypothetical individual who is like me—who resembles me in various respects, no matter how many—should ever be taken to be *identical* with me. Similarity is one thing and identity something quite different. The idea of *identifying* that otherwise anonymous but variantly described individual with me on the basis of the information at hand is absurd. Descriptive *similarity* is not and cannot be a basis for warranted identification—be it in this world or another. Nothing could be more alike than two carbon atoms. But that certainly does not make them the same.

Let us contemplate the situation of an (inexistent) world supposedly containing an (inexistent) individual of such-and-such a description, and that we now postulate another inexistent world in which something-or-other holds of

1. this very individual
2. yet another individual
3. an (or some) otherwise unspecified individual(s)

What is to be said about the cross-world identity of the individuals at issue? Clearly, three different things are at issue in our three different cases, as follows:

• With 1, a situation of identity will obtain *by suppositional stipulation.*
• With 2, a situation of difference, of nonidentity, will obtain—again *by suppositional stipulation.*
• With 3, a situation of vacuity obtains with respect to identity in consequence of which any claim to identity or difference will be untenable.

The situation that obtains in this third case is strictly analogous to that of fiction. Suppose a novelist discusses a mysterious stranger in chapter 1 and tells us about an unidentifiably mangled corpse in chapter 5. Are they the same person? Clearly, only if the author says so—there are no "facts of the matter" apart from those our novelist specifies. In the absence of such specifications, all that can be said about the issue of identity is—absolutely nothing. And the situation with hypothetically projected possible worlds is exactly like that. Absent postulational specification one way or the other, the issue of transworld identity *simply does not arise*.[14]

If we suppose that someone in another hypothetical world construct-ed a table, then irrespective of descriptive similarities it will not be *this* table that is at issue unless and until this identification is explicitly spec-ified in the world-projecting hypothesis at issue. The question "Is that world's *x* the same as this world's *y*" is uniformly negative save when a positive response is explicitly provided for. With respect to the question of what things are possible and impossible, logic is in charge. And with regard to the question of what sorts of things can (not just logically but realistically) exist or not exist in the real world, metaphysics is in charge. But with respect to what sorts of things we assume and suppose and postulate as objects of consideration—and their nature and interre-lationships—we alone are in charge. The objects that are projected for discussion are the discussant's prerogative. For the objects of supposi-tions have no independent characteristics—there just are no facts of the matter beyond what the assumer does or does not assume.

And just here lie the limitations, for the only possibilities with which we can deal are suppositional *de dicto* possibilities. Possibilities for ob-jects, *de re* possibilities—merely possible objects as such—lie outside our reach. We have no way to get there from here. For it is hypotheses and suppositions alone that carry us from the realm of the real into that of the merely possible. And such possibilities are always *de dicto*.

Of course, our world is contingent. Things might have been differ-ent. But what is at issue here is merely a matter of supposing differences for things and different orders of things. It does not involve that which we have not, namely, the resources for introducing different nonexist-ent things into the realm of discussion. For there just is no alternative here from dealing with particulars rather than schematic generalities. We have no means for operating at the level of the merely possible but nonexistent. (This, if you will, is the privilege of God alone.)

5. MORNING STAR/EVENING STAR

In dealing with the real world, it makes perfect sense to inquire whether or not two *incompletely described* items such as "Emma's hus-band" and "Tom's only brother" are or are not identical. Thus take Got-tlob Frege's example of whether "The Morning Star" (i.e., the star ap-

14. If nevertheless someone insists on pressing it, then we have no choice but to an-swer it negatively. With assumptive scenarios as with fictions we can go on the principle that if the author also meant the individuals at issue in his discussion to be identified, he would have told us so.

pearing in such-and-such a position in the morning sky) and "The Evening Star" (i.e., the star appearing in such-and-such a position in the evening sky) are or are not one and the same star. This real-world-oriented issue poses a perfectly meaningful—and resolvable—question. For in the real world partial descriptions can readily identify individuals so that we can—giving the contingently prevailing circumstances—particularize these incomplete descriptions by relating the items at issue to other, preidentified items (Tom and Emma in the one case and certain positions in "the sky" in the other).

But this is something we are altogether unable to do with supposed individuals in putative worlds. Here we are utterly and completely dependent on our stipulative and descriptive resources, the mechanics of connection to preestablished existents being unavailable. The question

Is such-and-such an (incompletely described) item the same as this-or-that one?

can make perfect sense with respect to the *real* world, where its presupposition that definitely identified items are at issue is readily satisfied. But this is emphatically not the case with respect to suppositional "items" in putative but nonexistent "worlds."

And so the issue of transworld identity actually poses no real problems: a resolution is automatically available. For in indicating that problematic individual of another suppositional world whose identity with some real-world item is in question, we would have to proceed either descriptively or by referential stipulation. If we proceed referentially, the issue of reidentification is settled automatically through the reference at work in the hypothesis at issue. And if we proceed descriptively, then there is no question of identity where nonexistents are concerned. Either way, the matter is settled automatically on the basis of the mode of individual specification that is at issue. And there is good reason why this must be so.

6. INFINITE DETAIL: THE BOTTOMLESS DESCRIPTIVE DEPTH OF THE REAL

The totality of facts about a thing—about any real thing whatever—is in principle inexhaustible and the complexity of real things is in consequence descriptively unfathomable. Endlessly many true descriptive remarks can be made about any particular actual concrete object. For example, take a stone. Consider its physical features: its shape, its surface texture, its chemistry, and so on. And then consider its causal background: its subsequent genesis and history. Then consider its multitude of functional aspects as relevant to its uses by the stonemason, or the architect, or the landscape gardener, or whomever. There is, after all, no end to the perspectives of consideration that we can bring to bear on things. The botanist, the herbiculturist, the landscape, the farmer, the painter, and the real estate appraiser will operate from different cognitive "points of view" in describing one selfsame vegetable garden. And there is in principle no theoretical limit to the lines of consideration available to provide descriptive perspective upon a thing.

Moreover, as we standardly think about particulars within the conceptual framework of our factual deliberation and discourse, *any* real concrete particular has more features and facets than it will ever actually manifest in experience. After all, concrete things not only have more properties than they ever *will* overtly manifest, but they have more properties than they ever *can* possibly actually manifest. The existence of this latent (hidden, occult) sector is a crucial feature of our conception of a real thing. Neither in fact nor in thought can we ever simply put it away. To say of this apple that its only features are those it actually manifests is to run afoul of our conception of an apple. To deny—or even merely to refuse to be committed to the claim—that it *would* manifest particular features *if* certain conditions came about (e.g., that it would have such-and-such a taste if eaten) is to be driven to withdrawing the claim that it is an apple. The latent implicit ramifications of our objective factual claims about something real is potentially endless.

Our characterization of real things can accordingly become more *extensive* without thereby becoming more *complete*. New descriptive features ongoingly come into view with the progress of knowledge (Caesar not only did not know, but in the existing state of knowledge could not have known, that his sword contained tungsten). Real things *are*—and by their very nature *must be*—such that their actual nature outruns any particular description of it that we might venture.

But wait! What about the distinction between the "intrinsic" properties supposed to constitute a thing's identity and its "disposition" in having effects on other things. Perhaps the former are merely finite and open-endedness enters in only with the latter. Alas, no go. The distinction does not work because *every* property of a thing marks its interrelationships with others. After all, if a property were wholly and entirely intrinsic, *we* could never manage to find out about it. The only properties one can ever warrantedly attribute are those one can discern *ab extra,*and they have to be dispositional by virtue of this very fact.

It follows from such considerations that we can never justifiably claim to be in a position to articulate "the whole truth" about a real thing. The domain of thing-characterizing fact inevitably transcends the limits of our capacity to *express* it, and a fortiori those of our capacity to canvas completely. In the description of concrete particulars we are caught up in an inexhaustible detail: there are always bound to be more descriptive facts about things than we are able to capture with our linguistic machinery—that is, the real encompasses more than we can manage to say about it, now or ever.

And so the fact remains that our actually formulated descriptions are always incomplete and, save for the real world alone, incomplete descriptions can never individuate. And incomplete descriptions are all that we can ever possibly manage!

7. NONEXISTENTS CANNOT BE IDENTIFIED DESCRIPTIVELY

It only makes sense to ask reidentification questions with respect to preidentified items. And the critical fact here is that we have no way to identify nonexistent items as particular individual things.

To identify (to individuate) an object within this *actual* world of ours we do not require complete descriptions: very incomplete descriptions will do because real things can be identified by ostensive placement. But this, of course, is not feasible with merely possible irrealia. As such examples as:

- that apple tree (pointing)
- the cat on yonder mat (pointing)

indicate, actual objects can be identified ostensively by pointing or using some other suitable ostensive gesture. But this sort of thing will *not* work with nonexistents. For partial descriptions will not do here: they yield no more than schemata for individuals and never individuals as such.

W. G. Lycan proposes to identify individuals with Leibnizian complete individual concepts—that is, saturated descriptions.[15] But authentic individuals could not *be* complete concepts, even though they should in theory *have* such concepts and be specified by them. And just here is where the difficulty arises because conceptual completeness is something that we cannot manage to provide. The level of detail involved puts them beyond our reach.

The difficulty with "nonexistent objects" lies not so much in their *nonexistence* as in their very *identity*, owing to the fact that the suppositional specifications are inevitably inadequate here. Thus consider the merely actuality-modifying case "Suppose one of the (perfectly real)

15. See William G. Lycan, *Modality and Meaning* (Dordrecht and Boston: Kluwer, 1994), p. 109.

coins in my pocket were placed on the table." What shall we say of this coin? Is it of copper (through being a penny) or is it not? We cannot say either way when various sorts of coins are in my pocket. And this is not because a rather mysterious sort of thing is at issue—a coin made not of copper, nor yet not made not of copper. But as long as our descriptive characterization of something remains incomplete, so does our identificatory specification of the thing at issue remain unachieved. Accordingly, if a *particular* nonexistent individual is to be at issue—that is, if there is to be genuine *individuation* (and not just abstract schematization)—then the properties of the nonexistent thing in view must be detailed with *complete* comprehensiveness.

After all, how could the individuation of objects proceed when one abstracts altogether from their spatiotemporal positioning by ostension or otherwise? It is clear that at this point our only recourse is to proceed by descriptive means alone. And this means that we would have to provide a *complete* description of an object for identification to be assured. But as long as our descriptions remain incomplete, they can never securely fix upon a particular object.

To be sure, "Hamlet" and "Ophelia" schematize different (and disjoint) *possibilities* for individuals but—barring historical attributions to actual people—they are not different individuals because such suppositional individuals are no more individuals than imaginary pigeons are pigeons.

To achieve reference to a particular individual is simply impossible in the case of nonexistents. Merely partial descriptive characterizations not supplemented by the prospects of experiential contact are of themselves unable to specify particular individuals. Since they are always incomplete—capable of even further elaboration—they cannot achieve individualization: the possibility of their multiple instantiation can never be precluded. When there is any sort of incompleteness, there will always be a plurality of alternatives—that is, a variety of different (because *descriptively* different) possible realizations of individuals that otherwise correspond to that incomplete description. The uniqueness essential to identification would be lacking, just exactly because descriptive blanks can always be filled in in several different ways. And just here lies the problematic aspect of those so-called fictional objects because descriptive completeness is something we simply cannot manage to realize.[16]

We could, of course, attempt the specification:

16. Already in the 1920s Rudolf Carnap pressed the question "How can it be possible to give a characterizing identification for objects within a given object domain without indicating any of them by an ostensive definition?" (*Logische Aufbau der Welt: The Logical Structure of the World* [1928], trans. Rolf George [Berkeley and Los Angeles: University of

Sherlock Holmes = the object that has just exactly those descriptive properties attributed to the protagonist of the Conan Doyle novels.[17]

But there are big problems here. One of them is that initial "the object," which presupposes a unique individuation—instead of the generosity of an object of a certain descriptive sort. And this use of the definite article simply begs the question. The second is that "exactly" of "exactly those properties," which comes to: those *and only those*. But, of course, there is not and cannot be an individual of which nothing except what has been explicitly specified is true—an individual, say, whose liver has no particular size or weight and whose breakfast coffee on a certain date had no particular temperature.

This point here revolves about a puzzle mooted in W. V. Quine's queries about the number of "possible fat men in the doorway."[18] The descriptive characterization at issue—"fat man in the doorway"—just does not identify any single possible individual; it is a descriptive *schema* to which many such individuals might answer. This plurality is due precisely to the *incompleteness* of the specification: it stems from the fact that we are dealing with incomplete and *schematic* indications. That suppositional fat man lacks descriptive substance (is he tall or short?) not because he is a peculiar sort of man but because there is not a he—no individual whatsoever has been identified. There just is no way to identify and individuate nonexistent possible individuals or worlds.

"But don't we get another possible world when we hypothesize just interchanging those two books on that shelf?" No, we don't. For a myriad of questions now arise regarding which anything worthy of the name *world* will have to decide. How did the books get interchanged? By moving them, by magic, by altering the fabric of nature, through changing the past history of the universe? What of the laws of nature that relate the present to the past? And what implications arise from the future course of events? And no matter how we decide this, a cascade of further questions will arise, each of which will have to be settled one way or another as a "fact of the matter" by any *world* at issue. We simply cannot provide the requisite detail here. The idea of a "merely possible" individual (or world) is something of which one cannot give even a single example.

California Press, 1967], pp. 25–27.) See also Ruth Barcan Marcus, "Dispensing with Possibilities," *Proceedings and Addresses of the American Philosophical Association* 44 (1975–1976): 45–46; esp. pp. 45–46.

17. Terence Parsons, *Nonexistents Objects* (New Haven, Conn., and London: Yale University Press, 1980); see p. 52.

18. W. V. Quine, "On What There Is," *Review of Metaphysics* 2 (1948): 21–38; reprinted in Quine, *From Logical a Point of View* (New York: Harper Touchbooks, 1961).

8. NONEXISTENTS AS MERE SCHEMATA

Nonbeing, of course, contrasts with being. Now being, as it relates not to abstracta such as numbers or statements but to things that exist concretely, is a matter of participating in the world's causal commerce. It is just this that makes such beings cognitively accessible to us as experiential givens. But nonexistent possible worlds and individuals are never *given* to us: only the real world is ever accessible in *that* sort of way. Insofar as we can talk about such worlds and individuals, we have to construct their descriptive characterization via assumptions, suppositions, hypotheses, or the like. And on this basis the only features they ever have are those that we impute to them—those that are explicitly or implicatively implied in our assumptions, suppositions, and hypotheses. Over and above this there just are no facts of the matter. And the circumstance of the substantive finitude of our assumptions (suppositions, hypotheses) means that such things are always schematic. They lack the prospect of identifiability on which alone a claim to having an identity—to being a concrete particular—could possibly rest. We can specify world-schematic *scenarios* but never merely possible worlds as specific particulars.[19]

Nonexistents can never be identified because with finite intelligences identification always calls for an element of ostension—of experiential contact—and only that which actually exists can figure in experience. The distinction between the real and the unreal is not an experiential but rather a referential distinction—the nonexistent cannot be experienced, it can only be thought of, talked of, and so on. In the face of the nonexistent we are never passive but only active: nonexistents can do nothing to us but we can be active in relation to them by way of conjectures, suppositions, and hypotheses. And such processes can only lead us to unrealized *possibilities (de dicto)* and never to unrealized *possibilia (de re)*, thanks to the inherent inability of linguistic mechanisms to realize the specificity of objecthood.

We are never just plunged into a merely possible realm by the presentness of Heideggerian *Dasein*. For unreal possibilities are never *Da*. Such worlds are not preexisting manifolds into which—lo and behold!—we find ourselves plunged. As David Lewis clearly puts it, "possi-

---

19. The recourse to complexes of descriptively incomplete but overlapping possible worlds—a superposition of full-fledged possible worlds—leads to the idea of a world type lacking the specificity of specific worlds. Such respect-indefinite world superpositions have been characterized as *scenarios*. See Nathan Salmon, *Reference and Essence* (Princeton, N.J.: Princeton University Press, 1981) and also *Frege's Puzzle* (Cambridge, Mass.: MIT Press, 1986). But note also the present author's earlier employment of this concept in his *The Logic of Commands* (London: Routledge & Kegan Paul, 1966).

ble worlds are *stipulated,* not *discovered* by powerful telescopes."[20] And
even this is going too far, since what we stipulate are possibilities *de dicto*
and never *de re objects* such as worlds or individuals. Worlds and individuals must have a completeness of detail that our stipulations can never
achieve. (Joyce Kilmer wrote that "only God can make a tree," but this
is just as true for individuals and worlds.)

The crucial point is that those fictional "objects" are no more objects
than ceramic owls are owls. They are, at best and at most, schemata for
objects. What we will effectively have here is not an *incompletely described
individual* but rather a *descriptively incomplete individual characterization*—
an individual schema which, in respect of certain features, is simply indeterminate. For that putative characterization fails to characterize an
authentic individual through refusing to make up its mind with respect
to a wide variety of descriptive issues, thereby doing no more than to
present us with a blending or superposition of alternatives.

Only a description that is saturated and complete could possibly
manage to specify or individuate a merely possible particular individual.
For any genuinely particular individual must be property-decisive,[21] and
a nonexistent possible individual can obtain this decisiveness only
through the route of descriptive saturation. Accordingly, if it is to be an
individual that is specified descriptively, then this description must be
saturated (complete): it cannot be vague or schematic but must issue a
commital yea or nay with respect to every property whatsoever. And no
such descriptions can ever be provided by us. Merely possible worlds
can only be discussed in the indefinite plural: we can never particularize. No simply particular nonexistent world can ever be specified. With
possible worlds there is, strictly speaking, no *it* but only *they.* One can
talk generally of a possible world of such-and-such a character, but never of *the* world of a certain specific character.

Nonexistents—as best we ourselves can ever indicate what is at issue
here—are simply not objects. For as far as we are concerned what they
lack, inevitably and crucially, is not just existence but identity.

9. INTENSIONAL OBJECTS?

A good deal of philosophical trouble has been occasioned by confusing the verbally or mentally intended reference to an object with an intensional object. For, of course, the discussion of an object does not en-

20. David Lewis, "Truth in Fiction," *American Philosophical Quarterly* 15 (1978): 37–46
(see esp. p. 44).
21. Cf. J. M. E. McTaggart, *The Nature of Existence,* vol. 1 (Cambridge, U.K.: Cambridge
University Press, 1921), sect. 62.

gender a discussion-object, the hypothesis of a unicorn does not engender a hypothetical unicorn save as an item of discussion or consideration, and such a "discussion-object" is no more an object than a paper tiger is a tiger.

Franz Brentano held that "John is thinking about a unicorn," while *informatively* significant has no *referential* function—there is no unicorn—be it real or inexistent—about which John is thinking; a contemplated unicorn is not a type of unicorn.[22] But Brentano's followers were not always so cautious and Alexius Meinong for one endowed "intensional objects" with a distinctly problematic objectivity.[23] He was prepared (incautiously!) to move from "John is thinking about a unicorn" to "there is a unicorn that is the object of John's thoughts." But, of course, thought and language are not instrumentalities of thing-production: in supposing an object of a certain description we do not engender a discussion-object of a certain sort.

As St. Thomas Aquinas rightly maintained, our cognitive commerce with nonexistents is *analogous* to our cognitive commerce with existents.[24] But like all analogies the parallelism is imperfect. The statement "Paracelsus sought for the philosopher's stone" does not come to "There is a certain object, the philosopher's stone, for which Paracelsus sought," but rather "Paracelsus *thought* that there is a certain object, the philosopher's stone, and Paracelsus sought to find it." And here the *it* at issue is not the (nonexisting) philosopher's stone, but rather the putative item that Paracelsus (mistakenly) thought the philosopher's stone to be." A suppositional being is just exactly that, the artifact of an interpersonally projected supposition or assumption. And such a linguistically engendered artifact is a pseudo-object that is no object at all. With finite beings, thought is not creative: the imagination or illusion of a lion does not engender an imaginary or illusionary lion. (A putative item is no more an item than a supposed witch is a witch or playmoney is money.[25])

---

22. See Franz Brentano, *Psychologie vom empirischen Stendpunkt* (Leipzig: Duncker & Humblot, 1874; 3rd ed., Leipzig: F. Meiner, 1924–1925), and *Kategorienlehre* (Leipzig: F. Meiner, 1933).

23. One can surely achieve an intersubjectivity of communication about a fictional being such as Sherlock Holmes without endowing this imaginary detective with objective *existence* of any sort—intensional or otherwise.

24. *De potentia,* 7c; *Summa theologica,* I.13.10. See also André Hayen, *Saint Thomas d'Aquin et la vie de l'Église* (Louvain: Publications universitaires de Louvain, 1952).

25. On the general history of intensionality, see Herbert Spiegelberg, "Der Begriff der Intentionalität in der Scholastik, bei Brentano, und bei Husserl," *Philosophische Hefte* 5 (1936): 75–91.

10. CONCLUSION

Once merely possible individuals and worlds are abandoned as specific items of deliberation, the entire question of transworld identification of nonexistents simply vanishes. Merely possible objects cannot be reidentified because they cannot be preidentified: in sum, they cannot be identified at all. And the reasoning at issue here hinges on two premises:

1. Descriptive hypotheses (assumptions, suppositions) afford the only entryway at our disposal for access to the realm of the *merely* possible.
2. Descriptive hypotheses (assumptions, suppositions) can never achieve the comprehensiveness of detail required to identify possible individuals and worlds.

Now where identification is impossible we cannot do more than deal in generalities; the specification needed to deal with matters of concrete detail is not realizable. With individuation impracticable, we literally do not—and cannot—know where of we speak. If to be is to be identifiable, then there just are no merely possible worlds as far as we mere knowers are concerned. Nonexistent worlds are nonexistent in more senses than one. It's not just that they don't exist, we cannot even manage to conceive of them in the detailed specificity needed for individuating identification.

With nonexistent worlds and individuals consigned to their merited nonexistence, other resources still remain at our disposal, namely, assumptions, suppositions, and so on, along with the scenarios and stories in which they are embodied. For merely possible states of affairs and scenarios are certainly things we can discuss and reason about meaningfully. And on this basis we can also come to terms with possible worlds and individuals at the level of abstract generality. But merely possible individuals and worlds viewed as particulars of some sort are not at the disposal of our latter-day modal realists; they are of such a character that the infinite depth of their requisite detail confines them to the province of God alone. Considerations of deep general principle indicate that only God can realize the idea of a nonexistent particularism. Possibilities are manageable but *possibilia* lie beyond our reach. And in this regard our latter-day theorists regarding modal semantics and metaphysics of possible worlds and individuals are in a position of seeking to obtain by theft that which would have to be the product of authentic—and for them unachievable—toil.

And so, back to the medievals. With regard to nonexistents the medieval mainstream thinkers sought to effect a compromise. On the one hand, their lack of reality, of actual existence, deprived nonentities of a self-subsistent ontological footing and made them into mind-artifacts, *entia rationis*. On the other hand, their footing in the mind of God endowed them with a certain objectivity and quasi-reality that precluded them from being mere *flatus vocis* fictions, mere verbalisms that represent creatures of the human fancy.

Confronted with this same issue of the status of nonexistents, secular philosophers of our own day face a dilemma because the Thomistic middle road of a God-underwritten quasi-reality is not open to them as a pathway to *possibilia*. For them the choice is all or nothing: either a (distinctly problematic) metaphysical realism of self-subsistent possibilities or else a (somewhat unappealing) nominalism of mere verbal possibility talk, of possibility not as a matter of genuine fact but merely the product of an imaginative fictionalizing by linguistic manipulations.

In effect the medievals resolved the question about the nature and identity of nonexistent objects with the response: God only knows. This is an answer that most moderns see as unavailable. But what they overlook in taking this line is that it effectively leaves them without any viable answer at all. Properly speaking, they have no business to conjure with possible individuals and worlds. All they are properly entitled to is possibilities *(de dicto)*, possible objects in the *de re* manner (worlds and individuals) are beyond their reach. To secure a plausible theory of possibility intermediate between the implausibly real and the dismissive imaginary, the modern secularist theorists of possible worlds and individuals require a functionally equivalent surrogate to replace the medieval recourse to the mind of God. And it is bound to be a massively puzzle and perplex where, on *their* principles, this is to come from.

REFERENCES

Adams, Marilyn McCord. *William of Ockham.* 2 vols. South Bend, Ind.: University of Notre Dame Press, 1987.
Adams, Robert M. "Primitive Thisness and Primitive Identity." *Journal of Philosophy* 76 (1979): 5–26. [Reprinted in Sosa, pp. 172–82.]
Chihara, Charles. *The Worlds of Possibility.* Oxford, U.K.: Clarendon Press, 1998. [See especially Chapter 2 on "Transworld Identity."]
Chisholm, Roderick M. "Identity through Possible Worlds." *Nous* 1 (1967): 1–8. [Reprinted in Chisholm, *On Metaphysics* (Minneapolis: University of Minnesota Press, 1989), 19–24; also reprinted in Kim and Sosa (1999), 149–53.]
Forbes, Graeme. "Origin and Identity." *Philosophical Studies* 47 (1980): 352–62.
——. *The Metaphysics of Modality.* Oxford, U.K.: Oxford University Press, 1985.
——. *Languages and Possibility.* Oxford, U.K.: Blackwell, 1989.

Hazen, Allen. "Counterpart-Theoretic Semantics for Model Logic." *Journal of Philosophy* 76 (1979): 319–38.

Hintikka, Jaakko, and Merrill Hintikka. "Towards a General Theory of Individuation and Identification." In J. Hintikka and M. Hintikka , eds., *The Logic of Epistemology and the Epistemology of Logic: Selected Essays*, 22–39. Dordrecht: Kluwer, 1989.

Inwagen, Peter van. "Plantinga on Trans-Worlds Identity." In J. Tombenlin and P. van Inwagen, *Alvin Plantinga: A Profile*, 101–36. Dordrecht: D. Reidel, 1985.

Kaplan, David. "Transworld Heir Lives." In Michael Loux, ed., *The Possible and the Actual*, 88–109. Ithaca, N.Y.: Cornell University Press, 1979.

———. "How to Russell or Frege-Church." *Journal of Philosophy* 77 (1975): 716–29.

Kim, Jaegwon, and Ernest Sosa, eds. *Metaphysics*. Oxford, U.K.: Blackwell, 1999. [See Chapters 22, 23, and 24 for papers by R. M. Chisholm, David Lewis, and R. M. Adams, respectively.]

Kripke, Saul. *Naming and Necessity*. Cambridge, U.K.: Cambridge University Press, 1980.

Lewis, David. "Counterparts of Persons at Their Bodies." *Journal of Philosophy* 67 (1971): 203–11.

———. *Counterfactuals*. Oxford, U.K.: Blackwell, 1973.

———. *On the Plurality of Worlds*. Oxford, U.K.: Blackwell, 1986.

Lycan, William G. *Modality and Meaning*. Dordrecht and Boston: Kluwer, 1994.

Marcus, Ruth Barcan. "Dispensing with Possibilities." *Proceedings and Addresses of the American Philosophical Association* 44 (1975–1976): 39–51.

Mondadori, Fabrizio. "Counterpuntese." *Historie, epistemologie, language* 5 (1983): 69–94.

Parsons, Terence. *Nonexistent Objects*. New Haven and London: Yale University Press, 1980.

Quine, W. V. "On What There Is." *Review of Metaphysics* 2 (1948): 21–38. [Reprinted in *From a Logical Point of View* (New York: Harper Touchbooks, 1961.]

———. "Worlds Away." *Journal of Philosophy* 73 (1971): 859–63.

Rescher, Nicholas. *The Logic of Commands*. London: Routledge & Kegan Paul, 1966.

Salmon, Nathan. *Reference and Essence*. Princeton, N.J.: Princeton University Press, 1981.

———. *Frege's Puzzle*. Cambridge, Mass.: MIT Press, 1986.

———. "The Logic of What Might Have Been." *Philosophical Review* 98 (1989): 3–34.

———. "Trans-World Identification and Stipulation." *Philosophical Studies* 98 (1989): 203–23.

Chapter 9

THOMISM
Past, Present, and Future

1 . THE PAST

The journey of St. Thomas Aquinas through the realm of philosophical history has gone along a rocky road beset with many ups and downs.

Within three years of his death in 1274, various propositions substantially identical with some of his main philosophical views were formally condemned as errors by Bishop Tempier of Paris. This episcopal condemnation was revoked a generation later in 1325, but Thomistic teachings nevertheless met with severe criticism in various quarters in the later Middle Ages—especially among the Franciscans. However, since Renaissance times, most of the popes have praised Aquinas's teaching, and St. Pius V provided for the first collected editions of St. Thomas's works alongside those of the Franciscan St. Bonaventure, diplomatically proclaiming both to be "Doctors of the Church." Already by the time of the Council of Trent (1545–1563) Thomas was regarded as the paradigm of Roman orthodoxy.

In 1879, in his encyclical *Aeterni patris*, Pope Leo XIII reemphasized the importance of the teachings of St. Thomas for Catholic thought, characterizing him as "the chief and master of the Scholastics." This led to the establishment of the Academy of St. Thomas in Rome and of the Institut Superior de Philosophie at the University of Louvain, both especially dedicated to the study of his thought. But, in consequence, Thomas suffered one of the most unfortunate fates that can befall an intellectual innovator: *his ideas became orthodoxy*. The crowning misfortune occurred in 1914 when a group of Catholic professors drew up a set of twenty-four propositions which—as they saw it—encapsulated the essentials of St. Thomas's philosophy. The Sacred Congregation of Studies then proceeded to publish—and Pope Pius X to approve—these "Twenty-Four Theses" as the canonical expression of the teachings of the Doctor of the Church. The poisoned chalice of official orthodoxy was pressed to the lips of academic Thomism with the unhappy result of a sterile formalization that has to be seen as a foregone conclusion. The philosophy of St. Thomas was widely accepted as standard fare in Catholic seminaries and institutions of learning, and its teachings were routinized into handbooks and manuals to create a neo-Thomism of a distinctly stultified character. And so matters came near to being the beginning to the end. But fortunately, as the twentieth century unfolded, various efforts were set afoot in Catholic intellectual circles to break out of this formalized and sterile mode of thinking and teaching. And while Catholic thinkers now also looked in other directions for sources of inspiration—above all to phenomenology, to existentialism, to vitalism, and elsewhere—nevertheless the influence of St. Thomas survived the disillusionment consequent upon that ossification of his teachings. The displacement of Thomism from the pedestal of orthodoxy has proved to be its salvation.

Just how does the matter stand at present? How fares St. Thomas in the contemporary marketplace of ideas?

It must be recognized that he does very well indeed. The existence of institutions is one straw in the wind. In North America alone, for example, there is a good deal of activity including a Center for Thomistic Studies (in Houston, Texas), an academic journal called *The Thomist,* two Aquinas colleges and two St. Thomas Universities (in Miami, Florida, and Fredericton, New Brunswick, Canada), as well as a University of St. Thomas (Houston, Texas) with another of the same name in St. Paul, Minnesota, thrown in for good measure.

Of course, institutionalism is not the real issue. More revealing is the matter of intellectual *engagement* within the larger philosophical community. The ongoing influence of St. Thomas is apparent not just in institutional terms but more vividly in personal terms as well. Such outstanding—and outstandingly creative—Thomists as Jacques Maritain (1882–1973), Etienne Gilson (1884–1978), Bernard Lonergan (1904–1984), and W. Norris Clarke (1915–) have produced a body of writing and teaching that has projected the doctrine as a live force well into the twentieth century through the ongoing efforts of their students, followers, and admirers. And independently of these influences, various other Catholic philosophers of religion continue to lean heavily on St. Thomas as an energizer for their creative efforts.

No less significant, however, is the fact that the work of St. Thomas has continued to exert a powerful influence on many first-rate thinkers who stand entirely outside the Catholic orbit. It is instructive in this regard to look at a handful of representative twentieth-century century classics. Such a demarche yields the following number of mentions of St. Thomas:

2—A. N. Whitehead, *Process and Reality*
3—John Rawls, *Theory of Justice*
1—Bertrand Russell, *Human Knowledge*
2—Ernest Cassirer, *Essay on Man*
2—John Dewey, *Reconstruction in Philosophy*
5—Hans-Georg Gadamer, *Truth and Method*
3—Martin Heidegger, *Being and Time*
1—R. G. Collingwood, *Essay on Metaphysics*
1—J. C. C. Smart, *Essays, Metaphysics and Mind*
3—C. S. Peirce, *Principles of Philosophy*
1—W. V. Quine, *Ways of Paradox*

To give some flesh to these skeletal numbers, let us consider a sampling of how these twentieth-century philosophers have taken the ideas of St. Thomas into account in their diverse deliberations.

In his classic tract on *Pragmatism* (1905), William James makes no mention of Aquinas at all. But in a fairly extensive outline for the pragmatism lectures that he presented at Wellesley College he cites St. Thomas (along with Aristotle among the ancients) among those who rejected what he calls "the false opposition of philosophy and science" and who deserve credit for seeing natural and theoretical philosophy as being of a piece.

In *Process and Reality* (1929), A. N. Whitehead makes two references to Aquinas. In the first of these St. Thomas is derogated as one of those philosophers who showed a prejudgment in favor of the deductive method of logic and mathematics. And in the second passage Whitehead contrasts his own view of the organic unity of mind and body as differing "from the Scholastic view of St. Thomas Aquinas, of the mind as informing the body" (p. 108). In both instances, Whitehead is not much interested in the positions of St. Thomas, but invokes his views simply as a reference point of contrast in expounding his own position.

In his *Essay on Man* (1949), Ernest Cassirer referenced St. Thomas twice. In the context of setting out his own view of "The Crisis of Man's Knowledge of Himself," Cassier pictures St. Thomas as holding that the Fall of Man obscured the original power of mankind's cognition, which now stands in need of illumination and grace, since it cannot recover its power and glory by use only of its own unaided resources. The second reference makes the supplemental point that St. Thomas sees those needed augmentations as avoiding and empowering reason rather than somehow conflicting with it: inspiration and revelation are suprarational and extrarational (and supranatural as well), but not irrational or antirational. It is clear from the context that Cassirer cites St. Thomas not to refute his views but to invoke them as affording enlightening insight into the nature of the human situation. He not only refers but defers.

In his *Our Knowledge of the External World* (1929), Bertrand Russell mentions Aquinas only once. The relevant passage runs as follows:

> To the schoolmen who lived amid wars, massacres, and pestilence, nothing appeared so delightful as safety and order. . . The universe of Thomas Aquinas or Dante is as small a speck as a Dutch interior.

All one can say here is that if the absence of safety and order in one's life environment constituted a cogent ground for adopting a cosmology, then the injunction "Back to Aristotle and Ptolemy" would currently have a good deal more impetus than seems to be the case. But the fact remains that even the utterly unsympathetic Russell takes St. Thomas's position as an orienting point of reference.

In a footnote in his *Theory of Justice* (1971), John Rawls lists Aquinas as one among various philosophers who accept liberty, opportunity, and a sense of self-worth as valid human goods. Additionally, in discussing the value of amusements and diversion, he approvingly notes the "although Aquinas believes that the vision of God is the last end of all human knowledge and endeavors, he [nevertheless] concedes play and amusement a [valid] place in our life" (p. 554).

In discussing realism in his *Essays, Metaphysics and Moral* (1987), J. C. C. Smart wrote:

> The scientific realist [such as Smart himself] looks at the facts . . . and asks why they are as they are. The answer "It is just a matter of fact" does not satisfy him. The theologian is not satisfied with an accidental world, as the scientific realist is not satisfied with an accidental . . . [world]. Aquinas, in his *Third Way*, concludes to a final cause, God, who was in some sense necessary. . . . [However,] Aquinas' argument depends on a notion of necessary existence which I find unintelligible. (p. 133)

In this passage Aquinas comes off with a draw. He gets applause for insisting on an explanatory rationale for the world's facts but draws disapproval for insisting on the necessary existence of an extramundane world-explainer.

But be all this as it may, our brief survey of some significant citation rationales indicates that St. Thomas continues to be read and noted in recent and contemporary philosophy. His work provides a point of reference and an expository resource for a wide spectrum of recent philosophers—including those who cannot by any stretch of the imagination be characterized as Thomists.

2. THE PRESENT

And so in answer to the question of where the philosophy of St. Thomas stands today, one could say that the issue of St. Thomas's current place, like Caesar's Gaul, has three distinct parts:

1. With regard to present-day Thomistic studies as such, much is astir and well. Spread across the globe there is a lively industry of diverse institutes, societies, journals, university departments, and the like devoted to the appreciation and study of St. Thomas's works.

2. With regard to the place of Aquinas in contemporary Catholic philosophy at large, the situation is decidedly mixed. To be sure, the heyday of rampant neo-Thomism exerting a preponderant influence on Catholic universities and seminaries is long past. But there is still a great bustle of learning and study in this area—in quantitative terms perhaps as much as ever. However, the buoyant state of Catholic philosophy on many other fronts has reduced Thomism's *proportionate* role to comparatively modest proportions.

3. Finally there is the matter of the place of Aquinas in secular philosophy at large. And here the issue is one of curious duality. On the one hand, there is a virtually total absence of secular neo-Thomists: theologically unattached philosophers who see the main source of their ideas and inspirations in the writings of Aquinas. But, on the other hand, virtually every major thinker of the period—irrespective of orientation—refers to St. Thomas in one connection or another, be it by way of invoking his authority or representing a position to be opposed. Aquinas accordingly serves as a point of reference for many—providing for some a signpost to truth and for others an indicator of the rocks and reefs of error.

All in all, then, it is unquestionably the case that the work of St. Thomas continues to be very active and astir over the last century even in general and substantially secular philosophy. Then too it could be said that St. Thomas is alive and well and living in cyberspace on the Internet. After all, the volume of "buzz" that an individual creates on the web reflects the extent to which he is alive and striving in the public mind where "to be is to be mentioned." A convenient entry into this Tower of Babble is afforded by such search engines as Google or Yahoo. And here it emerges that, as regards the Nietzchean dogma of "the death of God," it is both newsworthy and noteworthy as a counter to such Zarathustrian arrogance that at this writing (March 2003) the number of Google items for Frederich Nietzsche is 170,000 while that for St. Thomas Aquinas stands at 190,000.

3. THE FUTURE

But what of the future?

What are the prospects for Thomism? How will—or should—the thoughts of St. Thomas Aquinas figure in the future of Catholic philosophizing?

In addressing this question it helps to begin with another: What is it that a productive philosopher of one era can derive from one of an earlier day? There are many possibilities here. The principal sorts of things for which someone's own philosophical work can be indebted to a predecessor include:

- Concepts
- Problems and questions
- Doctrine and theses
- Methods
- Aims/goals/values

The first thing to note about this list is that it provides for enormous flexibility. One can fail to agree with a single one of the philosopher's doctrines and substantive conclusions and yet be deeply in his debt for concepts, questions, distinctions, methods, or aims. It is thus an error to think that Platonists alone profit from Plato's dialogues or that Thomists alone profit from the Angelic Doctor's intellectual toil.

Moreover, the fact that philosophy is not merely a kind of literature means that Thomism is something larger than the exegetical study of the writings of St. Thomas. If, as is indeed the case, Thomism is actually to represent a philosophical position, then its concern has to be with the ideas and arguments at issue in solving the philosophical problems and answering the philosophical questions posed by St. Thomas and not merely with the texts in which these were set out. Texts are historical fixities: their development ends with their production. But ideas, arguments, and positions have a life of their own. They evolve over time and become reconfigured in the wake of the responses they evoke. When philosophical illumination rather than text elucidation is at issue, it is the impersonal matters of cogency and truth rather than the thoughts of a particular individual that constitute the determinative consideration. The crux here is a matter not just of scholarship but of inspiration.

Moreover, philosophical doctrines and positions as such have a life of their own beyond the control of their inaugurators. They admit of refinement and development both in response to misunderstanding or criticism and in response to intellectual innovation on relevant issues. If they are not to be a mere piece of flotsam and jetsam of the past washed up on the shore of the present—inert driftwood, ready for decorative display—then they must be reexamined, refurbished, and reworked to meet the needs and opportunities of changed conditions and altered circumstances. Any Thomism worth its salt should be able to emerge healthy and fortified from an intellectual encounter with the ideas and methods produced elsewhere in the philosophical mainstream. A position of perennial value must not only be restated in the changed condition of a later different thought world, it must be reconstituted as well.

And one important consideration in particular must be stressed in this regard. There is one aspect of St. Thomas's great project that is clearly of transcendent value and ubiquitous utility, namely, its commitment to rational systematization. This theory and practice in the refusal to exile reason from philosophical theology carries a wider lesson. This may be favored in a regulative maxim: "Do not fragment and compartmentalize your thinking. Whenever there is no necessity for doing so, do not divide your thinking into separate and disjoined compartments. Develop your thought systematically, keeping all of its elements in productive contact and interaction with the rest." This is assuredly a positive and productive policy from which nothing but good can come. Commitment to cultivating the integrative unity of thought is of ever-increasing value in an age of specialization and division of intellectual labor. If *philosophers* do not strive for a synoptic perspective in the realm of human understanding, then who will? And just here we encounter one of the prime object lessons of Thomistic philosophizing.

Moreover, one of the most illuminating contrasts of medieval/ Scholastic thought is surely that between the Thomistic emphasis on the power of reason and the seemingly contrary emphasis of Nicholas of Cusa on the inherent limitation of the human intellect. But just here one can also see an ironic testimonial to the doctrine of the "unity of opposites" of my great namesake, since it must surely be counted as a remarkable token of the power of reason that it is able to recognize and clarify its own limitations and to elucidate their source and nature.

Of course, the future's detail is impossible to predict in intellectual and creative matters. Who can foresee where philosophy—or indeed even science—is going? The cognitive innovations of the future are hidden from present view. But one thing is clear. While the details of the future reception of Thomistic doctrines are well nigh impossible to foresee, the ongoing commitment to Thomistic ideas and methods of thought can be confidently expected.

Contemporary philosophers sometimes regard the pursuit of philosophical wisdom as aiming at "a form of understanding that should bring mankind peace of mind." But this envisions the decidedly unrealistic prospect of a completion or perfection. The reality of it is that the human situation cries out to be seen in a less optimistic light as a stage of struggle and striving. The battle against the forces of ignorance and incomprehension is unending. And, no less importantly, intellectual innovation also brings new challenges. Behind every "solution" there lurk further difficulties, behind every answer come further questions. The incompletability and imperfectability of our philosophizing is something with which we must come to terms. For in the intellectual as in the moral life we cannot manage to achieve perfection. The cognitive condition of man in this vale of tears is something we may come to view with resignation *(Gelassenheit)* but never with rational contentment *(Zufriedenheit)*. And so, while it is assuredly the case that Thomism can and will make ever-continuing contributions to the ongoing development of philosophy, nevertheless this does not—and cannot—alter the fact that there are no altogether permanent victories to be won in man's intellectual struggle for understanding.[1]

1. This section is an expanded and revised version of an essay originally published in *New Blackfriars* 80 (1999): 199–202.

Chapter 10

RESPECT FOR TRADITION
(And the Catholic Philosopher Today)

1. INTRODUCTION

Once upon a time one friend promised another that he would introduce him later that day to Grimsby, the versatile musician. The next day—after the foreshadowed encounter had transpired—that second friend reproached the first, saying: "How could you say that Grimsby is a versatile musician: on his own telling he can only play 'Chopsticks' on the xylophone." "Ah," replied the friend, "but his musicianship shows itself in the fact that he plays it well, and his versatility is manifest in his ability as a chef, a chessmaster, and a connoisseur of the metaphysical poets."

This odd little story conveys a lesson. It is one thing to be versatile *and* a musician, and another rather different thing to be versatile *as* a musician, that is, to be a versatile musician. And just this distinction applies in the present context as well: it is one thing to be a Catholic *and* a philosopher but something rather different—and more—to be a Catholic philosopher.

And the telling question that arises is: Wherein does this "something more" consist. What is it that is required for being a *Catholic* philosopher, and in particular for being a Catholic philosopher in our present place and time: in twenty-first-century America?

The issues raised by this question are complex and many-sided. The present discussion will address only one small part of the problem.

2. RESPECT

What is it that will nowadays demarcate the Catholic philosopher as such? In reading a philosopher's work, what features would lead one to suspect that it has issued from the pen of a *Catholic* philosopher? It seems appropriate here to single out five features above all:

1. Awareness of and respect for the great tradition of Catholic philosophy from the Church Fathers to the present day.

2. Concern for the big issues of philosophy and mindfulness that attention to matters of detail will exist for their sake. A reluctance to be caught up in the fashions of the moment.

3. A humanistic preoccupation with matters of morality, ethics, and philosophical anthropology—that is, with the fundamentals of how life should ideally be lived.

4. Care for the classics: special attention for the philosophers, moralists, and thinkers of Greco-Roman antiquity and their subsequent Latinate continuations.

5. Breadth of sympathies: A positive inclination to look for merit in the work of other philosophers at large. And correspondingly, a certain skeptical self-restraint through absence of cocksure certitude in philosophical matters.

What is at issue here is not, to be sure, a set of necessary and sufficient conditions for being a Catholic philosopher. But, nevertheless, taken together in collective conjunction, these items constitute a pretty strong evidential indication.

Thanks to the fundamental contrast between faith and philosophy, two distinct questions arise in the context of present concerns:

• Question 1: What does a Catholic philosopher owe to the Church and its teachings? Answer: Allegiance and acceptance.

• Question 2: What does a Catholic philosopher owe to the tradition of Catholic philosophy? Answer: Not allegiance and acceptance, but something else and rather different, namely, respect.

And, on this telling, the prime and paramount factor that characterizes the Catholic philosopher is a *respect for the tradition.* Accordingly, the focus of these deliberations will center on the question of just what this factor of respect for tradition is and what it involves.

The ancient Romans paved the way for the English verb "to respect" via their verb *revereor,* to stand in awe (or even in fear) of someone, to revere, and—in effect—"to look up" to him. However, with us moderns—who live in a society less given to hierarchy and subordination—the idea of respecting someone is something a bit different. It calls not so much for being awed by him as for being prepared to acknowledge his claims to some merit or positivity. Respect, as so construed, is thus less a matter of looking upward to something placed upon a pedestal, as one of esteem for what is at issue. "Respect" accordingly represents a value concept. "To respect" something or someone is to prize it or him in the way of admiration, as indicating the direction of what is to be striven for or emulated.

Respect even in this relatively modest sense is a concept that is not particularly popular among philosophers nowadays. In fact, they incline to preoccupy themselves with this conception today only and exclusively in one context—that of the Kantian issue of respect for personhood. A look at philosophical indices, textbooks, and handbooks shows that it is here and virtually here alone that *respect* figures on the philosophical agenda of the present day.

Now it must, to be sure, be recognized and acknowledged that respect for persons as beings created in the image of God is a central precept of the Judeo-Christian tradition. And this insistence on respecting the special dignity of the human person continued in the more secular age of the Enlightenment, where recognition of persons as the distinctive bearers of inalienable rights served as a focal idea. (Think especially of Kant in this connection.) All this, however, is a matter of an ethical respect of persons-in-general that abstracts from the issue of the distinctive particular individuals. And so this important issue of respect for personhood is not and cannot be the end of the matter. For it is—or should be—clear that we can and should respect not only personhood in general but also various people in specific. Such respect is a matter of the recognition of worth and merit—of the claims of other particular people to our recognition and consideration not on the basis of what they *are* but on the basis of what they *do*.

Those who by dint of talent, effort, and seized opportunity manage to accomplish great and good things in this world deserve not just our admiration but our respect as well. To be sure, such respect need not be indiscriminate; it can and should be more narrowly targeted. We can respect an individual as a talented musician while nevertheless deploring his bumbling incompetence in matters of social interaction. We can respect the able actor while condemning the unscrupulous womanizer.

And, of course, respect of this sort is not a matter of self-promotion. I can respect another not because of those features in which he agrees with or resembles me but because of features he may have that I neither do nor even want to have for myself. Personal respect is a matter of recognizing and appreciating someone's commitment to *his* project, not of vaunting my commitment to mine.

All the same, respect imposes a limit of egocentrism. After all, respect is the very reverse of self-aggrandizement and self-glorification. For insofar as we acknowledge the merits of others and their achievements, we cannot see the doings of ourselves and our congeners, cohorts, and contemporaries as holding a monopoly on worth and value.

To respect another is to admit that one is not oneself the pivot around which everything revolves—that others may have claims to a merit that is coordinate with and perhaps even superior to our own. In acknowledging the claims of others we assume the mind-set of being prepared—at least in principle—to see ourselves in a more humble light.

Respect, however, is not just a matter of subordination, submission, or obsequiousness. To respect someone is not automatically to see ourselves as their inferior. It is, rather, to see him as a bearer of value and thus in some respect as worthy of emulation. People we respect are those we are apt to see as role models. Respect is thus not a matter of self-debasement and kow-towing. This, after all, is not authentic respect, for in the end the only sort of respect worth having is the respect of those who respect themselves.

Then too individual persons quite apart, we can respect an office. Such respect may be marginal when the individual comes by the office without any specific merit-based claims—by lot, say, or by inheritance. But when the office is one that must be earned on the basis of talent and effort, and represents a locus of responsibility and trust, then that office as such merits respect independently of the flaws and frailties of its transitory occupants.

In general, then, respect will have a rationale since there will and must be factors of general principle that rationally call it forth. Specifically three sorts of considerations are paramount here:

1. Respect for what a being is *by nature* (e.g., a rational being) or *by fate* (e.g., a mathematical genius)

2. Respect for what a person is *by office* either natural (e.g., a parent), or customary (e.g., a king), or earned (e.g., a teacher or a magistrate)

3. Respect for what a person achieves *by effort*—dedication to the realization of positive objectives as instanced by such diverse personalities as St. Thomas and St. Francis

Of course, to respect a person or an office we need not *agree* with him or it. Respect does not demand endorsement. What it does call for is taking that individual seriously, exhibiting concern for his views, taking them under sympathetic advisement, seeking out and emphasizing the good strong points, the instructive lessons, the constructive examples. What respect demands, in sum, is not agreement but seriousness of affirmative response: it is not an alignment of opinion that is at issue but a consilience of values.

Yet another, more figurative, mode of the concept relates to respect for a principle, such as the law or the custom of the country. This is the sort of "respect" whose manifestation consists in "honoring" those laws and customs by way of following or obeying them. This should be seen as a figurative use of the term that rides in the analogy of emulating the practices and behaviors of those persons whom we respect—taking them as our role models, as it were.

There is, however, yet another potential focus of respect—over and above persons and offices—that needs to be taken into account. For there is reason for this narrowing of perspective. For while all of us *should*—and ethically sensitive people indeed *will*—respect rational beings as such, nevertheless, respect is possible and indeed required in other contexts as well. And it is this candidate for respect that will be the special issue for concern in our present context, namely, respect for a tradition. Let us take a closer look at this issue.

3. TRADITION

Just what is a tradition anyway? In general, tradition is a set of social practices hallowed by persistence over time. But what concerns us here is specifically an *intellectual* tradition. Such a tradition is defined by two interrelated components: (1) a set of texts (in the broadest sense of the term) constituting a commonality of knowledge, and (2) a set of issues, ideas, theses, and arguments that constitute a historic commonality of concern. Moreover, it should not be forgotten that a crucial feature of a philosophical tradition relates not just to teachings but also to problems and questions. For constituting the agenda of concern is as much a valid and proper form of traditionary commitment as is endorsing particular doctrines.[1]

Now in this regard what is definitive for the Catholic philosophical tradition is the unfolding of thought defined by the writings of Aristotle, his Christianizers among the Church Fathers, the systematizers of these ideas among the medieval Schoolmen (above all St. Thomas), as well as the host of Catholic thinkers from those distant times to the days of Jacques Maritain, Etienne Gilson, Bernard Lonergan, and beyond who strove to refurbish the relevant ideas of the bygone greats to the changed ethos of a modern world based on science, technology, and social massification.

What integrates this large manifold of thought and writing into a tradition is not its doctrinal uniformity but rather both a mutuality of concern on the part of the later workers for the work of the earlier workers and also—in a larger sense—a mutuality of involvement in a common

---

1. On the formative role of tradition in inquiry, see Alasdair MacIntyre, *Whose Justice; Which Rationality?* (South Bend, Ind.: University of Notre Dame Press, 1988).

project. This project is perhaps best defined through contrast and what it is not. It is not the Comtean project of dismissing religion as the characteristic product of an outdated era antecedent to the Age of Reason, nor yet the Kantian quest for a religion developed within the limits of reason alone, nor yet an "Averroism" that sees the work of religion and reason as "separate but equal" as it were, operating apart in distinct and disjoint jurisdictions of their own and having no bearing upon one another. Rather, it is the project of developing a perspective that enables reason and religion to exist in a holistic unicity that fructifies each through its interaction with the other.

4. RESPECT FOR A TRADITION

Against this background, then, there inevitably arises the question: What does a Catholic philosopher of the present day owe to this great tradition?

And here it seems sensible to take the stance that what we owe to the tradition of Catholic philosophy is not so much agreement as respect. Once nature and nurture have so conspired as to make someone both a Catholic and a philosopher, it is only right and proper that the great tradition of Catholic philosophy should to some extent engage this individual's interest and respect. And loyalty comes into it as well. Why, after all, should one align with any tradition at all? The answer is that this is part of our identity definition, of our self-definition as the individual we are. For being a person is a matter of having a personality—of acquiring an identity. And attachment to a tradition is one important pathway leading to this distinction of personality definition. After all, even those who might wish to avoid any such affiliation through this very circumstance take their place within the tradition of eccentrics and individualists. In philosophy, as in life, what sort of person one is is in the first instance a matter of how one relates to others. And here proverbial wisdom is right: "Birds of a feather flock together"—by their cohorts and fellow travelers shall ye know them. The situation of traditionary attachment is akin to that of a family, where even if we do not *agree* with one another we nevertheless do—or, ideally, should—*respect and care* about one another.

In sum, what the Catholic philosopher owes to these great figures of the tradition is not necessarily agreement with and endorsement of their teachings, but the sort of respect that any intellectual owes those whose talents and efforts have paved the way for his own work. One's duty as a Catholic philosopher, that is to say, is not so much to endorse this or that particular thesis or teaching espoused by the great figures of our tradition, as it is to adopt a certain stance as regards the relationship between their work and our own. In sum, what we owe to the shapers of our tradition is not so much to see them as fonts of authoritative truth as to see them as role models in defining the key issues and guiding us to ways in which they can be profitably addressed.

We need not agree, but we must seek out and draw upon threads of relevancy. When we respect a tradition we must be prepared to see the work of those who labor under its aegis as relevant to our own. We must, that is, be prepared to devote to the work of its exponents attention, consideration, sympathetic response, and, above all, care.

But just how is such care to manifest itself?

In addressing this issue it is useful to begin with an analogy, namely, that of architecture. How can one honor an architectural tradition? There are three prime possibilities here:

1. *Restoration:* reconstituting or re-creating a timeworn structure of the past with faithful reliance on traditional materials and modes of workmanship. Examples: colonial Williamsburg or Warsaw.

2. *Preservation:* reinforcing a structure with modern techniques. The visible finished result is virtually identical but the substructure is wholly different. Examples: fitting out the White House or Frank Lloyd Wright's "Falling Water" with an entirely new steel substructure.

3. *Inspiration:* creating entirely new structures but in a way that revises the sprit of the past. Examples: Prince Charles's support for traditional architecture in Britain or the "modern village" movement among sophisticated property developers in the United States.

And in philosophy too it seems that there are three substantially analogous approaches to the appreciation of past work:

1. *Restoration and revival:* rejuvenation of its *thesis and doctrines* in a changed environment.

2. *Preservation of issues:* reopening and reexamining its questions; addressing its issues and problems with the methods and techniques of a later day.

3. *Inspirational revivification of its spirit:* working in the same spirit and with the same style of concern and the same objective in view.

It makes sense to think that all three of these approaches—preservation, restoration, and inspiration—are perfectly appropriate and valid ways of honoring a tradition—an intellectual tradition included. Respect for tradition is in this regard a large tent that can accommodate a substantial variety of tenants. None has a monopoly of the project and there is ample room for difference. And irrespective of which approach we ourselves favor, there is no need and no justification for looking askance at those who have chosen to take a different approach. All three of these approaches seem to afford thoroughly appropriate and fitting ways of showing respect for the great tradition of Catholic philosophy.

How should a Catholic philosopher react when discord arises between hoary tradition and the moderns between the teachings of the past and the ideas of the present? What is appropriate here is a perhaps odd-sounding mixture of trust and skepticism. The larger issues of philosophy and philosophical theology are so deep and complex that we do well both to view our own ideas with some degree of skeptical tentativity and to expect instruction and insight from those whose thought and work has paved the way for our own.

To reemphasize, then, the unifying thread throughout is a matter of caring—of bringing to one's work a sense of communion with these earlier thinkers in the common endeavor of bringing reason to bear on issues that are figuring an intelligible framework of understanding in the realm in which we have been placed by nature and nature's God.

And here it must be noted that the concept of *authority* impacts upon that of *tradition* in a complicated way. For authoritativeness is a force that can flow in different channels. Perhaps the most familiar of these is the probative authoritativeness bound up with the idea of a proof text. Here an authority is someone whose say-so functions evidentially: what such an authority says is something that the rest of us incline to accept as true for this very reason. But over and above such an authoritativeness of truth there is also an authoritativeness of value. The issues that such an authority considers ought for this very reason to figure on our agenda of sympathetic concern: we need not necessarily agree with the theses of such an authority but we should be drawn sympathetically to the orientation and spirit of his discussion. The dicta of the authority will in this case constitute grounds for concern and consideration rather than grounds for endorsement and reiteration.

5. THE ASPECT OF VALUE

There are, after all, two somewhat different sorts of authority, to wit, authoritativeness with respect to *fact* and authoritativeness with respect to *value*. We can credit a person with *sagacity*—that is, see him as extensively informed with respect to certain issues. But we can also credit a person with *wisdom* or good *judgment*—that is, see him as having sound insight as to what the important issues are, what we would be well advised to attend to and think about. Both of these issues are aspects of authoritativeness in a larger sense. And so insofar as respect is a fundamentally evaluative matter, honoring a tradition involves prizing its concerns and in consequence looking to it both for ideas and for guidance for the conduct of our own philosophical efforts.

Respect for the tradition accordingly demands a sense of solidarity and colleagueship with those great thinkers who have formed this tradition that we respect. This certainly does not require agreement with the shapers of the tradition, who, after all, all too often do not even agree with one another. Rather, as with any colleagueship, we feel affectively engaged. To see them slighted and marginalized—let alone scorned—is something we feel offensive to ourselves. Allegiance to tradition is in this way not a doctrinal stance but a matter of community and spiritual affinity—of colleagueship and collaboration in a common effort at rational inquiry under the aegis of shared values. The situation is much the same as it is—or should be—with that of our teachers or our senior colleagues in our own fields of endeavor. We do not owe them agreement and an endorsement of their opinions but rather the respect that is due to those who have labored to make it possible for us to be who we are.

And so in essence what we owe to the great tradition of Catholic philosophy is a matter of acknowledging it as the source not only of a substantial problem agenda for philosophical inquiry but also as a role model for us in our efforts to grapple with the problems it poses.

An important aspect of the idea of colleagueship and community that should be at work here lies in the inherent implications of these very conceptions. For any sort of meaningful collaboration is predicated on foregoing any pretence to facile self-insufficiency in acknowledging that we ourselves are not the pivotal end-all and be-all around which it all revolves, but are only limited creatures constrained by difficult circumstances to do the best we can with all the help that we can get. There is a due sense of fallibility and incompleteness that recognizes that we are engaged in a large and difficult enterprise in which our own modest efforts are by themselves unavailing. In such a collaborative setting, we are prepared to welcome whatever help we can get in our attempts to wrestle with the difficult and challenging issues that preoccupy us in our philosophical concerns.

The salient point is that we do not merely *inherit* a tradition but that we must work to *appropriate* it. As T. S. Eliot puts it, "Tradition by itself is not enough; it must be perspectivally criticized and brought up to date."[2] And here, as I see it, we have the crux of what the Catholic

2. T. S. Eliot, *After Strange Gods: A Primer of Modern Heresy* (New York: Harcourt, Brace and Company, 1934).

philosopher owes to the tradition, namely, a caring that requires a perhaps somewhat confused-sounding mixture of metaphors, namely, a
recognition and acknowledgment that we both stand on the shoulders
of those who have formed our tradition and follow in their footsteps
along a road of deliberation and investigation for which they have
paved the way.[3]

3. This chapter served as the author's 2004 presidential address to the American
Catholic Philosophical Association.

Index